Behind the
Mask

Emma Sayle

WITH SUZANNE KERINS

Behind the Mask

Enter a world where women make – and break – the rules

HarperCollins*Publishers*

HarperCollins*Publishers*
77–85 Fulham Palace Road,
Hammersmith, London W6 8JB

www.harpercollins.co.uk

First published by HarperCollins*Publishers* 2014

1 3 5 7 9 10 8 6 4 2

© Emma Sayle and Suzanne Kerins 2014

Emma Sayle asserts the moral right to be
identified as the author of this work

A catalogue record of this book is
available from the British Library

ISBN 978-0-00-754616-9

Printed and bound in Great Britain by
Clays Ltd, St Ives plc

Prologue

Welcome to Killing Kittens!

MY TEN COMMANDMENTS

1. Members only.
2. Women make the rules and only women can break the rules.
3. No means no.
4. Men cannot approach women. They must wait to be invited before approaching or engaging in fun.
5. If there is something that is not right at any point in the evening, my team and I expect to be told. There may be times when one half of a couple is playing while the other is not, but guys should never look like they are on their own, flying solo – or hit uninvited on any of my women.
6. We expect the parties to be self-policing, and we want everyone to have the best time possible.
7. Behave within the Killing Kittens' remit – and make sure those around you are as well – and we will all have an experience to remember.
8. Don't forget your masks. A no-mask, no-entry policy will be enforced, and they must be worn for the first few hours (until they become too hot to wear – in more ways than one).
9. Strictly no mobile phones or cameras in the venue.

10. Dress code is sexy. There is a very large Jacuzzi for you to play in, so appropriate clothing is paramount. Large lockers and towels are provided.

And remember – enjoy yourself!

Eight years ago I decided I wanted to start a business running parties. These parties would not be professional events or corporate functions. I wouldn't be organizing leaving dos, work parties, birthdays or wedding receptions. No marquees, caterers or dozy DJs. Instead, I had the deliciously wicked idea of creating a very special private club, whose members were open-minded and where the atmosphere would be relaxed and friendly and, ultimately, intensely liberated. No one is getting hurt, no one is getting cheated on and every woman is being respected.

Twice a month a group of people who'd been accepted for membership via my website would congregate in cities across the UK for an evening where they could make their fantasies and desires come true. At my soirées, I would create an atmosphere of non-judgemental curiosity and acceptance. Nothing would be repressed or off-limits. If a woman wanted to dance around the bar in her underwear, or even totally naked, she could, knowing that she was not going to be either thrown out or jumped on. Partygoers would be able to toss their inhibitions aside and feel free to do whatever they liked. My parties would be for people at ease with their own and other people's sexuality, who weren't afraid to live out their desires with willing partners. Taking part would not be enforced: people would be free to watch, or to come as a monogamous couple, or even alone (if they were girls), to see what might happen and perhaps taste their own hidden desires without shame or judgement.

Now, I know this isn't the kind of soirée most party planners would organize. So I guess you're wondering why a normal girl from Surrey would choose such a wicked career path. Well, I was determined to make this vision a reality because, one life-changing night, I had seen for myself exactly how liberating it could be, when I witnessed an A-list crowd indulging in sheer, joyous erotic abandonment. I decided that it was my mission to help other people taste those delights and that freedom.

But this would not be a tacky swinging party, or an orgy fuelled by testosterone and male fantasies. My vision was to create a sophisticated environment where women were in control and felt comfortable. Anything could happen as long as it was initiated by women. My parties would be the first to be dedicated to female pleasure and feminine desires.

Some of my guests have told me that my soirées are like vivid daydreams where they feel as though they're floating on air. They tell me that it's intoxicating, captivating, titillating, thrilling, addictive and the most erotic experience they have ever had.

That makes me happy, because that's exactly what I want, and why I founded my Killing Kittens' parties in the first place.

And now I want you to experience it too.

Chapter One

'Once made equal to man,
woman becomes his superior.'
Socrates

I have two hours to kill before I am to host this evening's party. Tonight, it's in a stately home in London's exclusive Mayfair, and that always draws a particularly upmarket crowd, but my members come from all walks of life. For the most part they are young and curious, drawn by the glamorous settings and the enticing atmosphere of anticipation, for my parties are places where anything can happen. Members apply through my website and they must supply a photograph and some details about themselves (some like to send pictures that aren't strictly of their faces). Acceptance is not based on looks or wealth, but on a certain mind-set: will these people fit into the hedonistic environment and do they have the right spirit of fun and adventure mixed with respect for rules?

Tonight, 200 paying members will be attending my party. They expect something special and I intend to make sure they get it. As well as pleasing the regulars, I'll also be making sure the new members are having a good time and fitting in nicely. Anyone who doesn't play by the rules will be asked politely to leave. But thanks to the careful vetting process, there isn't usually a problem. A good time ought to be had by all.

Before then, I'm meeting a friend in Claridge's Fumoir bar. I'm not strictly following the dress code, but no one seems to mind my silky black sleepwear, which is a trademark of mine. If anyone has a discreet word, it will take me less than two minutes to whip on the chic Italian designer dress I've stuffed into my handbag. I love to be comfortable, but I never go anywhere without something smart I can slip on, just in case.

The glamorous Art Deco 1930s bar feels like a haven of tranquillity as I step inside. It's dark, sensuous, alluring and, best of all, tucked away behind a secret door, which appeals to my inner sense of drama. Inside, the decor is a rich aubergine with dark leather seating and low crystal lighting, and the walls are adorned with vintage photographs of beautiful women. I slip onto a seat near the horseshoe-shaped bar and order my wake-up call, a Bull Shot, which consists of vodka and beef consommé and tastes 10 times spicier and more potent than a Bloody Mary. 'And a bottle of rosé too, please.'

While I'm waiting for my drink, I get out my phone and start checking my messages. After a moment, I look up and see my friend Miss D striding slowly and gracefully towards me. I'm not the only one who's noticed the new arrival: all eyes are on her, which is just the way she likes it, and probably why she handed her coat to the cloakroom attendant before waltzing into the bar. She's wearing a sexy black strapless dress with sheer panelling down the sides that highlights her derrière to excellent effect. At first glance, she looks perfectly proper and very alluring with her bee-stung lips, olive skin and thick, glossy dark hair falling around her shoulders, but on closer inspection there's something missing. Her underwear! Typical. She's getting in the mood early.

'Hi, Ems!' she says, and gives me a kiss on each cheek. Before sitting down, she glances about the room, scouting out any attractive specimen who might be worthy of her attentions.

Miss D never misses a Killing Kittens' party. She's totally hooked. Her only stipulation is quantity – the more the better. 'I can't help it,' she'll say with a shrug, looking innocent. 'It's just that I'm a sexaholic.'

Miss D and I have known each other for years because our mothers were friends and fell pregnant at the same time. We were born just weeks apart, with me making my entry into the world first. Our friendship didn't have the best of starts: whenever we met, we fought. Later we went to different schools and Miss D became one of those girls with a high-octane social life and an expensive wardrobe, all paid for by her rich parents, who owned a townhouse off the King's Road in London as well as a sprawling country estate. She spent her time hanging out in Chelsea, dating boys from Eton and transforming herself into a real-life Sindy doll. Miss D adored Sindy, and by the time she was 13 she had manicured nails, a glossy pout, coloured hair and designer clothes. By contrast I was a complete tomboy and liked nothing better than playing with friends in our back garden. I adored hanging outdoors with my father. If he went fishing, I would try to fish, and if he was climbing a mountain, so would I. As a result, I was permanently clad in trainers and jeans and was pretty much continually filthy, much to Miss D's horror. Not that her disapproval put me off or dampened my spirits – in fact, it probably made me even more of a sporty and adventurous type. Then disaster struck for Miss D – her parents lost all their money and were declared bankrupt. Fortunately, her grandmother paid for her schooling, so she stayed at her boarding school, but her cool friends dropped her like the proverbial hot potato and her hoity-toity arrogance was completely deflated. One day, when she and her mother were visiting us, Miss D and I were sent off to amuse ourselves together. Instead, we listened at the door and heard her mother breaking down and sobbing like a baby as she confessed all about their woes. Miss D reached for my muddy hand and in that instance all was forgiven. I gave her a hug and we've been bosom buddies ever since.

A decade on, Miss D assures me money isn't everything when it comes to romance, but I have to remind her to stop waiting for her rich prince to gallop out of nowhere and rescue her. Luckily for her, an inheritance from her grandmother has provided her with enough to live on while she tracks down her prize, as she's incapable of holding down a job for long.

When we're sorted for drinks – Miss D with a glass of chilled rosé and me with my Bull Shot – she takes another sneaky glance around the room and says, 'So, how's your man, Ems? Is everything going well with the mysterious Mr Black?'

'Well …' I take a sip of my warm, spicy drink, playing for time. I don't really want to talk too much about him, not yet. 'It's very early days, so I can't say much except that we're enjoying each other's company.' I smile cheekily at her.

'Spill!' She grabs the wine bottle and tops up her glass. 'Will he be at the party tonight?'

I shake my head. 'Of course not! You know I need to keep my eyes on the ball when I'm working, young lady. And besides, it's a full-time job having to keep my eye on you once you get going. You don't have a stop sign, remember?'

'You're so lucky,' sighs Miss D. 'An older, single, eligible man. That's exactly what I'm looking for.' She takes a sip of her wine and then says hopefully, 'Does he have any friends? Really rich ones?'

'Stop with the rich, piranha woman!' I say, laughing but exasperated.

Miss D looks confused. 'Piranha woman?'

'Yes, you're a flesh-eating creature particularly attracted to anything with a bulging wallet,' I tease. 'Your type is lethal. The men get distracted by your pretty colours and don't see your razor-sharp teeth until it's too late.'

Miss D takes it in good spirit and laughs. 'You know me too damn well, Ems!' She smiles wickedly back. 'By the way, I've got something to show you before we head to the party.' She looks suddenly coy.

'What?'

'I've brought something special for tonight. Just warning you in case you discover me in a room upstairs later!' There's a very naughty light in her eyes.

'Come on then, what is it?'

She leans in and says excitedly, 'I've brought a grown-up toy to play with tonight!' And she reaches eagerly for her bag.

'Miss D, no! Not here in Claridge's!' I screech, trying not to laugh. 'Keep it in your bag till later, for goodness' sake! And talking of the party, we'd better think about making tracks. I promised Kitty I'd be early tonight. Pass me a glass of rosé, I'll help you finish that bottle.'

When we've made a decent enough inroad into the wine, I head to the ladies, smooth my hair, moisten my lips and fling on my dress. Now we're both ready for action, Miss D and I step outside where the doorman hails us a taxi, which takes us through the busy London streets, slipping around corners and gliding through the heavy traffic. There are people everywhere.

My BlackBerry beeps with a BBM from Trolley Dolly. She's a good friend of mine, a single divorce lawyer who's not to be messed with. At work, she's got a mind like a steel trap, and in her spare time, she oozes glamour and is the life and soul of the party, winning everyone over with her personality and her natural lack of social inhibition. She adores my parties and is certainly more tiger than kitten when it comes to sex. I've nicknamed her Trolley Dolly, as she never looks dishevelled, not even after a long-haul night at my parties. I read her message.

Hey. My car is still not ready so taking the bus! C u in 30.

I message back: *Cool.*

She replies a moment later: *Is it OK if I bring two guys along?????! I've met them in my local pub b4. They're good guys.*

I smile and text her back: *Sure.*

Back pings her reply: *Thanks! :) They're with me now. H-O-T!*

I wouldn't normally allow any stranger to turn up to my soirées without being vetted, but Trolley Dolly is part of my inner circle and a trusted friend, so I know I don't have anything to worry about. This is a one-off. She'll choose wisely when it comes to bringing new people to the parties. I just hope the men she's found aren't too innocent, or they'll be in for one hell of a shock.

*   *   *

We make good time through the traffic and arrive at the venue well before any guests.

'This place looks incredible tonight, Emma,' Miss D says as we walk through the double doors and into the palatial marble-floored hall. 'Such a brilliant choice, it couldn't be more perfect.'

'I know – it's fabulous.' I look about, pleased. I love this place. It's a rare eighteenth-century jewel, a Georgian town-house that is both incredibly grand and amazingly shabby, and the effect is perfect for my parties. There is beautiful art on the walls, and the exquisite rooms seem to go on and on, but the peeling paint and battered skirting add an air of divine squalor. This is my favourite part of the evening: soaking in the splendour of my surroundings, sipping a glass of champagne in the drawing room with Miss D and relaxing in the peaceful atmosphere before the real fun begins. 'You go and take a look around. I've got some work to sort out, then I'll come and find you.'

'Sure. See you later.' Miss D heads off up the huge staircase.

Kitty Kat saunters over armed with a clipboard. She's dressed in a sexy skin-tight black leather outfit and wearing a cute cat mask with pert black whiskers. Kitty Kat is in her early twenties, petite and has finely chiselled features and luscious lips. Her porcelain prettiness draws plenty of attention, even though she never seeks it. Tonight she looks *hot*.

'Here you go, Emma.' She hands over the clipboard with the list of names of guests attending tonight. There are almost 200. 'The candles have been lit, the rose petals have been scattered down the staircase and over all the beds, the mirrors have been polished and I've put out about a thousand condoms all over the place. You'll also notice I've strategically placed the "Please take a shower before Jacuzzi. *Seriously*" notice where it can't be missed.'

'Thank you.' I smile at her. I know I can rely on her precision and attention to detail.

'The canapés and oysters are ready. And the champagne's been chilling for a few hours, so it should be at the ideal temperature by the time everyone arrives.' Behind her mask, her eyes sparkle with a touch of mischief. 'Forty-five degrees Fahrenheit, of course.'

'Of course.' I'd expect nothing less from Kitty, who appreciates the finer things in life. By day she's a rising actress and has already appeared in films with some big Hollywood stars. She loves the arts, opera, theatre, classical music and French cuisine. But by night she's a dark, beautiful creature who prowls on my behalf alongside my security man, Jupiter. He's big, strong, suited and booted, and has a remarkable intuition when it comes to sniffing out trouble.

Kitty has other useful skills too: she studied martial arts and was taught how to box by a British ex-heavyweight champion, which is handy for my security staff and me, as she often spies the first hint of trouble. She also employs these skills to fend off men. Despite numerous attempts to set her up with some very eligible bachelors, she has point-blank said no. In fact, Kitty hasn't had sexual relations of any kind for three years, vowing abstinence after having her heart broken one too many times. Instead, she dedicates herself to helping me facilitate the pleasure of others.

I check the guest list as we take a stroll around the ground floor, looking over the set-up. It's all brilliant, and I hand back the clipboard with a smile. 'Thank you, Kitty, everything's immaculate down here. I'm going to make a quick inspection upstairs before people start arriving. I'll catch you later.'

'Of course,' she replies.

As I walk up the grand staircase, I can't help but absorb the house's dark glamour. It's an ex-embassy, and its eight reception rooms, billiard room, clubroom with Jacuzzi, ballroom and 24 bedrooms make it perfect for entertaining. It also attracts the world of show business: Kate Moss filmed a lingerie advert here, walking sensuously down these very stairs. Amy Winehouse shot her 'Rehab' video here as well. And it's also where Oscar-winning actor Colin Firth filmed his therapy sessions in *The King's Speech*. If it weren't so amusing, I would blush to think of the many Kittens who have enjoyed the kinkiest, acrobatic, down-and-dirty sex on the very furniture where Colin Firth, Helena Bonham Carter and Geoffrey Rush filmed their scenes. I can't help remembering one woman who screamed and orgasmed three times on that very sofa as she embraced her dark side with the tanned Swedish model she and her partner had selected for the evening. Sorry, Colin!

I find Miss D upstairs in the ballroom. In this splendid room, several huge leather beds covered with red Egyptian-cotton sheets have been pushed together to form one huge one underneath a massive chandelier. Around the sides are sofas, chairs and cushions.

'It looks lovely,' sighs Miss D, her eyes glittering with anticipation. 'I can't wait to see what happens here later.'

'Better keep your special toy handy,' I advise her, and we both giggle. 'Now – let's find a glass of champagne. It'll all start kicking off soon, and then I'll be hard at work.'

'Good idea,' says Miss D. 'I like your style.'

* * *

At 9.30 p.m. the first guests appear and then, suddenly, it's busy. The atmosphere is one of a slightly louche drinks party as guests start arriving. I'm busy at the door, ticking off names and making sure everyone is wearing masks – I have a few spares just in case. All the guests are attractive – some even beautiful – and distinguished-looking, but not intimidatingly so. They don't look like sex-mad orgiastic beasts, but like normal people, and any observer would think that this is just a normal party. Once inside, couples talk quietly together, glasses in hands, while groups chat around the bar as the champagne is served. The men are in lounge suits, and most women are immaculately dressed in cocktail dresses. The average age is late twenties to mid thirties. I wonder what they're all talking about – this is one gathering where guests are reluctant to discuss their jobs or much about their everyday lives at all. And why not? This is where they live out fantasies; they don't come here to dwell on the mundanity of existence. At this point in the evening, people are scouting for potential playmates. The more uninhibited are open about their desire to play – these are the ones who don't mind performing, or get a thrill out of being watched as they have sex, and who may be up for several encounters and group episodes. Others are shyer, some even a little awkward. Experience tells me they'll warm up. I've seen retiring, silent little birds turn into golden eagles when the play begins. Some are single girls looking for a couple or vice versa, or girls looking for one-on-one action with a man or a woman. Some are here to watch, perhaps while discreetly caressing their partner before going somewhere private to work off their inflamed passions. I notice two beautiful brunettes are wearing identical La Perla corsets made of pale-pink silk and boned into a hip bustle scattered with feathers. They are clasping hands, smiling, and give a hint of what is to unfold. I know exactly what these two will be doing before too much longer.

I watch as some people wander up the grand staircase towards the ballroom and wonder if the giant bed is seeing any action yet. At this point, I expect it's more like a sofa than a bed, a place for chatting and flirting – for now. The mood is one of playfulness and gentleness laced through with great expectations of the fun to be had. I'm pleased. This is precisely the good vibe I wanted when I originally planned my parties.

I hand the door duties over to Jupiter for a while and go downstairs, where some guests are sitting waiting for the Jacuzzi to open. I tell them that the Jacuzzi will be ready for playing in 15 minutes and remind them where they can leave their clothes. On the way back upstairs I pass Kitty doing her rounds accompanied by one of the security team. In a venue this size, I always have an extra couple of discreet big guys around in case anything kicks off, though they're rarely needed.

'Everything OK?' I ask.

'So far, all fine. No drugs. No guys on the prowl.'

Any Kitten caught with drugs is thrown out, no excuses, no exceptions. Even Miss D was once asked to leave when I spotted she had drugs in her handbag. I have a zero-tolerance policy.

'Great. I'll head upstairs and see what's happening.'

It's after 11 now, and the place is full of people. The noise levels are rising, and the party-goers are loosening up after a couple of glasses of champagne. I know that any second now someone will start something and then, with amazing rapidity, it will begin. I walk around the ballroom and check out the mood in the other rooms. It's definitely warming up. I can see people kissing, hands caressing, dresses unzipped, shirts unbuttoned. The regulars know the score and want to start enjoying themselves. Newcomers are a little less at ease, waiting to be transported out of their awkwardness by alcohol or lust, but also eager to begin.

By the time I return to the ballroom, that invisible switch has been pulled. It's started. Masks are coming off and there's a hedonistic, Bacchanalian vibe. The mood has swiftly changed to one of decadence, and what was a luxuriously relaxed drinks party 10 minutes ago has crossed the line into something else. Couples are on the bed, kissing, undressing one another. I can already see a beautiful naked girl sinking down to caress her partner's huge erection with her lips. Around the room, some people watch the scenes unfolding before them, others are getting down to their own action.

I notice that in the corner near me, two toned, tanned and leggy women are lying naked on a couch in the '69' position. They are devouring each other, as a beautiful young couple stands nearby, watching every erotic move. The couple look flushed, breathless, disbelieving. Then one of the women looks up and smiles at them radiantly. 'Hi,' she says invitingly. 'Why don't you come and join us?'

The young woman, dressed in a lavender draped cocktail dress, blushes and looks nervously at her partner.

He is handsome and impeccably dressed in a black pinstriped suit, and he gazes down at her, concerned. 'Do you want to stop this now? Shall we go home?'

She looks at war with her own desires. She takes a long gulp of champagne. 'No, don't let's go. This is what I fantasize about. You *know* I do,' she says, her voice quavering.

She seems to be looking for permission to do what she's longing for. Her lover takes her champagne glass, puts it down on a nearby table and wraps his arms around her tiny waist.

'You look incredible,' he says, his eyes gleaming as he takes in her form.

She beams. 'You don't look so bad yourself.'

He pulls his right hand from her hip and runs it up her leg, under her cocktail dress. He can tell that she's obviously turned on and ready for whatever is coming next.

'We could do it here. Just the two of us.' His voice is soft, but urgent.

She shakes her head, smiling now. 'I want to experiment – I want to see what it's actually like. Shall we join our new friends? We don't want to keep them waiting, do we?' Then, with a wicked smiled, she leads him over to the sofa, where they submerge themselves into the luxuriant pile. Soon, hands are undressing them, releasing their bodies, mouths are taking possession of their mouths and they are completely lost to the sensations they're enjoying.

Good, I think. Two more about-to-be-very-satisfied customers.

The huge bed is now covered with people having sex in every conceivable position, and the sofas around the room are occupied too. There are threesomes everywhere – two women and one man, two men and one woman, all kissing, licking, eating, caressing. One woman has invited three men to play with her. She looks like she is having a wonderful time.

A petite pale brunette is sprawled on the bed, her legs on her lover's shoulders as she invites him to penetrate her. Another young woman is kneeling on the floor, enjoying a man's huge erect penis like it is a giant lollipop. She is buxom, curvaceous, beautiful and sexual. Her breasts are swollen, her nipples hard and tingling with intense lust and need. She's expertly working her tongue down to his balls, licking, teasing, then popping one slowly into her mouth, followed by the other.

I know this man. He's a barrister who's made an absolute fortune from closely guarding the domestic and financial secrets of the rich and famous. He's tall and Draculine, with a penchant for blondes. His highly confidential, big-money business dealings are conducted in his glossy offices in London or New York. He's formidable, never loses a case and is certainly not to be messed with in the courthouse. But tonight, he's under my opulent roof, sprawled and thrashing about on my bed, totally defenceless. His fingers are tugging his lover's mane of perfectly tousled blonde locks; he's totally intoxicated by what she's doing to him. She's in complete control as she pulls her mouth away, grabs a condom from one of the many nearby baskets, expertly rolls it into place and then sits on top of him. She slowly bumps up and down his length, one hand on his chest, the other reaching behind her back to fondle his balls.

'Oh fuck, I'm going to come,' he says, panting and help-less, as she jabs him into her, deeper, quicker. She is setting her pace, fast and hard, as he writhes under her and then groans loudly as he reaches orgasm. I can tell that the woman is not finished yet. She'll be looking for her own orgasm, either from him or from someone else.

A masked gentleman walks in looking for his partner and finds her naked, gently massaging and kissing another woman's silicone-enhanced breasts. Slowly, her hands are wandering down the woman's neck to her nether regions, amid moans and gasps.

'Ah, there you are. *Naughty wife!*' he says, without a trace of crossness in his voice. 'I can't leave you alone for a second, can I?'

She smiles, inviting him to join in. He quickly unzips his trousers as both women prepare to welcome him.

'I'm glad you're back, darling,' his wife says, looking radiant, still kissing the other woman and stroking her breasts while she opens her legs wide for him. 'I want you to do me first, and then her. How about it?'

'Jesus, my darling, you are *naughty*! I am going to give you a good fucking now. I hope you're ready.'

Others are watching as he plunges into her, making her gasp with delight.

'Holy hell, watching this is the ultimate fantasy,' whispers a tall, good-looking man to his female companion, a bulge growing in his trousers. He has a look in his eyes I've seen before. It's a kind of wonder that's turning into arousal and a fervent desire to taste some of the pleasure that others are enjoying. His girlfriend gazes back at him with the same look in her eyes and I know that they'll soon surrender to the atmosphere of lubricity and the erotic stimulation of what is unfolding in front of them. This is no staged plastic porno with its relentless action and managed climaxes – these are real people giving and receiving real pleasure because they want to. The effect is liberating and highly arousing.

I've seen enough. I've grown used to scenes like this and I've taught myself to stay separate from it all. I can't afford to lose my head and join in; I've got to stay on top of things here. I head downstairs. In the hallway, two couples are flirting. 'We could go back to our house. It's round the corner and the children are away tonight ...'

In the other corner, a couple in their late thirties are look-ing for a female partner to join them.

'No, definitely *not* her,' says the woman. 'She's far too thin and will make me look like a *beached whale!* How about her?' She points to a tall brunette, who looks *very* familiar. Miss D!

'Perfect choice,' mutters the man, as they saunter over to Miss D.

I laugh inwardly. Miss D will have them for breakfast, lunch and dinner. Before my watch has clocked 60 seconds, Miss D is clutching both their hands, leading them up the winding staircase.

'I have a sex toy,' she's saying to her new friends. She smiles seductively at them. 'I think you might enjoy it! What do you think? Sound good?'

Oh, Jesus!

Just then I notice a commotion at the front door, but it's nothing to worry about. It's just Trolley Dolly arriving and making plenty of noise about it. She's wearing a mask and a Burberry mac with, I suspect, very little underneath. She's flanked by two gorgeous men.

Guests stop and stare. This is the power Trolley Dolly has when she enters a room.

'So you made it then.' I smile.

'Oh, Ems, Ems, I have. And look who I picked up at the bus stop of all places!'

'The bus stop?' I ask, bemused. Her companions are smil-ing nervously.

'Yes, the bus stop in Hampstead. No car, no cab in sight. So I decided to hop it on a bus, and I bumped into these two fine specimens. Aren't they just something? They liked my mask and said that I must be going to a pretty special party dressed like this. So I invited them along. And here we are. Gentleman, I introduce you to the hostess this evening, the glamorous Emma Sayle, my best friend and confidante.'

I say hello when she introduces her guests as Alfred and Kinsey.

There are blank expressions on their faces. 'Our names are *not* Alfred and Kinsey,' says one.

'They are tonight,' she smiles wickedly. 'It's in honour of my hero, Alfred Kinsey. Boys, I guarantee you are going to learn a *lot* here.'

They still look bemused. 'We've never heard of the man.'

'Listen and learn, boys. All you need to know is that we have him to thank for starting the sexual revolution back in 1953. If you can believe it, he was branded a Communist and investigated by the FBI – for saying that women have orgasms.'

One of the guys laughs in disbelief. 'Really? That's insane!'

Trolley Dolly shakes her head. 'I know. As crazy as claiming the earth is flat. Thank God we live in more enlightened times – but a lot of that is down to Kinsey.' She beams. 'So wear his name well, my friends, and let's see if you can prove his theory all over again! Follow me!'

She leads them off in the direction of the stairs. I suspect Trolley Dolly's prey have no inkling of the frantic activities unfolding upstairs, but they soon get the hint when she flings off her coat and reveals that she's wearing a black balconette Agent Provocateur bra, with flashes of hot-pink silk under the bust and along the straps, matching knickers and nine-inch killer designer heels.

'It's a Maddy bra. You like, gentlemen? Just call me Maddy tonight,' she purrs. 'See you later, Emma. I am going to show these lovely boys around now. I hope you don't mind. Catch up tomorrow?'

'Sure.' I wink back. 'Let's be in touch. Enjoy yourself.'

Kitty comes up and tells me that things are going well. It's in full swing now and won't start winding down for another hour or two. I'm no longer needed. The party will run itself, the staff is managing the bar, Kitty and Jupiter will clear up and lock up.

There is only one thing I can do now, as I am feeling restless, frisky and very playful. The scenes unfolding around me have affected me despite my best efforts. I take out my phone to make a late-night booty call to Mr Black.

I call his private number. He picks up on the third ring.

'Emma? It's two in the morning,' he says.

'You're still up. Is it a problem?'

'I never have a problem where you're concerned, Emma.'

'I want to come over. Just for a little while.'

'You can stay all night. Where are you?'

'Round the corner. Usual place. Mayfair.'

'My driver is on his way. Two minutes.'

I tuck my phone away. It's time to leave the party now: I know everything is going smoothly. I need a little action of my own.

Chapter Two

'It is never too late to be what you
might have been.'
George Eliot

I never got the chance to tell my parents myself about my new career in the sex industry. As far as they knew, I was a corporate PR girl promoting respectable businesses. So they were taken by surprise when the *Daily Mail* published an article about me with the headline: 'She's the Poshest Swinger in Town'.

I had only been running Killing Kittens for a few months and hadn't yet spread the news to my nearest and dearest. I was sunbathing on Bondi Beach in Sydney, Australia, when Mothership called me, obviously furious. I could practically hear her blood pressure rising and her nervous system going haywire.

'Emma, I've never been one of those mothers who yells and spanks their children. But if you were here, I would smack you right now for being such a risk taker!' she shouted.

I had no idea what she was talking about, but once she'd managed to draw breath long enough to calm down and read out the *Mail* piece to me, I felt terrible, filled with guilt that my parents had had to read about me like that. I tried to apologize but Mothership was having none of it.

'How could you, Emma?' she cried, her voice cracking and sounding like she was about to cry. 'Don't you know how this makes us feel?'

'I was going to tell you, I promise!'

'When, exactly?' she snapped back.

'As soon as I got back to London.'

'The phone has been ringing off the hook all day. Your father is furious. The *Daily Mail* called us. Don't you realize how this could affect us all? They say you run orgies for wealthy liberated couples and single women. Is it true? And if it is, why did you have to leave it to the *Daily Mail* to inform us?'

'I'm sorry, I really am,' I replied, thinking it must have been Chinese whispers, my story getting passed around and eventually ending up in the press.

'The whole world knows before we do. Oh, Emma, really! Your father and I have decided the only good news is that, according to the *Daily Mail*, you're not getting involved in these orgies yourself.'

'That's right,' I said calmly, trying to soothe her. 'It's business for me.'

'Well, that's a relief at least. Thank God for small mercies.' But she still sounded angry. I crumbled on my sun lounger, wondering how I was going to clean up this mess and make it up to my parents.

The 10,600 miles between Sydney and London bought me some time for everyone to calm down, but a week later I faced the music. I stopped in London only long enough to dump my luggage at my flat, and then I went back home to my parents' house, arriving so late that they'd gone to bed. I made my appearance the next morning, trying to get back into the good books by bringing my mum and dad (other-wise known as Mothership and Colonel) tea in bed, along with two baseball caps embroidered with slogans. One read 'Poshest Swinger's Dad', the other 'Poshest Swinger's Mum'. To their credit, they laughed. As they sipped at their tea, a little less stony-faced than when I'd come in, I offered them my overdue apology for the shock and embarrassment I'd caused, and tried to explain exactly why I'd taken this particular path in life. They made an effort to understand, but I don't think they did.

'I'm sorry for not telling you first,' I said. 'I should have. But it's only been a short time and I'm still finding my feet.'

'But honestly, Emma – sex parties?' My mother still looked scandalized. 'Why? What makes you want to do it? Look what they're saying about you.'

I shrugged. 'I don't care what the newspapers write about me. Remember what you said to me once? "A tiger doesn't lose sleep over the opinion of sheep." I live by that motto. Besides, this is what I want to do. It's an excellent business opportunity, I'm providing a service people want and I intend to make the most of it. I'm not going to be derailed by the groaning hypocrisy of people who'd like nothing better than to come and see what's going on for themselves.'

Colonel burst out laughing. 'Emma, you're a stubborn creature, aren't you? You're probably right. And your mother and I would be lying if we said we were truly shocked. You've never failed to surprise us.'

I could see that they both understood that I had made up my mind and that there was no point in trying to convince me to follow a different path. I smiled at my parents. 'You always said to me you wanted me to be the best at what I do. This is what I'm going to do. Now watch me.'

Looking back, I can see now that I was never going to do things conventionally. I've always had a desire to take risks, do things out of the ordinary and forge my own path. From the moment I could walk, I wanted to run away from home. Every opportunity that presented itself, I'd have my little wheelie case ready so I could flee the nest. It wasn't that I didn't like home, I loved my family deeply. I was very fortunate: I had a privileged upbringing with nice homes and private schooling, but I always knew no matter how comfortable my life was, I was never going to take the usual route and do things the easy, mapped-out way. I never liked taking orders and I was keen to win my independence and get on with life's adventures. Childhood was an irritating inconvenience and I couldn't wait to grow up.

My sense of adventure began early. I was born in Guildford, Surrey, but when I was one, Colonel's army duties took us to Belfast. My father was brilliant and academically gifted; he had read Classics at Magdalene College, Cambridge, and was fluent in German, French, Italian and Latin. After becoming a Fellow of his college, he'd left for a career in the Army and then the Diplomatic Corps, which meant his family was destined for a life on the move. He was talented and successful, but nonetheless he always looked a little ordinary next to my beautiful mother. She was glamorous, leggy and olive-skinned, with ash-blonde hair, blue eyes and a smile that could calm a raging ocean. She was a devoted wife and a great asset to my father, as she charmed everyone she came into contact with at the same time as raising her little family all over the world.

My sister Georgie was born during our two-year stay in Belfast. By the time I was three, home was the Rheindahlen Military Base in Germany, where my brother Johnny was born. I was seven when we moved back to England, where we set up home in Somerset. When I wasn't at school, I spent my young days hanging upside down out of oak trees or lining up my toys in height order with OCD military precision (I still have a mania for order). At eight, I was sent to Hanford Prep boarding school for girls in Dorset. I spent most of my free time reading, devouring the books of Enid Blyton, Arthur Ransome and Willard Price. Adventure appealed to me, and my literary heroes and heroines gave me the sense that anything was possible. When I outgrew these books I moved on to the spy novels and books about war and religion that my father read.

I was a real Daddy's girl; I worshipped my father and always longed for his attention and approval. Attention I got by causing mischief, and approval I tried to win by impressing him with my school reports and athletic prowess. I was impish and prone to getting into scrapes, but I also did well at school. I didn't mind lessons and I was good at games; at 10 I was tall for my age with long legs that made me a natural runner and captain of the netball team.

Although I was away from my father in term time, I was desperate to be with him in the holidays. Wherever Colonel went, I followed, which meant flying out to join the family wherever he had been posted. He'd become a leading liaison officer and was sent to Berlin in 1989, so I was there when the Wall came down. I was only 11, but I remember that night vividly. People everywhere were jumping up and down, crying and laughing with joy. My parents and I joined the crowds by the Brandenburg Gate and cheered on every East German Trabbi that drove through to the West. I also took a hammer to the Wall like everyone else, knocking off chunks of history and stuffing them in my bag. With everyone rolling into the West, we went to East Berlin's flea markets and I stocked up on Russian dolls and fur hats, which I bought for next to nothing. I was nicknamed Del Boy Trotter back at school, as I sold my bits of Berlin Wall, fur hats and dolls and made a fortune.

With the Cold War coming to an end, my mother started organizing food and medicine convoys to Russia, and when I was home for the holidays I helped her. Once we were filmed by ITN as we sat in one of 10 trucks on the 1,454-kilometre trip from Berlin to Smolensk. I felt humbled by meeting orphans, some of whom were the same age as me. To be able to hand out the clothes and sweets that I took for granted made me determined that when I was older I would set up my own charity and carry on doing what I could to help others and relieve a bit of the misery in the world.

For the next two years, I hammered away at the Berlin Wall in the holidays and continued to sell the chunks to my school friends in term time. I gave half of the proceeds to charity. At 13, I left Hanford Prep and went to Downe House, a girls' boarding school in Berkshire. Any girl who makes it into Downe has fought to be there and, as result, the school is full of strong, competing personalities and a lot is demanded of the students (including the future Duchess of Cambridge and her sister, who were there at the same time as me). I loved it – I was born a fighter.

I made strong friendships at school and took an enthusiastic part in the healthy tradition of practical jokes (in fact,

I'm told that some of my most notorious pranks are still recounted to this day). I also fell in love for the first time. The object of my passion was one of the school gardeners, a lad of about 17 who looked deliciously tanned and muscular as he trimmed the bushes. I was completely infatuated with his impressive masculinity, and he always stopped work and stared when he saw me too. Our romance was fuelled by love letters, passed between us by his boss (who perhaps ought to have known better), but when we actually managed to meet, it was a disaster. Close up, my gorgeous gardener was far less impressive than I'd thought, as he stared cow-eyed at me and fumbled for my hand. His love letters had seemed sophisticated, but in person he was sickly sweet with a squeaky voice. Everything I felt for him withered and died in an instant.

Although I enjoyed myself at school, there were times when I felt isolated. I was not one of the 'London Trendies', as we called them – the girls from rich families with opulent pads in the most expensive parts of London. They were real-life Barbie dolls, with a skinny look and the right designer clothes; some of them not only wore Versace or Alexander McQueen, but also had photographs in the dorms of them-selves clutching their favourite fashion designer's arm. While I was on Russia-bound medicine-and-food convoys, their school holidays consisted of private jets, Bentleys and exotic locations. By the time I was 16, I began to feel the difference so keenly that I developed eating issues and secretly started taking laxatives. I wanted to be as thin and glamorous as those girls, with their effortless confidence, fantastic clothes and gorgeous boyfriends from Eton and Radley. Despite all the privileges I had and all of my outward confidence, I still felt inferior and thought I could control it with food, as though that would somehow be a route to social success. The eating issues that started then would take a long time to conquer.

When I was 14, my father was made the British Defence Attaché to Kuwait and Egypt. Home was now Cairo, and that was the same year that we all went to Buckingham Palace to watch Colonel being invested with the OBE for his services during the Falklands War, Northern Ireland and Berlin. I watched in awe as the Queen pinned the award on my father's jacket and congratulated him. Mothership squeezed my hand and whispered, 'All right, darling?'

I didn't say anything in reply. I was too proud of my father to speak.

Despite my sometimes-shaky self-esteem and on-going eating problems, I was developing a keen interest in another side of life: boys. My passion for the gardener was long dead, but I had other objects of fascination now. Although I was at an all-girls school, I had a brother, which was an advantage as I was able to snog a few of his friends. Otherwise I met boys at parties or through my parents' friends. I met Ed at a party during the summer holidays, and he became my first boyfriend. The romance had an expiration date, but I loved holding Ed's hand and kissing him (we're still friends). There were other boyfriends after him, and at 16 I went further than ever before. Sex was not on the menu, but there was plenty of exploration and I began to unravel the mysteries of what men were like and what happened when things got steamy, and it's safe to say that I liked it.

As I got older, I became wilder and more reckless. I was still kicking over the traces, keen to get on with life and taste everything that adults enjoyed. It could have disastrous consequences, like the time I got properly drunk for the first time, aged 16. Colonel was hosting a lavish dinner party at our Cairo house for the Canadian Ambassador. Unknown to everyone else, my endless glasses of Sprite contained double shots of vodka and after a couple of drinks, I became convinced the 28-year-old army officer sitting to my right was deeply in love with me. Colonel noticed my odd behaviour and said, 'You can try a tiny glass of wine, Emma. It may calm your nerves.' He wasn't to know that the wine would prove the proverbial last straw, and my flirtation came to an abrupt end as I threw up violently all over my plate of beef Wellington, stunning the other guests into horrified silence. Colonel dispatched me to my bedroom with military efficiency. He did not offer me a glass of his beloved Châteauneuf-du-Pape for years to come after that.

I lived up to my final Downe House school report from one teacher, which read: 'I have found Emma to be cheeky, over-excitable, opinionated and thoroughly obnoxious – she'll go far.' I thought it was a fair point.

Colonel hoped I would follow in his footsteps and apply to Cambridge University, where he had been both a fellow and bursar of his college, but I decided that wasn't for me. Instead, much to his disappointment, I chose Birmingham University, to read Sports Science. Before then, I took a gap year paid for by my Del Boy Trotter trust fund, and my first stop was Africa. Colonel had now been sent to Kuwait and was busy with his new posting, while my mother was resettling yet again, and I reassured them by telling them I had a job lined up in Cape Town. The truth was that there was no job, and all I managed in the first week was to get my belly button pierced and lose my memory for most of it after being offered hash cakes. I was mugged in the street and had my passport and purse stolen. When I went to the police station to report the incident, I was groped by a burly Afrikaans copper, who kept muttering, '*Gee my jou hand. Ek hou van jou,*' while he pawed me. Translated, he was asking for my hand and saying he liked me. I'd had enough of Cape Town, and I swiftly packed my wheelie case and headed to Kuwait to join my parents. They had lined up a job for me at a holiday resort, but I was sent packing within two weeks after I encouraged most of the Filipino staff to go on strike because of their appalling pay.

With time on my hands, I turned my focus to boys and began dating a man. Losing my virginity never felt monumental to me: I knew it would happen when it felt right. That moment came during one date, while we were sunbathing at a poolside. I suggested that it was the right time to do it. He was surprised but willing, and we lost no time in going somewhere private to do the deed. As I was an 18-year-old virgin, I had no idea what I was doing, but pretended I did. Luckily I didn't expect it to be a magical event – after all, I had no strong feelings for the man, I just wanted to do it – and sure enough, it wasn't mind-blowing. It was awkward and it hurt, but I was glad I'd done it: I felt more grown up and confident, and I sensed potential. This time might have been a damp squib, but I knew it could be much, much better.

My motto for that wild year before university – and ever since, if I'm honest – was to let go of any inhibitions I had and push the boundaries to the limit. For me, it was part of my journey to self-exploration and finding myself, but I went beyond reckless sometimes. It helped that being a daughter of a diplomat came with privileges and immunity:

my diplomatic ID card gave me quite a safety net and turned me and a few other English and American diplomat kids into reckless risk takers. Once, Colonel took me to a party on board a US warship in Kuwait and I enjoyed a marathon kissing session with a handsome Lebanese man there, until my father discovered his family was part of the Lebanese mafia and nipped that in the bud at once. Another time, I was dared to climb on board a superboat belonging to the ruling family of Kuwait. Never able to resist a dare, I gave it my best shot and managed to get on and off without being caught, but the British Embassy heard of my little exploit and my father was ordered to get me under control. Another time I was thrown into jail for being a potential spy after being car-chased by Saudi patrolmen along the Kuwait–Saudi Arabia border. The truth was, no espionage was involved. It was dark, I got lost and I'd forgotten my diplomatic ID card. Colonel had some choice words to share with me when he picked me up from jail.

I wanted fear, risk and exhilaration, but I soon learned that pushing boundaries could have consequences, and not just for me. I was dating an American marine who was a member of the US Embassy security staff. Deciding that Kuwaiti hotels, the beach, army barracks, tankers, helicopters or warships no longer had the thrill factor, we decided the rooftop of the massive, fortress-like US Embassy was *the* place to have sex. Now that my virginity was out of the way, I had taken to this pleasant new activity with gusto and loved having sex with my hunky marine as often as possible. As we exchanged that devilish look on the rooftop, we both relished the excitement of doing something so daring and forbidden, and that made us throw caution to the winds. But the loud groans that followed meant that it didn't take long for us to get caught with our pants down. Moments later, security guards armed with rifles swarmed like ants across the rooftops and it was only my marine identifying himself that stopped a full-scale military shootout. Colonel was summoned to the US Embassy for a stern dressing down, and once more I was in big trouble. But he was learning by now that I was headstrong, difficult to control and determined to play as hard as I could.

My crazy gap year came to an end and I headed to Birmingham University to take up my place to read Sports Science. I reluctantly left my marine and we made promises of mutual devotion, but in my first week of university, a friend in Kuwait called to tell me that no sooner had I left than he'd jumped into bed with someone else. So that was that. Despite the activity and excitement of Freshers' Week, I was miserable, but my heartbreak was swiftly dispelled when I met Aidan. He was tall, dark, athletic and handsome, and his intense piercing blue eyes won me over before he said 'hello'. We fell in love almost at once, but it was a tumultuous, rollercoaster ride of a relationship and it came with the condition that a break-up never really meant 'it's over'. For three years, our big love affair was punctuated by frequents splits and passionate reunions. I loved being with Aidan, but when we were apart, I didn't slow down. University was mostly a blur of sports, some studying, drinking, making friends and having sex. I made sure that I broadened my horizons, with sex in particular. A foursome with a guy I'd been seeing, his best mate and a girlfriend of mine became a threesome when my friend did a runner, leaving me with two very hot, ripped rugby boys. I tried the other kind of threesome when I was having a drink in a bar with an ice-hockey player and another girl joined us. She and I shared a drunken snog, which was quite fun, and my boyfriend, clearly enjoying the show, suggested we go back to his place. When we got there, he told me he'd like me to go down on our new friend. I was game for anything, so I did, but I decided then and there it wasn't for me. My boyfriend ended up shagging her, which was fine, but we didn't last much longer after that, and Aidan and I got back together yet again.

When graduation came, Aidan and I went our separate ways: I headed to London and he moved to Sydney to become a high-flying corporate psychologist. But we stayed good friends and made a promise to each other: if we were both single by the time we hit the big 4–0, we would marry.

But for now, I had to decide what I was going to do with my life. The last thing on my mind was organizing orgies, but Fate was soon to intervene with a spectacular experience.

Chapter Three

'Whenever you find yourself on the side of the
majority, it is time to pause and reflect.'
Mark Twain

The real world was an unpleasant experience after the high
jinks of university. I had no idea what to do next and I
drifted to London, where I shared a flat with a friend and
looked for a job. I worked for the *Independent* newspaper selling advertising space, but I hated the targets, the pressure
and the long hours trying to convince people to spend
money. It was a relief when I managed to get into financial
and entertainment PR, but even though this was a bit
better, I had no real interest in using my feminine assets to
build superficial relationships with clients, or in writing
fluffy press releases about celebrity parties or products I
didn't give a toss about. It was a job, though, and it brought
me into contact with lots of different worlds where surely
I'd find new opportunities. At times I was asked to represent people and businesses in the adult industry, and I went
to a couple of those big trade fairs held at Earls Court or
Olympia and saw what a huge business sex could be.
Hundreds of stalls sold thousands of products and mountains of equipment, or offered myriad services from sex
parties to fetish gatherings. I was awed by how much was
on offer but surprised that the whole thing appeared to be

run by men. Women were used in advertising, of course, and some businesses claimed to be female friendly, but the truth seemed to be that it was all aimed at men. I'd seen porn movies while at university, and my girlfriends and I had agreed that, for us, it just wasn't sexy. All that bright light, the massive penises and the endless pounding, anatomical action where the woman was not much more than a collection of willing orifices, taking it all in while she groaned in fake ecstasy – it was not a turn on. If anything, it was the opposite. And yet *Sex and the City* was causing a new sexual revolution, showing women in control of their sexuality and pursuing what they wanted in life, without shame or judgement. The message was that we could be in control of sex, enjoy it and not be judged for promiscuity. But none of that was reflected in the adult world as far as I could see. I believe in equal rights for women, and the truth is, male-dominated porn just doesn't work for our differently wired brains.

Then one day I got the call that was set to change my entire life. In her quest to find a rich man, my old friend Miss D had started working for one of the most successful wedding planners in the world. From chartered jets to private islands, couture gowns and 10-tiered cakes, nothing was impossible for Miss Wedding Planner.

I was bored with city life and my job, lonely and missing Aidan. The call could not have come at a better time.

'It's rainy, dark and miserable in London. You are so bored, Ems, stuck in that office. Come and have some fun with me,' Miss D wheedled.

'I'm a responsible adult now,' I replied matter-of-factly. 'I have a job, press releases to write, important meetings lined up. I have commitments.' I looked around the bleak, climate-controlled office. Colleagues slouched in their chairs. Some were furiously tapping away on their keyboards. Others stared blankly at their computers pretending to be busy. Sedentary work was sapping the life out of each and every one of us.

'Well, be irresponsible for once. Get out of that bunker and take a sickie. Just for a couple of days? Please, Ems?'

'I'm not sure … It's not exactly going to help my career if I'm caught.'

'Do it for me,' she pleaded. 'There's a seat on a private jet leaving London and taking us to Ibiza tonight for the most amazing wedding you'll ever see. That seat has your name written all over it.'

How can anyone resist an invitation like that?

Before our jet took off, I sent a text to my boss telling her I had food poisoning and not to expect me in the office. It was a lie that caused me a frisson of guilt, but I didn't regret it. Instead, I felt alive again as we stepped off the jet and were chauffeured to a private villa on the beach for a party to celebrate the wedding of Mr Filthy Rich and Miss Socialite that was taking place the next day.

I knew it would be a smart, glamorous party and I expected a hedonistic vibe, but I could never in my wildest fantasies have imagined what was going on inside those doors. Apart from the music and the ocean, the only sounds I could hear were of total ecstasy as Miss D and I stepped inside the villa. The party was already in full swing. Inside there were around 200 beautiful guests, most completely naked, some wearing glittering eye masks.

Mesmerized, I gratefully accepted a glass of Dom Perignon champagne as I took in my lavish surroundings and the erotic events unfolding before my eyes. It was like a scene from *Eyes Wide Shut*: naked people were everywhere, their bodies entirely exposed in every state of arousal. There were couples exploring each other, groups meshed together as one. This was a real-life masked secret society that indulged in ritual orgies, but unlike in *Eyes Wide Shut*, there was no jealousy, revenge or obsessiveness, and there was no sense of exploitation or shame.

I was drawn to the most exquisite moans coming from deep inside the house. Hypnotized, my heart sprinting, the air rushing from my lungs, I searched for where these whimpers of delight were coming from and was led to a glossy white kitchen. There, sprawled on the granite top, was a world-famous actress. She was naked, gazing dreamily and utterly ravishing. The clinical white of the kitchen would highlight any blemish, but she was flawless, looking just as perfect in real life as on her alluring glossy magazine covers, apart from her cheeks flushing with colour when she groaned with pleasure. A man's fingers were deep inside her and the scent of her arousal filled the room. Every time she moaned, the man responded by pressing deeper while massaging her clitoris with his other hand, evidently delighting her when he did. Then, the man withdrew his fingers, stepped back to admire her tiny waist, the erect nipples and her luscious lips before sliding his huge erection into her. Both of them began to moan and gasp with pleasure as he picked up pace. Soon he was plunging deep and frantic, like an animal possessed. For someone who looked so fragile and tender, this actress could keep up with her suitor, taking all he could give and begging for more. Her sexual appetite obviously had no bounds and soon they were both shouting and crying out as he thrust harder, deeper and faster, until eventually he shuddered on top of her, and she finally climaxed around him. But almost at once, she seemed ready to go all over again. As he withdrew, 10 hungry, handsome men patiently waited their turn, their eyes flaming with desire, all totally focused on the glamorous woman sprawled out naked for them to enjoy. Meanwhile, she made her sexual desire look erotic and totally captivating. This fiercely talented and acclaimed actress was no porn star looking for a world record for having sex with the most partners in one day. She was taking her time, relishing her sexual desire, *loving* every second of her time on stage, albeit a granite kitchen top.

'Have you been outside?' an attractive, naked brunette whispered in my ear, smiling as I nodded no. 'Follow us,' she added, as she walked off outside with a fine specimen of a man close behind her.

Curious, I left the actress to her pleasure and followed the brunette outside. On the beach, guests were dancing around a huge bonfire, some in designer underwear, some in bikinis and some naked. All of them were grinding, smiling and moving like the stars above us, twinkling like flames in the night sky. The waves rolled in and drenched people making love on the sand, revelling in the atmosphere of lust and passion. This type of lovemaking is normally forbidden – but why, when all these guests looked so happy? I was turned on, but I didn't want to join in. I was happy just watching and soaking it all in.

Later, I saw the actress again. I froze. She looked fresh-faced and innocent as she danced around the fire in a fuchsia-and-violet toucan-printed maxi dress with a white orchid blooming in her hair. The bride and groom were by her side.

Captivated by her all over again, I watched her laugh, chat and sip champagne with her two friends, who were going to become man and wife on this very beach the following day. She casually slipped her hand inside the bride's top and tenderly kissed the groom. Her cheeks began to flush with colour once again and her nipples tightened through her dress as she teased them both. This time, though, she wanted somewhere more private as she smiled and pointed to a luxury super-yacht in the distance. She giggled as the bride and groom chased her across the moonlit beach towards the huge pleasure boat.

It was pretty obvious what was going to unfold once the threesome climbed on board.

Miss D may not have found the rich husband she wanted, but I spotted her lying on the wet sand in a passionate embrace with a man, sharing in the amazing laissez-faire atmosphere.

The morning after, the guests sat outside in the sun, recovering and drinking Bloody Marys. People were idly discussing who had got with whom in a relaxed way that showed just how normal it was for this glamorous, hedonistic crowd to indulge in their pleasures.

'I guess we killed a lot of kittens last night,' said one man. When I asked what he meant, he told me that, according to a well-known US college joke, whenever someone masturbated, God killed a kitten. The joke had escalated so that any orgasm now had the same result. The table laughed, and so did I. Little did I know what a role those words would play in my life …

* * *

I was amazed and liberated by what I had seen in Ibiza. All the hidden furtiveness of sex, all the embarrassment and shame so many of us associated with what was supposed to be a pleasure – it didn't have to be like that. It could be given and taken with joy. In an atmosphere of security and happiness, sex could be shared with one or with many, with true and exquisite abandonment, and without fear.

I had loved seeing women relish their sexuality and the pleasure they could both give and receive.

Then it hit me, catching me totally off-guard. My mind was made up: the minute I got back to London I was quitting my PR job and setting up my own business. I would bring this beautiful, joyous experience to others through elite parties where anything was allowed.

I had never been more sure of anything.

Chapter Four

'For most of history, Anonymous was a woman.'
Virginia Woolf

Back from Ibiza and that incredible wedding, I was fired up with enthusiasm for what I'd seen. I'd decided I would quit my job the moment I returned, but once I was actually back and facing the reality of my life in London, it didn't seem as easy as I'd imagined. By Monday, I was back behind my desk, working away at my corporate PR job and wondering how I would go about setting up a sex-party business. I didn't have a clue, and researching sex parties while at work didn't seem a particularly wise move.

It might have ended there, but Fate took a hand.

A friend of a friend approached me to ask if I would do PR work for a company called Heat Bomb, which specialized in sex parties. This was the perfect opportunity to get some experience and I jumped at the chance. Now I would discover a little more about the mysterious world of free love that I was sure existed with far more prevalence than anyone suspected. The thing I had taken away from the wedding in Ibiza was how accepting everyone was, and how keen to take part, either as a monogamous couple or in a more adventurous, exploratory way. It wasn't confined to just a few people. And that made me think that this phenomenon must be happening everywhere.

I didn't know much about this particular company, but I had the feeling that very few parties were going to match the glamour and beauty of the Ibiza wedding. I had visions of bored, middle-aged couples swapping partners while dressed in comedy S&M gear, but while it wasn't as utterly seductive as Ibiza, it wasn't like that at all. The first sex party I attended was the reverse of the tacky, suburban scene I had anticipated. It was held in an apartment in London and 60 people attended, all aged between 25 and 50. They seemed like professional, sophisticated people, the men in suits and ties and the women in smart dresses and heels. You would never guess from looking at them that these people were about to break down all the normal barriers of social convention and start having sex with each other, but that was exactly what happened. Gradually the mood of the evening changed and became more highly charged, and then it kicked off. Soon, clothes were dropping to the floor, people were openly kissing and caressing each other and then more. The vibe was free and uninhibited, and I saw couples allowing each other to experiment and indulge themselves with others, or just letting the atmosphere charge them up to a peak where they wanted to have fierce sex with each other, turned on by what they were witnessing.

This was my first taste of what was on offer in the UK and I wanted to know more. I decided to go freelance so that I could be more in control of how I worked and concentrate on those areas of most interest to me. I helped promote quite a few of Heat Bomb's parties, which were always held at the same venue, and I began to understand their appeal. I saw many couples evidently in strong relationships but wanting to spice up their erotic life. By dipping their toes into the swinging scene, they could do so with honesty and safety. Sex parties allowed couples to experiment and satisfy their desires without the deceit and underhandedness of an affair. If anything, as far as I could see, it kept them together. And if a couple made that decision and were happy with it, then who were we to judge them?

I soon discovered there are hundreds of clubs and hotels up and down the country that exist purely for sex parties. Most of the people who go to them look perfectly ordinary. You could be sitting next to someone on the bus and never suspect that the night before they'd had sex with six people or more at one of these private orgies. Obviously it's not for everyone, but there are many 'normal' people who want to explore this side of life – and why shouldn't they? We've all been given the amazing gift of sex and the pleasure and enjoyment it can bring, and life is short. There are plenty of people who tell us it's bad and wrong, but as long as it's between consenting adults and we don't hurt anyone in the process, why shouldn't we enjoy ourselves? People are complex and fascinating, capable of living and loving in many different ways, and I don't think we should judge each other for making different choices.

Heat Bomb's parties never replicated that incredible vibe I'd experienced at the Ibiza wedding. The truth was that men still dominated and I sometimes got the feeling that they were busy making sure their own private fantasies got enacted, as though they were directing and starring in their own personal porn films. There was also an element of fetish; at one foot party, the men paid to have women walk all over them and be allowed to suck their toes. Fine if that floats your boat, but not exactly fulfilling for the women (unless they got off on having their toes sucked), and I wasn't keen on that kind of dynamic.

I couldn't understand why no one was aiming these parties more at women and what they wanted. The Ibiza wedding had been about women pleasing themselves at least as much as men and had provided the kind of deliciously glamorous atmosphere that could stimulate female sexuality, but no one here seemed to be catering for that.

Then I was asked to do some work for a group of US women who'd formed a company called Cake that put on sex parties for women. They wanted to launch their business in London. At last, someone was doing the kind of thing I had in mind. I went out to New York to attend a party and enjoyed myself enormously. It was a brilliant and highly entertaining night, but it wasn't at all what I'd envisaged for a female-friendly sex party. The founders of Cake had done women's studies at university and their parties were a feminist statement, a riposte to the male-dominated porn world. Men could only attend with a woman and everyone was wearing all manner of hilarious and outlandish fancy dress. The pole dancers were men, and generally men were put in subservient roles. It was great fun and very amusing, but it was too aggressive for me, too interested in making a point to be successful as a really erotic experience for women. It was more like burlesque with a very hard edge to it. Working on the London launch of Cake was good fun, but still there was no one putting on the kind of parties I envisaged.

Meanwhile, my relationship with the organizers at Heat Bomb had run into trouble. The guys wanted to run a really huge party and get media attention for it. I told them I thought this was a bad idea; the papers were bound to try to reveal the identities of the attendees. They wouldn't listen, though, and insisted that we went ahead with getting publicity. I did as I was told and when the *Sunday Mirror* did a front-page splash headlined 'VIP Orgy', naming everyone involved and trying to speculate on who had been at the party, the guys at Heat Bomb did not like it one bit. So I decided to leave, with the plan of taking them on at their own game and turning my vision of that glorious night in Ibiza into a reality. I would beat them by miles and show them all how it could be done.

Whenever I wonder whether to do something or not, I try to imagine the worst-case scenario, and if I think I can handle it, then fine. If I started my own sex parties, what was the worst that could happen? I would have to put all my savings into the venture, which meant that if I lost everything I would be made bankrupt and would have to go back to working in PR. Well, neither of those things was the end of the world. I could cope with that. The start-up costs would be low, so the risk wasn't that huge, and I already had a lot of experience and contacts to draw on.

I remembered the *Eyes Wide Shut* atmosphere of the Ibiza wedding and decided I would have the masks, and I set out my party rules like the *Fight Club* rules. It was fun, almost jokey. If it worked out, fine. If not, I could live with it.

I drew up the ethos of my parties – first, in order to attend, people would have to be members of the club, which meant I'd be able to vet applications. That way I'd be able to keep out people who might want to subvert the parties for their own ends, and I'd make sure I could keep the environment as safe as possible. It also meant that guests were likely to meet people with the same mind-set as their own, and the more comfortable everyone felt, the more likely they were to have a great time. I knew from experience that the organizers of some parties didn't mind if the party-goers went to extreme places, indulging fetishes and some of the more niche practices. But I didn't want that. My parties would be more normal, if that's the right word, where people who were not into particular scenes would feel at home. I would charge £150 for a couple to attend, and £50 for a single woman; no single guys would be allowed. It may cost more than your average Saturday night out, but the price included canapés and free bubbly till midnight, and was designed to ensure that only those willing to play attended.

But what would I call my new enterprise? I remembered the college joke I was told about the morning after the Ibiza wedding party, and I decided I would call my business Killing Kittens in tribute to that night when everything changed. It felt just right – it was intriguing, naughty and would keep people guessing. I set the date for my first Killing Kittens party. First, I needed a location. With the help of friends, I found a sauna bar in the middle of London. It was perfect, with a large mosaic-tiled spa, lounge bar, sauna room, steam bar, wet room and a dozen private rooms – small dark cubby holes with massage tables in them. It had a friendly atmosphere and, most importantly, the owners and staff were discreet. It was going to cost a bomb to hire it for the night, but I was prepared to take the gamble and I used all my savings to do so. Then I invited 40 guests. I had built up a database of contacts from all the parties I had worked for, the kind of people who'd be interested in parties like this, and I emailed out the invitation to them. I didn't broadcast the fact that I was starting a sex-party business, but I invited a couple of friends I thought would get into the spirit of things: Miss D, of course, and another good friend of mine I'd nicknamed Plaything. He'd been my friend since childhood, and now that we were both living in London, we saw each other all the time. He was my best male friend and my wingman, always looking out for me. He was also young, handsome and very keen to party, and I knew he would be just the right kind of person for Killing Kittens. Word spread fast and soon I had people emailing me, asking where and when the parties were held. Before long, my guest list was full.

Now I had the most important things in place: a venue and a set of ready and willing people who'd paid good money to attend my party. Even though I was sure it was going to be a success, I was still nervous. I'd been at enough parties by now to know that people would get into the spirit of things, but I worried that this time no one would lose their inhibitions sufficiently to start the action going. Would I be able to create the right vibe?

I needn't have worried. I had the sauna bar looking perfect – sophisticated and welcoming in the bar area, where candles flickered and trays of drinks awaited the party-goers, and a little more steamy and enticing further on, where the large pool and darkened areas promised pleasures to come. Baskets of condoms were placed discreetly around the place; I'd ordered hundreds to make sure that, whatever happened, we couldn't run out. A security guard stood on the door to ensure that only invited guests were allowed in – I didn't want anyone straying in from the street by mistake. People began to arrive as soon as the doors opened at nine o'clock, and I was delighted to see that they looked fantastic, dressed in glamorous evening clothes and wearing glittering masks. This was what I wanted – sophistication and style. And, of course, I wanted to see those glamorous clothes well and

truly off by the end of the night. I certainly did. The atmosphere of a smart drinks party changed subtly until it was
sexy and permissive. People sought playmates and found
them. By midnight the entire club was full of naked people
and wherever I looked, I could see unbridled enthusiasm for
the sex that was taking place everywhere. Couples, groups,
threesomes, foursomes, together in every variety. Some were
partakers; others were watchers. I saw one man happily
observing his girlfriend as she fucked another man fast and
hard in front of him. I saw girls caressing each other, kissing
and making love for their own pleasure, not so some man
could enjoy it (though some did, of course). I saw all manner
of high jinks and sport in the pool, the sauna and in the
recesses of the cubby holes: if the doors were left open, then
the participants welcomed being watched or even wanted
more partakers.

Miss D and Plaything launched themselves wholeheartedly into the action, getting into each other first and then
exploring a wilder side of things with two other girls. It was
kind of strange seeing my two old friends getting down to
full and frank sex, throwing themselves into the whole
thing with gusto. But it was also strange how quickly I got
used to it. Nudity is natural when everyone is carefree,
uninhibited and accepting, and even the wildest sex soon
ceases to be shocking when you've witnessed it for a while.
The main thing was that people were happy and enjoying
themselves in safety and comfort. There was one hairy
moment when security was temporarily breached – a
photographer had sneaked into the club, trying to get some
snaps to sell to the press to cause a scandal and put the new
members off the club, but my security chased him away and
nicked his film. After that, everything ran smoothly. The

fun and games went on until the early hours when, at last, exhausted and satisfied, the final party-goers left.

Killing Kittens was up and running. I was now a bona fide sex entrepreneur.

Chapter Five

'You have your way. I have my way.
As for the right way, the correct way, and the
only way, it does not exist.'
Friedrich Nietzsche

I've met a few people in the sex business and a lot of them are dreadful, ruthless, cigar-chomping men driven solely to make money. Some are among the wealthiest people in the country. More often than not, they treat their money with more respect than they do their employees, most of whom are women. They lure young girls into the industry and exploit them until their appeal is gone, then chuck them out in favour of younger, fresher replacements. It's about using women to service men's desires and fantasies, and it can be an unpleasant business that I can't help feeling is related to darker activities such as prostitution and sex trafficking.

I am not interested in that side of the sex industry and I'd be horrified to be like those seedy men getting rich on exploitation. My business might be about sex, but my aims were always to offer pleasure and entertainment, where safety and control were paramount. Besides, I was happy to start small and see what happened. When it comes to business, in my opinion slow and steady *always* wins the race.

* * *

At the beginning I kept my sex soirées small and intimate. I continued to use the venue in the middle of London, with between 50 and 100 people attending the parties. They all kept on coming back for more, and I got ever more enquiries from the one-page website I'd set up. It simply asked anyone interested in Killing Kittens to submit their email address for more information, and from there I went through the process of vetting my applicants. I didn't make the mistake of over-expanding by allowing everyone who wanted to attend to come to a Killing Kittens' party, and I made sure, as far as I could, that people fitted my criteria for membership. They had to accept that these parties were for the open-minded but not suitable for specific tastes or niche pleasures. Most of all, they had to get the fact that they were primarily designed for women. I had plenty of candidates to choose from. New Kittens flocked because of existing members and word spread fast – especially among women – that there was never a dull moment once darkness fell and the masks came off. My BlackBerry soon started beeping off the hook with calls and emails from people keen to join in. The monthly parties in Covent Garden were generating a real buzz. Every party turned a profit, even if it was just a small one. I still did freelance PR to supplement my income, but I was hopeful that it wouldn't be long before I could begin to run Killing Kittens full time.

As word of the parties spread through networks of friends, Killing Kittens began to be noticed by the established world of sex parties and I was surprised to get emails from people offering their opulent homes for hire as a venue. They all set out their need for discretion in this area, but it was clear that if I was in the market for stately homes, lavish hotels and penthouse apartments, and was able to keep the owners' names out of view, then there were plenty of wonderful places available. Naturally I assured everyone that I was a very discreet party organizer – no whisper of any participation would ever leave my lips – and soon I found I was being offered some truly magnificent venues. I knew a somewhat notorious businessman who, through some interesting circumstances, had become the owner of a magnificent mansion in central London. It was in great demand as a backdrop for photoshoots and films and as a party venue. When he heard about Killing Kittens, he offered me the mansion as often as I wanted it. I jumped at the chance. It was a beautiful venue, and I could have bigger, more interesting parties there. It went down a storm with my members, who adored the shabby opulence and the aura of decadence. More than 100 guests partied and played under crystal chandeliers and in front of vast marble fireplaces, with naked bodies writhing around in Georgian splendour. The fact the house had played host to some of the most famous faces in the world gave an added frisson to the activities. All 15 of the bedrooms were made good use of – not to mention the grand staircase. I hoped that before too long we would be able to make it the permanent home for Killing Kittens. As my parties grew more popular and membership of Killing Kittens increased, word spread to Fleet Street and the press started knocking on my door. National newspapers and glossy magazines including *Cosmopolitan, Elle* and *Glamour* became fascinated by this new sexual liberation. They couldn't believe that educated and affluent young women were flocking to join a secret society that hosted anything-goes sex parties, and I was inundated with requests for interviews. I was happy to oblige. I had no problem with being the face of Killing

Kittens, or with promoting it as much as I could, and the press seemed very interested in the story of the public-school girl who was unashamedly working in the sex business. People seemed to believe that this somehow made me a nymphomaniac, but that was all right. I didn't mind; I just laughed it off and carried on.

My family and friends were right behind my chosen career as a bona fide sex tycoon. They knew there was no stopping me once I'd put my mind to something. Even Colonel was quietly impressed with the way my business was growing stronger by the day, even if I was stirring up controversy. My parents were getting used to the fact that I was attracting publicity and making headlines. Now, a year since I'd started, I had 1,000 members and a growing number of applicants keen to join my club. I was sure there would be 3,000 Killing Kittens members by the end of my second year. I was ready to expand.

To celebrate a year in the sex business, I decide to spend the evening with my parents, followed by drinks with Miss D and the gang later.

Colonel is in fine form tonight. He's not wearing his 'Poshest Swinger's Dad' baseball cap, but he's no longer shooting me down with unsupportive words as he pours me a glass of his beloved Châteauneuf-du-Pape. I'm back in his good books. The atmosphere is convivial, and the wine and conversation flows as we tuck into Mothership's perfectly roasted lamb in the kitchen. We're nearly finished when my father calls for silence and lifts his wine glass.

'A toast to Emma,' he declares proudly, and looks over at me with a glint of amusement in his eyes. 'Here's to your ability to never fail to amaze me.'

I'm touched. Growing up, I hungered for Colonel's love and approval. Time has softened that craving, but I digest his every word all over again, even though I got it through unlikely means. My mother and I raise our glasses as well. 'Thanks, Pa.' I take a sip of the rich red wine. It's lovely that my dad is proud, but if he knew about the special Killing Kittens Valentine's party tomorrow night, he might think a little differently. I try not to giggle at the thought and instead say, 'Thanks for dinner, Ma, it's delicious.'

Mothership shoots me a mischievous look, then lifts her glass again. 'And now for my toast to Emma.'

I look at her, surprised. The dust has settled since the tabloid exposé on me, and my mother seems a lot more at ease with my chosen career, but even so, I didn't expect her to toast its success. I think secretly she still hopes that I'll give it all up and do something a bit more respectable.

Mothership looks back at me with a smile. 'My toast to you, Emma, is about something else entirely. I'm so proud of your new project.'

'What's this?' Colonel asks, looking wary. I expect he thinks I'm starting some scandalous new venture that will bring yet more unwanted attention to the family.

'Emma's going to raise some money for charity.' She looks at me. 'Tell him, Emma.'

'It started in a silly way,' I explain to my father. 'A drunken bet in a pub with some boys. They're planning to row across the English Channel in a dragon boat to raise money for charity. So I told them that I'd get a gang of girls together and race them to France. They're calling them-selves the Brotherhood, so we're going to be the Sisterhood. And we're going to raise just as much money as they do, if not more.'

Colonel frowns. 'That's going to be tough, Emma ...'

'You know me, Pa. No challenge too great. Besides, I've already emailed friends I think will be up for it, and you'd be amazed how keen they are.

'We're going to start training as soon as possible,' I add. 'Some of my girls are rowers, but they're used to going backwards. It's a whole new skill to paddle a dragon boat and face the way you're going.'

My father looks impressed.

'Have you decided on the charity you're going to support?' asks Mothership.

I nod. 'Yes. The Ben Hollioake Fund – it supports hospice care for children. And Babes in Arms, the Norfolk Park charity. We want to raise £50,000.'

'The Channel is extremely busy with shipping,' my father adds. 'Crossing it is not exactly straightforward.'

I nod. 'It's going to be very tricky – we'll be dodging ferries and whatever all the way over. I'm going to do my research on that, don't worry. We'll have lots of support as well.'

'Well done, Ems. You'll pull it off, I know it,' my mother says.

'Thanks, Ma!' I lift my glass again, delighted that the hurt and embarrassment I caused my mother a few months ago seems to have evaporated.

Just then the phone rings and my father goes to answer it. As soon as I hear the shrill tones coming down the line, even at this distance, I know exactly who it is. My mother and I exchange looks: it's someone in my father's family I'll call Annoying Distant Relative, known for her delight in sticking her nose into other people's lives and stirring it all up as much as she can. I think she's toxic through and through and I would happily avoid her for the rest of time. As it is, I can hear every word she's saying down the phone to my father.

'How are you coping with all this sex-party scandal?' she bellows, not caring if I'm in earshot or not. She's always been unfazed by people hearing her negative opinions of them, and she's certainly in venomous form tonight. 'People are still talking about it, and I saw Emma in the paper again only last week. The shame of what she's been up to! You must be devastated.'

'Devastated?' Colonel replies calmly. 'Actually, I'm rather happy at the moment. Emma's here, as it happens, and we've just had a very nice dinner together.'

This isn't quite the answer she'd hoped for by the sounds of it. She goes on: 'You're being very brave, but you must be absolutely appalled at her behaviour. Oh, I pity you, I really do. You spent all that money on her, giving her the best education and start in life … and look how she's repaid you. The sex industry. So sordid! I'm disgusted and shocked and I expect you are too. Silly girl! The whole country has read every vile detail.' My Annoying Distant Relative has evidently taken this very personally from the anger in her voice. She thunders down the phone, getting quite carried away. 'This whole thing is seedy and plain wrong. You must make her see sense. This could end in disaster; it could destroy the family. It reminds me of the Profumo Affair.'

'Now, now.' I can hear frustration simmering in Colonel's voice. 'Stop being so ridiculous. It's hardly comparable to that.'

Mothership is staring intently at me, as if to gauge whether I'm hurt by what I'm hearing. She refills our glasses with wine, then gets to her feet and says coolly to Colonel, 'Give me the damn phone.'

My father hands it over, looking apprehensively at my mother's stony expression.

'Good evening,' she says softly down the phone. 'How nice of you to call. We appreciate your concern, but everything's fine.'

'I strongly disagree, I'm afraid,' Annoying Distant Relative barks back.

My mother says slowly and clearly, 'Emma has thought it all out and is working very hard to make her business a success. She has a dream and she intends to accomplish it. If we don't accept what she does, we could risk losing her and I'd never be prepared to allow that.'

There's silence. I wonder if my Annoying Distant Relative has lost her voice. Then there's a massive grunt and she starts again.

'Sex parties! It isn't a real job, a normal job. This *isn't* what normal people do. You should be doing everything to make her see sense. Lock her up if you need to,' she roars. 'I'm perfectly happy to help you. I'll stand guard if that's what you need. We've got to make her see sense.'

'Normal? I can't see Emma being content living in Normalville, working a nine-to-five office job for the rest of her life. There's nothing wrong with it, but Emma would find it incredibly suffocating. Who are we to judge if she says an emphatic no to keeping her life safe, simple and predictable?'

'But it's wrong; you shouldn't tolerate it. You should whip some sense into her if you have to.'

Mothership finally loses her patience. It's obvious that nothing she says will make any difference. 'The simple fact is that it's none of your damn business. I don't care what you think about my daughter, or me, because I've never been able to stand you or your nasty opinions. I have waited over 30 years to say this, but honestly, why don't you just … FUCK OFF!' She hangs up and re-joins us at the table. Colonel and I are smiling.

'More lamb, anyone?' she asks, as if nothing has happened.

'I'm done, Ma,' I say, laughing. 'But thanks.'

My mother smiles back. She knows I mean thank you for more than just the dinner. 'Oh, she's an awful old bag! Don't let her get under your skin. Now off you go and join your friends. They're probably all waiting for you.'

I turn up to Kouar Bar, a club in West London. It's one of my favourite playgrounds when I'm in the mood for a late night. Inside, there's an aura of decadence created by the red walls, dark leather sofas and seats and the low-level lighting that conjures up an intimate atmosphere. I spot Plaything and Miss D at once, sitting at our usual table in the corner and deep in flirtatious conversation. They've not exactly been an item since the first Killing Kittens party, when they got down to business in the Jacuzzi, but they're on very friendly terms, especially as they both love to attend as many KK parties as they can, sometimes amusing themselves together and sometimes not. Both of them are too much in love with playing the field to confine themselves to each other, even though there's no doubt they find one another attractive.

As I approach, I notice that Plaything has a supportive collar round his neck.

'Evening,' I say, sitting down and picking up the glass of champagne that's awaiting my arrival. I gulp it down in one go.

'Whoa, slow down, Emma. The night is yet young. You need to pace yourself,' says Plaything, watching me.

I signal to the waitress to bring us a bottle. I'm still in the process of obliterating the Annoying Distant Relative from my mind – although my mother's sparky defence of me has cheered me up. I'm sure now that she's on my side and all is forgiven. I give Plaything a sideways look. 'And you know all about pacing yourself, I suppose? What's with the neck brace? Have you been up to your usual tricks?'

Plaything grins. 'Well ...' He takes a sip of champagne, then reaches up to rub his neck, grimacing at the soreness beneath his fingers. 'I blame it entirely on you, Emma.'

'Me?'

'Yes, you. You're the one who bought me a box of glow-in-the-dark condoms.' He smiles cheekily, then takes a packet from his pocket and drops it on the table.

I raise my eyebrows. 'Gosh, Plaything. Heard of subtlety?'

'Want to see my glow stick, ladies?' he jokes.

'You're not in a fit state to look down long enough to get it out,' I retort. 'Now put them away, for goodness' sake. How did you stuff up your neck? I'm guessing some kind of awkward sexual manoeuvre?'

'You could say that.' Plaything's expression takes on a blissed-out quality at the memory. 'I pulled one hell of a fiery American girl last night. I was her English knight in shining armour, apparently. She was quite keen on bouncing on top of me while she grabbed my neck and buried my face in her tits. It was great, of course, but when she came she gave me a particularly violent tug and ...' He winced at the memory. 'I am as you see me now. It was bloody amazing, though.'

I laugh. 'That brace is going to be a bit of a hindrance tomorrow night, isn't it?'

'It'll be off by then,' he says confidently.

Miss D is running her eyes over Plaything's fine form. He's a modern-day Cary Grant: young, tall, dark and handsome. Our friendship blossomed when we were children and now Plaything lives in London and works as a body-pump instructor. His piercing blue eyes and lean, toned body have hypnotized hordes of women into bed. Luckily for me, I've always been immune to his charms and he's never tried to seduce me either. I think it's the secret of our long and happy friendship. Miss D, on the other hand, seems to be in the grip of her primal instincts – as usual. She's twirling her hair around her finger, wetting her glossy bee-stung lips and fluttering her eyelashes at Plaything. She slowly begins to stroke her champagne glass up and down with her index finger.

I frown at her. 'Stop flirting, D. Where's your self-control? Besides, can't you see he's injured?'

She laughs, a mischievous sparkle in her eyes. 'Sorry, I can't help myself. You know that sex is the very core of my existence, Ems.'

Plaything says, 'And she's only human, Emma.' He winks at Miss D.

'The sex party is tomorrow and you can do what you want then,' I say sternly. 'Let's keep it clean tonight, shall we?'

Just then, Trolley Dolly comes striding up to our table. She drops her bag on a chair and slips off her coat, revealing one of her immaculate business suits underneath. By the look of her no-nonsense expression, she's had a long, hard day. 'Hi, Emma. Sorry I'm late,' she says. 'Have you started?'

'The champagne's just arriving,' I say as she kisses my cheek. The waitress is bringing the bottle I ordered in an ice bucket. Trolley Dolly greets the others as the glasses are filled and we are left to enjoy it.

'Right, first things first.' Trolley Dolly sits down, lifts her glass of bubbling golden liquid. 'Here's to Emma and the first anniversary of Killing Kittens.'

'Thanks,' I say, smiling. I tap her glass with mine and take a sip. 'I can't believe my little business is already a year old. I started with one party and 40 members. Now I have a party every month and I have over 1,000 members. I'm going to be making enough profit on the membership and the parties to work at it full-time soon.'

Trolley Dolly goes on: 'And this is just the beginning, right? I think Emma could be on her way to world domination. After all, look how quickly two cats can become 80 million.'

'Can they?' asks Miss D. She always goes a little quiet when Trolley Dolly is about; she's in awe of the other woman's top-flight legal career plus a hunger for sex to rival her own.

'Oh yes. If you let two cats breed at will, and allow their offspring to breed at will, these two cats will become 80 million within a decade.'

'No way. Seriously?' Miss D looks stunned. 'That's a lot of cats!'

'Thank goodness for neutering,' I say drily, casting a look at Plaything.

'That's assuming two litters per year and 2.8 surviving kittens per litter,' Trolley Dolly adds matter-of-factly.

'Wow!' Miss D is all wide-eyed at the thought.

Trolley Dolly sips her champagne and turns to me. 'So, what's the plan for the upcoming year?' she asks.

'Killing Kittens is going to get bigger,' I reply. 'More members, more parties, added glamour and craziness. And I'm thinking of expanding into new areas too.'

'Oh?' Trolley Dolly looks interested. 'You mean like the French Letter Days?'

A few months ago I began to offer adult experiences on my website, which has grown from the initial one-page email catcher I started with. I was inspired by the Red Letter Days that meant people could buy things like a day's racing at Silverstone or a trip in a hot-air balloon, either as a gift or a personal indulgence. I decided I could give my Kittens the opportunity for marvellous experiences, like filming their own porn movie, or fulfilling fantasies of bondage or sex in a plane, or whatever. It's expensive and not always easy to arrange, but I love challenges and my French Letter Days add a bit of spice to life.

'Yeah – I definitely want to do more of those,' I say. 'And I want to expand the site. Perhaps offer merchandise.'

'Sounds great. Another step on the path to ruling the world!' Trolley Dolly smiles at me. 'Well, if you're taking requests, then I've got one for you. It's short notice, I know, but if you can manage it for tomorrow night, I'm in the mood for something exciting. I was thinking of a three-some, preferably with a married couple. And if the wife could be blonde and curvaceous, so much the better. Do you think you can do it?'

Miss D's eyes start glittering with excitement at the thought. She knows that even if she doesn't fit the bill for taking part, she'll probably be able to see at least some of the fun.

I think about it, running the latest membership lists through my mind. I know we've had some lusty couples join the club lately and I'm getting to know some of them a little better. 'Actually, I can. I have the perfect couple. They're new to KK and just back from holiday. Let's just say that despite being married for 10 years and having three young children, they're very well rehearsed in the Kama Sutra.'

Trolley Dolly laughs. 'Brilliant! Thanks, Emma. Just wait till you see the Victoria's Secret number I'll be wearing.' She turns to Plaything. 'Order another bottle, will you, darling? Let's get this celebration going.'

Chapter Six

'Though the sex to which I belong is considered
weak you will nevertheless find me a rock
that bends to no wind.'
Elizabeth I

I wake up late the day after our celebration of Killing Kittens' first birthday. I had a skinful of booze last night but feel fine: no apocalyptic headache, no anxiety, no problem. Thanks to forgetting to set my alarm, I've slept off any potential hangover. I have plenty of time to enjoy my snack-attack of sardines on toast and open the two Valentine cards that have arrived.

One is from Aidan in Australia and he's written:

Happy Valentine's, Em!
I miss you and I'm still waiting for you.
Love Aidan. P.S. There's a surprise coming your way.

I can't help feeling warm and fuzzy when I read it. Even though we've broken up and live on different sides of the world, we'll always share a special bond. The attraction between us has never faded, and I can't help wondering how things would be if he were living in London. Would we be together? Maybe even married? But his life is over there, and mine is here.

I tuck Aidan's card away and open the other one. It has a huge red heart on the front and it's been signed inside: *Mr B*. I stare at it, wondering why I don't feel any cupids flying round my head, or as though I'm soaring to the dizzy heights of love. It might be because his PA picked the card and probably even signed it too.

Stop it, Ems. You don't know that. Mr B has made a romantic gesture. And it's early days. Cut him some slack.

Tonight, there'll be romance in the air: champagne, oysters by candlelight, chocolates, sexy pillow talk and smoochy music – just not for me. I've laid on all this for tonight's Valentine's party. The fourteenth of February might be the festival of love, but I have the first anniversary of my business to celebrate with my Kittens, so love – and Mr Black – will just have to wait.

I jump into the shower and get ready for work. I fling on a slinky black mini-dress, opt for minimal make-up with just a hint of eyeliner and lip gloss, and moisturize my legs as they're on display tonight. I jump into a cab and head for the financial heart of London: the City. Heavy clouds cover the skyline and the journey is an arduous one: my driver is a snail and I try to calm myself as he catches every red light while his meter keeps on clicking away. I finally arrive an hour later, £50 poorer.

The venue for tonight's Killing Kittens' party is a funky retro-modern boutique hotel. I've booked four lavish pent-house suites at the excellent price of £1,000 for the whole evening. The owner is dating one of my members, so he's thrown in the bar downstairs for nothing, which means people can gather somewhere before the party gets going. I walk through the busy hotel lobby to the elevator and press the penthouse button. I ride to the top floor and when the door slides open, I find Kitty Kat waiting for me, looking stunning in a skin-tight red all-in-one PVC outfit and mask, and armed with a clipboard.

When I started the parties, I knew I would need help. I could do all the organization myself, but I needed security and someone on the door. At first I corralled friends and family into helping me. My sister even spent a few months as my door girl, on the firm condition that she stayed on the door and didn't venture into the humid depths of the Covent Garden sauna. I met Kitty Kat through a friend of mine and we hit it off right away. She was working as an actress and needed to supplement her wages, and she was organized and open-minded. It was a perfect match and she happily agreed to become my permanent part-time door girl, helping me run the monthly party. Now I can't imagine how I would cope without her.

'Good evening, Emma.' She hands over the clipboard with the names of those attending. 'I sent an email last night to the guests informing them of tonight's venue. We're expecting 100. My only concern is that there's no private elevator to the penthouse. I'll have to make sure we don't get hotel guests straying up here by mistake.'

I laugh as I scan the list of names Kitty Kat's given me. 'Can you imagine?'

'Don't worry. Everything's under control.' She flashes me a reassuring smile. I have nothing to worry about with Kitty Kat on the prowl.

Jupiter, my security, comes down the corridor towards me, greeting me with a breezy hello. He's a tough, burly guy, always immaculately suited and with an unexpectedly sweet smile and a cute sense of humour. He patrols my parties and makes sure that there's no trouble. The three of us make up the core of the Killing Kittens' family. 'Great place,' he says, nodding with approval. 'I'm going to keep nimble, with four suites to look after, but we'll be fine.'

'Great. Thanks, Joop.' I smile at him. He's open-minded, which is a must, but also completely level-headed. I've never seen him bat an eyelid at all the goings-on. He's also very sensitive to atmosphere, sensing when there might be a need to have a quiet word, calm someone down or escort them discreetly off the premises. 'Right. I'm going to do my check.'

Tonight, in honour of the occasion, I've renamed the suites Heart, Rose, Cupid and Lovebirds. Hearts will be beating fast tonight, and even some of my shy and retiring Kittens will turn into bold lovebirds, cooing at others to join them in bed once the action starts. We walk through the suites, inspecting the set up. Kitty Kat is spritzing the rooms with a scented spray and scattering rose petals over the coffee tables.

'It's lavender. It creates a sense of warmth,' she says with authority. 'And did you know that rose petals also represent confidentiality? In Ancient Rome, a wild rose was placed on the door of rooms where confidential matters were being discussed.'

'Very fitting for tonight,' I reply.

Kitty Kat's eyes sparkle behind her mask. 'Are you happy with the suites?'

'Absolutely. They're perfect.' All four rooms are smart and modern, with sitting rooms furnished with white sofas and chairs, glass tables and lamps. The beds are large and inviting, made up in crisp white linen. Each suite has a view of the glittering city skyline. Outside are private terraces so guests can go out if the atmosphere gets too steamy inside. One suite has a private hot tub on its terrace.

'It's great,' I say. 'And a bargain too, which makes me happy.' I check my watch. 'People should be arriving around now. I'll go down and see what's happening.'

Downstairs guests have already started turning up. The men are smartly dressed in suits and the women all look wonderful, most wearing cocktail dresses. Their masks are on and they are sipping champagne.

I clock Miss D at the bar in deep conversation with a man. She's wearing a red strapless dress designed to grab attention. I'd expect nothing less. But I have a feeling it won't be long before she's slinking upstairs to take it off.

I walk among the guests, greeting the ones I know, and then sit at the bar to soak up the flirtatious atmosphere. A pretty young woman comes up. She's wearing a red floral-print dress and seems full of confidence. Her handsome companion looks the total opposite: he is full of nerves and out of his depth. They take a seat next to me at the bar. She immediately gives him a glass of champagne, which he holds in shaking hands.

'Just drink it,' she says. 'It'll calm your nerves. You're acting like a virgin.'

'Nonsense,' he snaps, looking mildly flustered.

'No, it's not. You look like Dustin Hoffman in that film *The Graduate* when he goes to sleep with Mrs Robinson for the first time. Seriously, get a grip. I don't know why you joined KK if this is how you feel.'

He shoots her a look. 'You know why.'

She sighs. 'Listen, it was fun, but we're not getting back together. We're just friends now. That's why I find it slightly odd that you wanted to join. But as long as you're here, please try to man up, OK? And try not to be jealous.' She frowns. 'I'm just not sure this was a good idea. I mean, I'm used to this. You're not.'

'It's OK, I can handle it.' The man still looks nervous, though, and he takes a big gulp of his drink. 'It's just a bit weird, that's all. I'm going to need a bit of Dutch courage.'

I want to congratulate my new KK virgin, the Graduate, for making it to his first sex party and encourage him to relax and enjoy it, but just then he chokes on his champagne and I turn to see Trolley Dolly sauntering my way. She's got all eyes on her, as usual. She clearly meant business when she said she wanted to play with a married couple: she's wearing a blue lacy corset and a double-tiered ruffle skirt with a matching wedding veil and garter. No wonder he's a bit taken aback. He can't stop staring as she comes up to me and kisses me on each cheek.

'I do. I do. I do!' she says between kisses. 'I'm the Victoria's Secret sexy little bride tonight. So where are Mr and Mrs?' She scours the room for her playmates.

'Patience is a virtue, Trolley Dolly,' I reply, giggling.

'Oh, I'll wait all night if I have to. I'll keep my eyes open, but no doubt they'll find me in my bridal attire!'

'You won't be disappointed,' I promise.

'Neither will they, I can assure you,' she smiles. I realize that three beautiful young women are staring at her across the bar. Trolley Dolly is just irresistible to my members; she has amazing sexual charisma.

'I've got to go,' I say. 'I'll send Mr and Mrs your way when I see them. Have fun tonight.'

I leave Trolley Dolly in high spirits, the Graduate and his friend still staring, and head back to the lift. I ride up to the penthouse with a young woman in her early twenties who's wearing a black glittering eye mask, and her partner, who's sporting a flamboyant red Venetian one. Clutching her lover's hand, she turns to me and asks in a thick French accent: 'Have you been to one of these parties before?'

'Yes, many times,' I reply, smiling reassuringly. She seems more curious than frightened, though.

'Am I too young for this?'

'No. As long as you're over 18, you're fine. You'll find all ages here.'

She whispers, 'Do people really start having sex?'

'Yes, some do. But not everyone. It is really down to you.' The lift stops and the doors open. 'Just enjoy your evening,' I add as I step out.

I head to the Heart suite, where the party is already in full swing. It hasn't taken long for people to lose their inhibitions tonight. Perhaps it's the inviting beds with their stretch of white linen and room enough for plenty of people to play together. In one corner of the bed, a curvaceous naked woman is on her hands and knees. Her long blonde locks cascade over her back and her bottom looks very round in this position. She is fully exposed as she looks over her shoulder, smiling happily at her partner, who's still fully clothed and masked. She wiggles her hips to signal that she's ready for him to have his way with her, and he quickly unzips his trousers, too aroused to do more than free his huge erection. He pauses only to tear open a condom wrapper and slip the condom on before he slides his length into her. She begins to wail in ecstasy as he digs his hands into her waist and thrusts into her, starting slowly and then picking up speed until he is penetrating her hard and fast. They seem to be having a splendid time, and they're not the only ones. All around, couples are kissing and caressing, and on the bed there's a tangle of limbs and mouths and stroking hands.

A young Asian man is standing by the side of the bed watching five women in various stages of undress but all with their heels on, playing with each other. Next to him is a pretty brunette in red silk underwear who's passionately kissing another girl with a short peroxide-white haircut. His eyes are glazed and I can tell that he's trying hard to control his breathing, but it quickens as the brunette slides off her red silk knickers just inches from him and moves her legs slightly apart to reveal her swollen lips. She asks in a sweet voice if her girlfriend would like to kiss her somewhere else altogether and the peroxide pixie-cut girl wastes no time in diving downwards to start pleasuring her.

The young man looks fit to burst, but he can do nothing else other than watch.

She's naughty, I think, smiling inwardly. I know the pretty brunette is his girlfriend, as I rubberstamped their joint membership. She's loving Killing Kittens' golden rule: men must wait to be invited. Women make the rules and only they can break them. The more she moans as her female companion pleasures her, the more he desires her, and the greater his arousal. He can't keep his hands off her when she finally reaches for him, her smile promising sex as she undoes his belt and carefully lowers his zip, before pulling him onto the bed to join them both.

I'm glad to see that all's well so far.

I need some air.

I head to the Cupid suite, which has the largest terrace. It's chilly outside with a fierce wind buffeting the rooftop, but a couple in their forties are sitting outside in the Jacuzzi. They look blissfully happy, chatting and laughing. Through the glass doors of the suite, I spot the young

French lady sitting on a sofa in the suite, watching the mass of naked flesh on the bed. Apprehensive no longer, she's now relaxed and aroused, her hands touching her lover's body as he frees her breasts from their bra and fondles them lovingly.

I head along the terrace and go into the Rose suite, but turn around and head straight out when I spot Plaything with a woman in the Japanese bath having full-on sex.

I think I'll leave him to it. Glad to see the neck brace is off, though. I'm sure that adds to his pulling power.

I bump into Jupiter, who's been on patrol. 'How are things?'

'Fine. No trouble. It's the men I have to keep an eye on more than the girls, but they're all playing by the rules, even the new members. No need for any reminders yet. But you ought to talk to Kitty Kat.'

'Really?' I'm worried at once. 'Why?'

'It's Miss D, I think. Kitty Kat's near the lifts.'

Sighing, I make my way through the throng to the corridor where Kitty Kat is standing, still armed with her clipboard.

'Jupiter told me you're worried about Miss D,' I say, going up to her.

'Yes, I'm afraid so. She's acting a little erratically. And she's made more than one trip to the loo in the last 20 minutes.'

My heart sinks. I wish Miss D could learn to control herself. I also wish that she'd respect my friendship and my rules, but she seems incapable of it. If I weren't so fond of her, she'd drive me mad. What am I saying? She does drive me mad. 'Is it drugs?'

'I think so.'

'I can't believe she'd be so stupid. She knows how I feel about it, and what the consequences could be.' My fury starts to grow. 'Where is she now?'

'She's in the bathroom in the Lovebird suite, I think.'

I head there, marching along with my eyes blazing, Kitty Kat following on behind. When I get there the door is locked and I rap firmly on it.

'Miss D! Come out right now. If you don't open the door, Kitty Kat will break it down. I'm going to count to 10.'

A voice floats out from behind the door, its tone unconcerned. 'Ems, is that you?'

'You know it's me. Now open up!'

'Just checking. Better to be safe than sorry!'

'If you don't open up, you'll be *very* sorry!'

'Give me a sec, Ems,' she says, her voice wavering a little now. There's suddenly a lot of noise and activity going on inside: the loo flushes, the taps are on and I think I can hear the sound of fast and frantic snorting.

I narrow my eyes and say loudly, 'That's it. Your time is up. We're going to break the door right now.'

The door opens and Miss D peers round it, all wide-eyed and innocent. 'You want to speak to me?'

'Cut the Miss Innocent act. Exactly what have you been taking tonight?'

'Oh! Er … nothing.'

'What's with the straw you're carrying in your hand then?' I ask, grabbing it from her. She knows the game is up and looks sheepish. 'All right, Ems. I've had a bit of coke. I only brought a gram with me. It's no big deal.' She rolls her eyes as if to indicate that I'm making a big fuss out of nothing.

I'm really angry now. 'Well, it's a big deal to me. I'm afraid you have to leave.'

'Leave?' Miss D blinks at me, astonished. 'Come on, Ems. It's gone. I've just finished it all.'

'No,' I reply flatly. 'You know the rules. Anyone taking drugs is thrown out, no excuses, no exceptions. Kitty Kat, please escort Miss D out.' I can hardly look at her, I'm so cross. 'We'll speak when I've calmed down.'

'There's no need for the escort. I know where the door is.' She sighs as she looks wistfully over at the bed and then up at the mirrored ceiling where the reflection shows an athletic man doing some jackrabbit moves to a writhing, hip-bucking girl. Miss D knows her playing is over for the night. She heads for the door, Kitty Kat close behind to make sure she really vacates the building.

I watch her go, wondering what's going to happen to my old friend. She just doesn't have an off switch. She's dedicated her life to the pursuit of hedonistic enjoyment with the vague idea that she'll land a rich husband on the way, but I worry that she's going to get herself into serious trouble, or else one day wake up alone and in need of some kind of job. And the way she's going, her looks and sex appeal are not going to last forever. But I just don't know how to help D find her way when she's her own worst enemy.

I head back to the bar. My party is in full swing. There are only a dozen masked guests sipping champagne downstairs. I watch things unfolding and the atmosphere heating up as more and more people let go of their inhibitions and start to give in to the hedonistic vibe. They're here to sample delicious pleasures. Out in the real world, restaurants will be awash with couples who began their evening whispering sweet nothings but may now be running out of things to say to each other on what surely is the worst and busiest night to dine out. Right now, my Kittens have stopped with their whisperings and started peeling each other's clothes off. Out there, plenty of singletons will be crying into a bottle of wine alone or with their girlfriends, cursing men. Here, singletons are moaning and crying out with joy.

I don't have to worry about Trolley Dolly, who I spot huddled in a corner with Jupiter. He's introducing her to Mr and Mrs, the married couple I've earmarked for her, and she's very happy with my choice of playmates judging by the smile on her face. I can't blame her. Mrs is ripe blonde, her plunging hot-pink dress showing off large breasts and ample curves. She means business, rising from her chair and reaching for Trolley Dolly's hand. They get up together. They're going to find somewhere private or even head home together. Mr follows them into the elevator. He is one lucky husband.

Another satisfied customer!

Armed with a glass of champagne, I head back upstairs, where my guests are occupied with giving and receiving pleasure. No one seems to have noticed the drama earlier tonight with Miss D, and everything is proceeding well. I check out what's happening in the Cupid suite, where there's quite a crowd. Some are on the bed and others are watching the action unfold before them. The nervous guy in the bar is now centre stage, playing with two women and without any trace of his earlier reservations. He's in charge now, massaging and teasing his female companions' bodies into a state of panting desire before he slips on a condom and digs deep into one while pleasuring the other with his hand.

His ex-girlfriend from earlier in the evening walks in and stops dead when she sees him. I laugh inwardly. He doesn't need her now, judging by the power he's commanding in the room.

Another Kitten, lithe and pretty, standing nearby murmurs to her: 'Gosh, he's some shark, isn't he?'

His ex-girlfriend can't say a word, or take her eyes off the action. She stands there with her mouth open.

'I'm going to join Sharky,' declares the Kitten. 'The best way to learn is to play! I want to be there when he reaches his end,' she adds, her skirt slipping to the floor. Then she dives into the pile. The groans and screams become even louder as he continues to pleasure all three now while his ex watches in amazement, probably wondering what she's missing out on.

My eye is caught by a movement outside. I see that the couple are still in the Jacuzzi on the terrace. They've been there a long time. I hurry out to see if they're OK.

'Hi, guys,' I say chirpily as I reach them. 'You've been out here all night. I'm impressed, but aren't you cold?'

They smile up at me. The woman says, 'We would like to get out, actually.'

'Well, why don't you? There's nothing stopping you,' I say.

The man looks embarrassed. 'Yes, there is. We've haven't got any towels. We left them in the suite, and we are a bit too shy to walk about naked.'

'Shy? Even with all that going on?' I ask, gesturing at the action taking place behind the glass doors.

The woman nods. 'I know. It's silly. But it's our first time at a party like this and we just felt a bit awkward about it. It's so steamy in there. I thought we'd look a bit daft if we walked through naked and said, "Don't mind us, we just forgot the towels."'

'Wait right there!' I pop inside and come back out with towels and robes. 'Did you at least have some fun in the tub?' I ask, handing them over.

They take them gratefully. 'Oh yes,' says the woman, 'lots of fun, thanks.' She smiles fondly at her partner.

'Good. Well, you two have been very adventurous outside tonight. Maybe next time, try the bed,' I say, smiling.

Parties like mine take all kinds. But it's after 1 a.m. now and I'm ready to hand over the reins to Kitty Kat and Jupiter and call it a night.

As I leave, my phone beeps with a text. Mr Black always likes to suggest I visit him the same night I've organized a party. He knows I'll be primed for a little fun myself.

How about a little Valentine get-together? Come over now. I want to see you.

I gaze at the text. It's a little while since I've seen Mr Black and I'm feeling restless. I'm in the mood for him tonight. He may be wrong for me in some ways, but our bodies fit together very well indeed. It's not my style to trot along obediently when I'm summoned, but I don't think I can resist tonight.

I text back: *On my way.*

Chapter Seven

'Switzerland is a country where very few
things begin, but many things end.'
F. Scott Fitzgerald

I'm what you might call an enthusiastic participant in sex.
I like it, and when I do it, I like to do it wholeheartedly.
I've never been one for mentally writing a shopping list or
thinking about the housework while my man goes at it. Mr
Black and I have always enjoyed an active, involving and
ultimately very satisfying sex life, but tonight I'm not
getting there. I'm surprised to find that my mind is working overtime in a completely different direction. I can't
help wondering if this is a sign that I'm with the wrong
man.

Mr Black and I are kissing in his smart central-London
flat. His home is beautiful, with nothing out of place. The
place is lit by the soothing glow of expensive lamps, music
is playing and we're on his sofa getting down to some serious snogging.

I've been dating Mr B for nearly two months, ever since
Trolley Dolly introduced us at a dinner party. Work takes
him overseas a lot, which suits me fine. He is 51 years old to
my 28 and has never been married. He has a sophisticated
palate, great taste in clothes and, when he chooses, can be an

excellent conversationalist too. He's handsome, witty and urbane. He makes me laugh and likes to spoil me.

Mr B loves women and work. He's a high-flying American entrepreneur, born in New York but educated in England at Eton and then Oxford University, which he chose over Harvard. When his fingers are not all over me, they are stuck in many pies – land, property and the stock market, among others. Business aside, he's also good between the sheets, as he's done it plenty of times before, and he enjoys feeling challenged by a younger woman. He ticks all the boxes.

Why shouldn't he be my Prince Charming? And yet …

'You're gorgeous,' mutters Mr Black. 'Let's go to bed.'

'Not yet. Let's savour the moment. I know you've been waiting for this,' I whisper. I begin to kiss my lover on his neck again, knowing that each soft, moist kiss is sending powerful pulsations through his body. But for some reason I can't stop thinking about the golf lesson I had yesterday.

I wish this felt as right as I want it to. I'm about to have sex with my boyfriend. I ought to be far more into this than I feel right now.

That thought makes a wave of sadness flow through me, but I push it out of my mind. Immediately I imagine I'm back on the golf course.

'Keep focus,' says my golf teacher.

Mr Black is powerful, strong and reliable – qualities I find attractive. His money doesn't interest me – his masculine strength seduced me into bed. I like the fact that he's so much older than me, and secretly I'm convinced that I'm better off dating an older man, as the younger ones are immature. Men reach full maturity in their thirties, whereas women have ticked that box by the time they are 21.

There's my golf teacher again. *'Concentrate. Always look at the ball, Emma.'*

I slowly work my way down Mr Black's neck to his collar. *But is he really the right man for me? ... Oh God, I wish this voice in my head would shut up.* 'Clear your mind and commit,' *commands the instructor.*

'Oh, darling—' Mr Black's voice is low and insistent. 'I want you now.'

'Not yet. You'll have to wait.'

'Wait? Why do I have to wait?'

I don't answer and continue to shower him with kisses, undoing his shirt and gently exploring his tanned, beautiful body. He pulls me up and pushes his tongue into my mouth. This catches me off-guard but I respond to the kiss, massaging his tongue with mine. He wraps his arms around me and pulls me close. I slowly start to kiss him on the collarbone again, then move downwards over his hard, toned chest. It's smooth, with no trace of hair. I reach his right nipple and start caressing it with my mouth, sucking, licking and rolling it with my tongue.

When both of his nipples are well tended to and as stiff as tiny bullets, I move my kisses down to his stomach, putting my hand in his boxer shorts and gently stroking him. I pull my hair back into a ponytail before I launch into a full-on attack.

Now this feels good. I'm enjoying it. But here's my golf teacher again, his voice floating into my head: *'Keep your head down, your bum out and remember to keep your hands down on the club.'*

I fall to my knees, unbutton his trousers and unzip the fly. I pull his trousers down.

'*Keep a strong wrist but don't grip too tightly. On a scale of one to 10, the grip should be seven and firm on the shaft.*'

He's fully aroused as I start gently caressing his shaft with my hands and then, with a shower of gentle kisses, I take him in my mouth, just the first two inches, and start expertly rolling my hungry tongue around his bulging manhood, sucking softly, teasing and driving him crazy. I know that with each kiss, he is feeling different kinds of sensations. I'm working my magic on him, driving him into a frenzy of need as I tease with my lips and tongue. Then, when I know he can barely stand it a moment longer, I wrap my lips around him and engulf him completely. I can feel his presence in the back of my throat as I let him enjoy the warm tightness of my mouth.

I like this … I like him when he's at my mercy.

'*Always look at the ball, Emma!*'

'Oh, darling,' he says with a gasp.

But I do wish he wouldn't call me darling. '*Don't go too quickly. You don't want to kill the baby bird, Emma!*'

I hear his moans even over the loud classical music and I know he's savouring every moment. His hands are on the back of my head as I let his masculinity slide in and out of my mouth.

'Darling, you are such a naughty girl! And you're all mine. Oh my God, you're good at this.'

His voice changes to a grunt as he gazes down at me with admiring, wanting eyes, watching his shaft move between my lips. I begin to suck him faster and harder, holding his thighs with eager hands. His moans are animalistic as he thrusts himself into my mouth, his muscles flexed, his body shuddering.

'Oh God … Please, not yet. Let me have you now,' he hisses.

I acquiesce, taking my mouth from his iron-hard penis and standing up. I'm aroused by what I've been doing to him and the lust I've inspired in him. I'm ready to enjoy a little pleasure of my own in return.

He leads me to his Gothic-inspired four-poster mahogany bed. It's bold and majestic, carved with intricate patterns and with a silken roof detailed with cloverleaf cutouts. He quickly unzips my dress, letting it fall to the floor, and then pulls my lacy knickers down. I step out of them.

'Keep your sexy heels on,' he orders.

'He's going to go deep and put it in the hole!'

He lowers me onto the bed and nudges my thighs apart with his. Desire is etched on his face as he presses the tip of his manhood into me. I shudder as he pushes forward, entering me firmly, filling me up as he sinks deeper inside me. Our bodies are completely joined now. I feel positively villainous and aroused as I catch a glimpse of movement in the mirrors – one a full-length cheval glass tilted towards the bed, the other on the wall – both strategically placed to capture this moment. I'm tingling with excitement.

I buck my hips hard and fast against his. I can feel his hard, muscled back as he moves back and forth against me. I thump my hips hard into him, enjoying him inside me. My body shudders every time he slides in, out and back in, and out again. When he touches my magic spot, waves of pleasure meld into an intense solitary one that envelops my entire body. His manhood is swelling and hardening as he thrusts again, faster and harder. Mr Black's pleasure wave is starting to build up judging by the intensity all over his face. He looks a little scary, so I close my eyes. We are both close now. I can't take much more myself – I can tell I'm on the brink.

Our mouths are inches apart as we exchange moans. Our climaxes approach, each of us urged on by the other's growing desire, and then we reach the tipping point at the same time, exploding together.

Exhausted, he collapses on me. Our naked bodies are sticky and scented with sex.

'Darling, that was sensational,' he says.

'Mmm. It was.' I smile at him, feeling thoroughly tired out. I'm exhausted, I realize. Within a few moments, Mr Black and I have rolled apart and I'm sound asleep on the cool, crisp sheets.

When I wake up, it's early. Mr Black is not lying beside me but standing naked in the middle of the room, staring at the reflection of his body in the freestanding mirror. His eyes are scrutinizing every inch, an anxious expression in them.

'Darling, do you think I look old?' He turns to me with a beseeching look. He wants my approval, a validation from me that his body passes muster.

'No,' I say reassuringly as I stretch my legs. 'And good morning to you too.' I hope we're not going to start all this again. He's obsessed with how he looks and has a morbid fear of ageing. We regularly have to discuss it at length and no matter how much I tell him he looks great, he won't believe me.

Mr Black ignores my greeting and says anxiously, 'Are you sure?'

'Yes, of course I'm sure.'

'Do you think I'm handsome?'

'Yes. You most certainly are.'

'Oh, thank you, darling! But …' He won't be so easily satisfied, I know that. '… do you think I have wrinkles?'

'Wrinkles on men are attractive. They give you character.' I smile encouragingly.

'So you *are* saying that I have wrinkles! You think I look old.' He seems shocked, mortified, even angry.

'No, I'm not. You're twisting my words.' I roll my eyes in frustration. Mr Black would be a lot easier to be with if he weren't so paranoid.

I am spared having to prop up his ego further as we are interrupted by the ring of his mobile phone and the moment he picks it up, I'm instantly forgotten. His back is turned to me as he listens. I can tell it's a business call when he says coolly, 'I want to snap up that land.'

When the person on the other end replies, he says, 'No is not in my vocabulary.' Then, his voice becoming slightly menacing, he adds, 'Can't is not in my vocabulary either.'

As he does his tycoon act down the phone, I get up and start gathering my things together. I'll have a shower and head home. No doubt Mr Black will be on his way to work within half an hour. He won't have time for a leisurely morning in bed.

It didn't take me too long to figure out that Mr Black has never married because he's incapable of loving anyone but himself. When we're between the sheets, we've been having lots of fun, and I've excused Mr B's vanity and narcissism, as I suspect the insecurity bug is biting him. Although he's sharing his body and his bed with me, I am still someone relatively new in his life. He is exceptionally sensitive to the fact of his advancing age. In a quest to get his youth back, he runs eight miles daily and 15 at weekends. He does vigorous weight-training sessions with his personal trainer and has facial treatments to guarantee his skin's longevity. Sushi is his favourite food. He could gorge on it for breakfast, lunch and dinner. He has made it his mission to sample his beloved sushi everywhere he travels in an attempt to find the best sushi in the world. According to Mr Black, Japan, the birthplace of sushi, is still the best. New York is second, with sushi restaurants springing up around most blocks in the Big Apple. London is third – solely because of the restaurants Nobu and Zuma. The portions may be on the small side, but the taste, he tells me every time he takes me, is 'really something special, Emma'.

So is he my Prince Charming or not? The problem is that in fairy tales Prince Charming has good looks and money and not much else. I need wit, charm and brains or the deal is off. Mr Black has those, but can I take the relentless self-obsession?

I stand up and stretch my limbs. Mr Black's bedroom is a warm, masculine space. He likes dark colours. All his furnishings match the mahogany bed, even his walk-in wardrobe. The gleaming hardwood floors sparkle as brightly as his mirrors. But there are no family photographs. That part of his life remains a mystery.

Mr Black is still talking into his telephone. 'Gold aside, good old-fashioned land is the best investment. Stocks disappoint. Currencies go to war. Food prices go through the roof. America has got a lot of land and I want a piece of it. Ted Turner is gobbling it all up, but he can afford to share some of the action. Do you know how much Ted owns? ... Well, let me tell you. He's got land in Montana, South Dakota, Nebraska, Kansas and a hunting reserve in Florida. We are talking two million acres of land. And all I'm asking you to do is to secure a fucking apartment block in Manhattan.' His tone is menacing as he says, 'Just make sure you snap it up for me at the auction. Goodbye.'

He hangs up and turns his attention back to me. 'Hello again, darling.' His eyes are twinkling now, all trace of his anger gone. 'I see you're getting up. I want to whisk you back into bed and keep you there.'

Mr Black has a remarkable ability to change his mood with lightning speed. From menacing to charming, within seconds.

'Oh, by the way, I've got a surprise for you,' he says, smiling.

'Really?' I ask.

'Yes,' he replies, looking very proud of himself. 'What are your plans for this weekend?'

'Nothing much.' The month's party is done and dusted. I have some freelance work to do for some of the clients who keep me on retainer, but other than that, my time is my own for a while. Unless you count all the organization I'm doing for the Sisterhood, marshalling more than a dozen girls and trying to coordinate timetables and training slots. I've been emailing like a mad thing for the last week.

Mr Black smiles happily. 'Fantastic! As your work kept us apart on Valentine's day itself, my PA has arranged something special for us.'

I say nothing. Mr Black's work takes him all over the world all the time and he never feels the need to apologize to me for it, so I'm not about to start grovelling to him. Besides, he likes to needle away at me on the subject of Killing Kittens. He's always pestering me to take him to a Killing Kittens' party, where he's convinced we'll have a threesome. I always refuse, no matter how often he tries to wear me down. He doesn't seem to realize that I don't take part; it's business for me, not pleasure. So my tactic is never to respond when he mentions my parties.

'I want you to meet me this afternoon. We'll fly to Switzerland and stay at my chalet for the whole weekend.

We'll have a very romantic time – dinner, skiing, saunas. You'll love it.'

'How wonderful,' I reply, surprised. It does indeed sound rather special. At moments like this, when Mr Black is sweet, thoughtful and romantic – even if it has involved a little help from his PA – I think there's hope for us. I remember why I liked him in the first place. 'What time should I be at the airport?'

'Don't fret, darling. My driver will collect you from your house. Just pack some things and be ready for four o'clock.' He comes over and kisses me. 'In a few hours, we'll be making love in front of an open fire.'

Mr Black is as good as his word. His driver collects me on time and by late afternoon I'm at the airport. After a comfortable flight and another car journey, I find myself cosily ensconced in a beautiful Swiss chalet. Mr Black feeds the roaring fire with logs, while I lie on the Persian rug and sip red wine, relaxed after a bout of vigorous lovemaking in front of the flames.

'I could watch the fire all night,' I say, watching it flicker and dance.

'Could you really?' He looks surprised.

'Yes. Have you ever noticed that everyone tends to stare at the fire when the TV is switched off?'

'I can't say I have.'

'Watching fire is far more relaxing than watching TV.' I smile at him. 'It inspires intimate conversation.'

'Does it?' he says doubtfully. He leans over and pours me some more wine, smiling. 'OK then. So ... do you like my chalet?'

'I love it,' I say honestly. He gave me the grand tour when

we arrived, and I have to admit this place is impressive. It's full of beautiful furniture, objets d'art, indulgent hand-embroidered linen and Hermès toiletries. As in his London home, there are no family photographs. There is every imaginable creature comfort: attentive staff who know when to make themselves scarce; an outdoor hot tub; a sauna; a cinema room with comfortable sofas and state-of-the-art surround sound. He even has a treatment room complete with massage table. If it were mine, I'd be slipping off to Switzerland for a bit of après-ski all the time.

'It's wonderful to share it with you, Emma,' he purrs. He reaches out a hand and strokes my leg. 'You're a fabulous girl.'

'Thank you,' I say, smiling. 'You're being very sweet to me. I appreciate it.'

'Nothing but the best for a woman like you,' he replies. 'Now, how about we get dressed and go out for some dinner? I know a wonderful place—'

He's interrupted by the sound of his mobile ringing from the side table where he left it before we got down to business. I'm surprised he can get a signal up here in the mountains. He goes over, picks it up and when he sees the number on the screen, he suddenly becomes fidgety. 'Oh,' he says, frowning. 'Um ...'

'Are you OK?' I ask.

'Darling, do you mind if I go to my office and take this call? It's a big business deal I'm working on. I won't be long. Promise.'

'Of course,' I reply. Mr Black is almost surgically attached to his BlackBerry. He can't be separated from it, often taking it to bed. I'm used to business calls intruding on life's most intimate moments.

'You go up and get ready. We'll go out as soon as I've finished,' he says, trying to look casual and cheery as he slips the still-ringing phone into his pocket and heads for the door.

'All right,' I say. A luxurious bath with some of the Hermès bubbles sounds very appealing.

I go up to the master bedroom, which is draped with fur throws and offers the most beautiful views over the mountains from its floor-to-ceiling windows. I run a bath while I wait for Mr Black to finish his call. He's on the phone for almost an hour, but I don't mind. I love the hot scented water on my skin and the luxurious feeling of well-being that only comes after a good bout of satisfying sex. I think I'm going to enjoy myself this weekend, and revel in being looked after and indulged, even if it's only for a little while. Maybe this is what Mr Black and I need to get back on track.

My positive attitude towards Mr B takes a battering during dinner at a nearby restaurant when he says idly, 'You should think about having babies, Emma. You'll make a good brood mare.'

I gape at him in astonishment, hardly believing what I've just heard. 'What?'

'You heard me. You should give up this ridiculous business of yours – it's just a fantasy and you know it. Have some babies. That's why you've been put on the planet.'

I can't quite believe what I've just heard. 'Watch this space. Killing Kittens will be a huge success,' I reply calmly, hiding my annoyance at his assumption that my sole purpose in life is to breed. 'You'll be surprised, I guarantee it.' I smile angelically at him. 'And as far as babies are concerned, once I find a suitable stallion, I may use his sperm. It's just I've got terribly high standards. In the meantime I'll continue practising.'

He laughs, leans over the table and kisses me. 'I like you, Emma. You make me laugh. You're a smart cookie, aren't you? Whenever I toss a ball at you, you smash it right back.'

'Yes, I do. Dare I remind you of your frequent requests to come along to my parties?' I add mischievously.

'Oh darling,' he snorts. 'That's an ace you've just served me.'

'Indeed. Game, set and match.'

'I met a young woman a while back who used to go to your parties.'

'Really? What's her name?'

'I can't remember. She's seeing a friend of a friend of mine and has given up your parties because of him.' His BlackBerry beeps from where it sits on the table between us and he eyes it warily. 'I'd better read that.'

'Sure.' I take out my own phone and check it while he's busy with his. I've missed three calls from Miss D, but I have plenty of grovelling 'I'm sorry' texts to make up for it. I'm going to let her stew for a bit before I forgive her. I'm really cross with her this time and I have to be sure she's not going to use narcotics at one of my parties again. Just then, my phone rings. It's an unknown number. Mr Black is still absorbed so I answer it. 'Hello?'

'Hi – Emma?' It's a familiar voice, but I can't quite place it. An old friend? A work mate from the old PR days?

'Yes.'

'It's Kate here. I'm calling about the Sisterhood. I want to take part, if you'll have me.'

Kate? I'm blank for a moment and then it floods in. *Kate Middleton. My old mucker from our school days at Downe House.*

She's recently split up from Prince William. No doubt she wants to distract herself with a new challenge. 'Of course! Let's talk ...'

While Mr Black carries on texting and emailing, I have a chat with Kate. She wants to be part of the first all-woman crew to cross the Channel in a traditional Chinese dragon boat in the race against the Brotherhood. I tell her I am delighted to have her on board, but can't help being concerned that the minute the press find out it will become a Kate Middleton and Killing Kittens' story. I ask her to seek advice from Clarence House. She assures me it's fine and that she wants to get involved. It's a good cause and she's keen to contribute.

By the time Mr Black is ready to return to our meal, my chat is over. I keep the identity of my caller to myself.

Out on the slopes the next day, Mr Black is not amused when I bomb down the hill and beat him. His mood deteriorates even further when he overhears our young, handsome ski instructor ask if Mr Black is my father.

'No!' I giggle. 'I'm using him for sex – he has a massive penis.'

As soon as we're out of the instructor's earshot, Mr Black turns to me and says furiously, 'Emma! Really!'

'Sorry – should I not have mentioned your penis?'

'It's not that! You should have said I'm too young to be your father!'

I roll my eyes. Some men are never satisfied.

*   *   *

I'm home the following evening after a whirlwind 48 hours of skiing, sex and luxury. It was great fun, but I had the feeling all the time that Mr Black was somehow absent. I don't feel I know him any better than I did before. Perhaps it was because he spent so much of his time shut away on business calls. As a result, I'm still no wiser about where this relationship is going.

I've only been back five minutes when there's a knock on my front door. A delivery man is standing on the doorstep with an extravagant bouquet of the finest lilies with long ivory trumpets and dark furry tongues of orange pollen. Mr Black has timed it to perfection. I feel my BlackBerry vibrating in my coat and fish it out. *Oh, he's good!*

I answer the phone, saying in a teasing voice, 'Is this Prince Charming?'

'Do you like the flowers?' he asks in a business-like tone. 'Yes or no?' He's obviously not in a romantic mood. It makes the flowers and the call seem a bit of a hollow gesture.

'Yes, I like them.'

'I remembered your favourite, see? I asked for them specially.'

I look at the flowers. 'You did? How sweet! What are they?'

'Huh?'

'My favourite flowers. What are they?'

He says nothing.

'I told you over dinner. Remember?'

'Er …'

'They're roses.'

'Yeah. Of course. Roses.'

'That's right. But these are lilies.'

He snorts something.

'What?'

'My fucking PA fucked up.'

'Charming! So nice to know you chose them yourself,' I coo.

'No one has time to order their own flowers, Emma, you know that.'

I feel terribly sad all of a sudden. Aidan bought me flowers, choosing them himself, knowing what I liked and going to special efforts to make sure he got them for me. Mr Black makes the right gestures, but somehow the heart isn't there.

'I know,' I say. 'It doesn't matter. Thanks anyway.'

We say our goodbyes and I hang up. I look at the beautiful bunch of flowers, but they mean nothing to me now. On impulse, I take them next door and give them to the astonished woman who lives there, telling her they've arrived by mistake and I don't want them. I'm glad that they brighten her day.

Somehow they've made mine darker.

Chapter Eight

'Common sense is not so common.'
Voltaire

'Hello, Wonder Woman.'

'Hello,' I answer. I recognize the timid, tremulous voice. He usually calls at the worst times, when I'm with Ma or Pa, and once when I was in church attending a friend's wedding. Today I'm standing in a ridiculously long queue in Sainsbury's. A heavily pregnant woman and her small daughter are in front of me. The woman grins awkwardly as her daughter gives me a big 'Hello' and begins to show me every item in their shopping basket.

'I don't have much time.' His voice is becoming a whisper. 'I'm about to chair a board meeting.'

'I see,' I reply. The little girl is offering me one of her liquorice sticks.

'I want to be kidnapped.'

'When?' I ask. I smile at the girl and accept her generous offer with a whispered 'Thank you!'

'Today. Six o'clock. I want Batman to kidnap me. Marilyn Monroe will save me and then fuck me, with extras. Marilyn must be all Hollywood.'

'All Hollywood?' I ask. 'You mean, accent?'

'No! I am talking hair. Not upstairs – downstairs hair. She must be clean for my lips.' His breathing is becoming heavier.

I look at my watch. Six o'clock is less than three hours away and I have no car. 'It's very short notice.'

'But you're Wonder Woman. You can do anything.'

'OK.' I boast that I can fulfil any fantasy, anywhere, at any time. So now I'll have to prove it. 'Where?'

'Outside the Pistol Panties shop.'

'Where's that?'

'Westbourne Park Road. Notting Hill.'

'OK.'

'Make sure Batman has a pistol too,' he quips, then he hangs up.

'I want to be just like *you* when I grow up!' says the little girl, eyes like saucers, looking back at me with a wave while her mother leads her out of the supermarket.

Since I added French Letter Days to the Killing Kittens repertoire, making people's fantasies come true has become a big part of my business. More and more young men and women are willing to dig deep into their pockets to turn their dreams into realities. Normal life is simply not enough for them and they see no shame in paying for thrills and excitement. Using models, actors and escorts, I often conduct fake kidnappings, muggings and sex with superheroes. Each and every model, actor and escort I use is not just doing it for the money. They're doing it because they get a kick out of it too. They're part of my exclusive fantasy-kidnapping club. They all love the naughty games and sex with strangers, fulfilling their own secret desires at the same time as the client's. It turns out a lot of people want to spice up their lives with a little bit of danger and fantasy. And why not?

*   *   *

It's 5.30 p.m. and Miss D and I are outside Pistol Panties warning Japanese tourists and two pensioners that a fake kidnapping is about to happen. Armed with cameras and smartphones, the Japanese tourists ask if they can take photographs and immediately start snapping away, even though it's only Miss D and me so far. The flashes make me feel dazed. Meanwhile, Miss D is trying to explain things to the pensioners. After a lot of penitent promises that she won't bring drugs to my parties again, Miss D is back in my good books, although I'm not sure I expect her good behaviour to last indefinitely.

'Kidnap!' gasps the old lady. 'Did you hear that, George?'

'Shall I call the police?' asks the man, his eyes full of concern.

'It's not a real kidnap.' Miss D smiles reassuringly. 'No need to call anyone. None of us want to be getting into trouble with the police now, do we?'

'Why would George get in trouble?' the old lady asks, clutching his arm. 'He's done nothing wrong!'

'We'd all be wasting police time. The kidnap is a fake kidnap.'

'Fake kidnap?'

'Yes, fake. It's not real. So please don't worry.'

'Oh,' replies the little old lady, finally understanding. 'So is this some stunt TV show you're doing?'

'Yes!' Miss D replies enthusiastically. 'I'm quite a famous TV presenter. It's all perfectly safe, but it may be a good idea for you to cross the road. We don't want you to get caught up in it.'

The old man looks about, his initial panic being replaced by confusion. 'But where are the TV cameras if it's for a show? And where's your microphone?'

'Good question, George!' Miss D replies flirtatiously. She touches his shoulder and gives him a flutter of her best come-to-bed eyes. 'I have no need for a mic,' she says, licking her lips. 'My mouth is big enough. You can watch me in action and judge for yourself if you like.'

'Watch?' He looks uncomfortable, perhaps even afraid of Miss D.

Oh no. This could end in disaster. His wife does not look happy.

I roll my eyes, take Miss D's hand off George's shoulder and smile at the couple. 'We're using a tiny secret camera so as not to cause a fuss and get in the way,' I state matter-of-factly. 'I do apologize for the work-experience girl. By watching, she meant if you'd like to watch, it would be best if you sit down over there.' I point to a bench across the road.

'Ah. How kind of you.' The old lady smiles at me, but she's got a dagger stare aimed at Miss D. 'But I think George and I have heard quite enough – you don't want me to cause an emergency.'

'You might cause an emergency?' I stare at her, concerned she could have a heart attack at any moment.

'The ambulance will be for your friend, my dear, if I have to stand and watch her gawp at my husband for another second. Hands off! Now come on, George, let's go.'

I can't help smiling as she walks off with her husband, their arms linked. I have a sudden vision of Colonel and Mothership in years to come, out together like this elderly couple, perhaps looking in a shop window at baby clothes for their future grandchildren. It's a comforting image. I wonder who I'll be with when it's my turn. I can't imagine Mr Black as my life partner somehow.

'Aren't they so cute?' says Miss D, watching them go.

'You really are something else!' I roll my eyes again.

'Are you rolling your eyes at me?'

'I sure am. He was at least 80 years old. Is no man safe in your company?'

Miss D grins. 'I was only playing, Ems!'

'I'd tell Batman to throw you into a dungeon, but it would probably turn you on, so on balance I'd better not. I don't want to make matters worse.'

'I'm happy to oblige, Ems. You can throw me in with Mr Kidnap. I can't believe you've never introduced me. Is he handsome?' she asks, back on the prowl again. She's always looking for her next catch.

'You'll have to wait and see.' Teasing Miss D is the best way to punish her. She can't stand delayed gratification; she's all about now.

'Is he rich?' Her curiosity is piqued.

'All will be revealed shortly. Just be patient.' We head over to our car. Usually I hire a van, but with so little time to plan, the Batmobile is Ma's Golf. I've also had to lean on a friend to play Batman: Plaything. A fitness and *Batman* fanatic, he's always volunteered his services, and given the short notice, I've decided to give him a trial run. He's sitting in the back dressed in a two-tone grey jumpsuit with a black-and-yellow Batman logo printed on the chest. I have several Batman costumes in different sizes – it turns out he's a popular fantasy. One of these days I want to get the full outfit in shiny black rubber. Until then, this will have to do.

'Right, guys,' I say in all seriousness as I open the door and climb in. Miss D gets into the passenger seat beside me. 'We've got to make this feel real for my client, or I will be fucking pissed off.'

'Just call me Batman from now on,' says Plaything in a deep voice and a strong American accent.

'Put your mask and cape on, Batman. Today you're a baddie – but repeat after me: thou shall not kill.'

'I shall not kill. Not today!' he replies with a wry smile.

'Miss D, I want you to put on a vaguely German/Eastern-European accent. You're Batman's vicious sidekick.'

The other two giggle. It would be nice to laugh with them, but my business head is on and I'm in the full swing of it. Mr Kidnap pays me well for these fantasies and it's important that they work for him.

'What does my victim look like?' asks Batman, gazing out of the car window and looking up and down the street.

'I'll point him out when I see him.' I glance in the rear-view mirror. Lots of people are heading home from work, but there's no sign of him yet. Then suddenly I spot him. He's an average-looking man with a penchant for thrills, adrenalin and a little element of fear. Mr Kidnap is the only client who always insists on his superhero abducting him. It's either Marilyn Monroe or Anna Nicole Smith who save him.

I say loudly, 'I see him, guys!'

I'm nervous, I realize. My heart starts to race. I want this to go well and there's so much potential to fuck up.

'Which one?' asks Plaything, his head swivelling round. He seems a bit nervous now, despite the superhero suit. He starts to pull on the mask.

'The short bloke in the pinstripe suit.'

'Holy fuck!' Miss D says, disappointed. 'He's got good taste in suits, but damn, I'd have to rule out wearing heels. He is single, right, Ems?'

'Beauty is in the eye of beholder, D. But yes, he's single and happily so, and pretty rich too.'

This news is music to Miss D's ears and she instantly cheers up. 'My primary goal when it comes to love is to help my significant other be better than he was when I found him. I can save the lonely duckling. Watch me work my magic on him.'

I flick a warning glance at her. 'Zip it, D. We're here to kidnap him, not plan your love life. Batman, when you get out there, throw the sheet over him and just chuck him over your shoulders. Leave the car door open when you get out so it'll be easier for you to get back in. I want lots of shouting and swearing when we're on the move. OK? Right – let's go!'

Plaything opens the door and leaps out. Apart from the camera-laden Japanese tourists who start oohing and ahhing and snapping away when Batman emerges from the car, no one else bats an eyelid. They're world-weary Londoners used to craziness on the city streets. They don't want to get involved and instead walk past like Batman is not even there.

Mr Kidnap has been acting very casual up till now, but when he spots Batman sprinting towards him, wings flapping, huffing and growling, he looks a bag of nerves.

'Batman, you're my favourite superhero, because you're the only one who's not a real superhero. You have no powers!' he gulps, trying to keep his voice strong.

'Shut the fuck up! I'll show you power,' growls Batman.

A sudden panic sweeps across Mr Kidnap's face when, in one swoop, Batman throws a white sheet over him and hoists him over his shoulder. He's kicking and screaming.

It's going well. Plaything's doing a brilliant job. I start the engine. Miss D is totally hooked, her eyes wide and her mouth open.

'*Holy shit!*' she squeals excitedly. 'This feels so real.'

'Get a grip, D. This is what he's paying me for! Remember, fireworks when he's thrown in the car.'

The next moment, Batman hurls Mr Kidnap into the back seat, climbs in beside him and we're off. Mr Kidnap begins to scream like a baby under his white sheet and starts scrabbling about. In the rear-view mirror I can see Batman tighten the sheet around his head.

'Don't fucking move, you prick!' he says menacingly. Plaything's Batman voice is impressive.

Mr Kidnap carries on scrabbling. Batman slaps him hard across the thighs. 'I. Said. Don't. Fucking. Move. Prick,' he repeats calmly.

'But I should be wearing a seatbelt! It's illegal not to,' Mr Kidnap says, his voice high and shaking.

Batman takes his head and jams it into his lap, just in case the police are lurking and spot the commotion taking place in the back of my car.

Miss D speaks in a Russian-style accent, her voice now authoritative and sexy as hell. 'You bad boy! Shut up and listen to Batman. Otherwise you will be in even bigger trouble!'

'Yes, boss!' he whispers from his bent-over position. 'Where are you taking me – Gotham City?'

'Shit city.' Batman's menacing tone sends shivers even down my spine. 'Now shut the fuck up or I will *kill* you.'

There's a little whimper from Mr Kidnap.

'No!' Miss D snaps back. 'Put your pistol away, Batman. The boss said no. Driver, keep your eyes on the road.'

Right on, guys. I'm pleased. Everyone's playing their part beautifully.

I slam my foot on the accelerator and weave the car through the rush-hour traffic. I cannot be late as the owner of the boutique hotel is waiting for us at the back entrance so we don't alarm any of his guests. I slam on the brakes when I reach the back entrance. The owner is standing outside looking bemused as Batman climbs out of the car, drags Mr Kidnap out from behind him, throws him over his shoulder and rushes into the hotel.

Miss D and I climb out and follow him.

The owner hands me the room key. 'Penthouse suite at the top.'

'Thanks!' I take the room key he's holding out as we hurry past. 'Can I leave the car there for a bit? Won't be long!'

We ride the lift to the penthouse suite, Mr Kidnap wriggling and squeaking under his sheet until Batman orders him to be quiet. He's hustled along the corridor and into the room, where his sheet is removed and Miss D orders him to strip and put on a pair of tiny leather black underpants. When he's done that, Batman ties him to the four-poster bed.

'Sexy!' growls Miss D, eyeing Mr Kidnap's prone body. 'Can I have him, right here, right now, Batman?'

'No!' Batman barks. 'The boss said we're not to touch him!'

Mr Kidnap asks for water and they let him sip from a glass before throwing the rest on his stomach. Miss D is relishing her role as torturer, dropping a few ice cubes on his stomach and watching him groan and writhe. She's in fine form.

'Shall we shoot off his big toe? We could sell it for witchcraft.' Miss D cackles with evil laughter.

'No, please!' cries Mr Kidnap. He's cold, wet and looks terrified, but I can tell by the muscular movements in his pants that he's finding it all very sexy. 'Oh Marilyn, Marilyn, where are you?'

'Marilyn?' growls Batman. 'Who the hell are you talking about?'

'The sexiest woman in the world – Marilyn Monroe!'

'Shut the fuck up!' snarls Batman. 'Marilyn Monroe is dead, you fucking idiot. She died in 1962.'

I make a cross face at Batman. Marilyn is not dead! That's not part of the scenario.

'Or did she?' improvises Batman. 'She'd better not be alive, or I'll be furious.'

I stifle a giggle. This is getting ridiculous. I just hope my Marilyn is waiting for her cue. She didn't mind the last-minute booking, but she still had to get ready for it. She ought to be here by now. I glance anxiously at the door.

'Give me your finger,' demands Miss D.

'No! No! No!' he squeals, but she grabs his thumb and gives it a bite, just hard enough to make him squirm.

'Ah!' he screams. 'You wait, Marilyn is very much alive and she'll rescue me!' He goes on in this vein while Batman and Miss D enjoy themselves, inflicting some low-level torture on him. I check the time. Where are you, Marilyn? I don't know how long we can string this out.

Suddenly the doors fly open and Marilyn is standing there, wearing her iconic white dress and high heels. She's got platinum-blonde hair and red lips and looks astonishingly like the real thing. All hell breaks loose. There are screams from Miss D as Marilyn flounces into the suite shouting, 'Pow! Pow! Pow!' and 'Take that!' as she tussles with Batman. After a few frantic moments, the kidnappers vanish into thin air, leaving me to watch Marilyn uncut Mr Kidnap's ties. He's overwhelmed with gratitude and love.

'There, there,' she says breathily. 'You're safe now. Were those kidnappers very unkind to you?'

She sweeps her tanned arms around him. Suddenly, he bursts into sobs like some abandoned child and clings to Marilyn's ample breasts. They stare deeply into each other's eyes. Then, slowly, Marilyn stands up, unzips her dress and steps out of it to reveal some lacy underwear: love is born.

'You asked for extras,' she says, smiling. I hand her a basket containing a vibrator, lubricant, a butt plug, hand-cuffs, a collar and nipple clamps.

'Yes, yes, yes, I did.' He's breathless with excitement. His squeals of terror will, I predict, shortly be squeals of delight.

'Ssh! You must love, honour and obey me,' says Marilyn, flashing her biggest Hollywood smile. Mr Kidnap stares in excitement as Marilyn grinds her hips and runs her fingers across her breasts, taking the journey down to her exposed private regions.

'Mmmm,' she moans teasingly. She kneels down next to him and begins to squeeze, pull and twist his nipples. She then puts on the nipple clamps, only to take them off and back on again. Marilyn is taking great pleasure in torturing his nipples, driving him wild. His pants look like they're about to burst. She bites his lobes and whispers into his ear, 'What must you do?'

'I must love, honour and obey you.'

'That's right. I've got something to remind you that I am your mistress and you are *mine*.'

'I love you, Marilyn.'

'It's a bondage collar. You have to submit to everything I say. You are my slave. No moaning, just obeying,' she says coolly. Marilyn puts the collar tightly around his neck, attaches the leash and pushes him on his back. She pins his arms over his head. Click go the cuffs around his wrists.

'Now you're going to eat me,' she purrs, and she prepares to slip off her lacy knickers.

It's time I took my leave. I tiptoe to the door and slip out, closing it behind me. In the downstairs bar I find Miss D and Plaything, now out of his Batman costume. The bartender is serving them Mojitos and they order another one when they spot me.

'Holy shit!' says Miss D, grinning broadly. 'That was awesome, Ems.'

Plaything is amused. 'And spill with the rest, Miss D.'

She looks sheepish. 'I've slipped a note into Mr Kidnap's wallet with my telephone number.'

'We don't call you piranha woman for nothing,' I reply. I take a long sip of my drink. My phone rings and I take it out. I don't recognize the number. 'Hello?'

'Hello, it's Mr Black's assistant here. Mr Black is taking you out for dinner tonight. Nobu at nine o'clock.'

I look at my watch. It's 7.15 p.m. I reply through gritted teeth: 'Tell Mr Black that if he wants to go out for dinner with me, he can pick up his phone and call me himself.'

'I'm afraid I couldn't possibly say that,' the PA says, sounding flustered. 'He would bite my head off! He's a busy man.'

'In that case, I suggest you send an email and explain that I'm not speaking to his PA to organize a date. Bye.'

I hang up. Miss D and Plaything congratulate me for speaking my mind. I've got no wish to be rude to his assistant, but Mr Black has to understand that there are ways you just don't treat a girl.

'The problem is, I'm losing my patience with Mr Black,' I say, feeling exasperated. 'I am dating a narcissist who is madly in love – with himself. All he cares about is his own feelings and he has zero empathy when it comes to dealing with others.'

'So are you going out with him tonight?' asks Miss D.

'Nope, he knows my terms.' I can be pretty stubborn when I want to be. There's no way I'll be invited out to dinner by someone's assistant.

'You know you're risking him ending it?' Miss D stares at me. If she had a pet millionaire, she'd do anything to keep him happy, but I'm not like that. I need to have the feeling. As I gaze at her, I suspect that I will never have the feeling for Mr Black. Any man who is a long-term prospect has to make me feel at least what I felt for Aidan, or there's no point.

'Is your heart really in this, Ems?' Plaything asks.

'I'm not sure. It's fun, we're dating – I guess it's not a great deal more than that.' I remember some of the good times I've had with Mr Black, and how sweet and charming he can be when he wants to be. He likes to spoil me, he's great in bed and he's got that all-important older-man thing going on too. 'Maybe I'll give it a bit longer.'

'You're treating him mean. He's bound to be keen!' Miss D says and takes another drink. 'Do you think Marilyn is finished yet?'

'Does Batman need to rescue *her*?' Plaything says hopefully.

I laugh. 'You wish! Come on, let's finish up and get out of here before they come back down.'

Chapter Nine

'Why are women ... so much more interesting
to men than men are to women?'
Virginia Woolf

All women need time-out from men occasionally. I choose
to spend my day off with my girls. Our waitress never needs
to take our orders for a full English breakfast as we've been
coming here for years. We've gone through all our heart-
aches in our local cosy little café. We always try to make
time for each other, even when life gets in the way. None of
us want to get lost on that monotonous hamster wheel,
mindlessly running but going nowhere, with life simply
revolving around the man in your life.

'Can I have another full English with two slices of butter
and toast?' I ask the waitress.

Trolley Dolly fires me a suspicious look. 'I know we're
forgetting about calorie counting and indulging ourselves
today, but haven't you had enough? Or are you *pregnant?*'

Miss D gapes at me in shock. 'You're having a baby! Mr
Black's baby!'

'Goodness gracious. No. *Never!*' I laugh. 'He did tell me
that I should give up my business and have a few babies.
Apparently, I'd make a great brood mare and that is why
I've been put on this planet.'

'Are you serious?' Trolley Dolly stares at me in horror. 'I'd choose a sperm bank any day over a male chauvinist.'

'Me too,' I giggle.

'I told him you were a good catch when I made the intro-duction. You're a keeper. But maybe it's time to throw him back into the water. There's plenty of fish in the sea, after all.'

'I'm using him for sex.'

'Good,' Trolley Dolly says.

'But the best thing about him is his bank balance,' D says matter-of-factly.

'Zip it,' barks Trolley Dolly.

'Why?' D asks, her eyes wide with hurt.

'Chill, D,' I say. 'We all understand each other around this table and that is why we are not worried about telling each other to zip it when one of us is talking rubbish.'

'Yes,' Trolley Dolly says drily. 'We love you, but money doesn't talk. So zip it.'

A waitress delivers a plate of bacon, eggs, sausage, beans and hash browns to our table when Mrs waltzes through the doors in her gym kit, looking all flustered.

Trolley Dolly looks happy with my big breakfast surprise. Her expression takes on a blissed-out quality at the memory of her threesome with Mrs and her husband at my Valentine's party.

'Hi,' Trolley Dolly gushes. 'What a wonderful surprise. So the full English is for you! It's nice to have you with us outside in the real world.'

'It's nice to be here,' Mrs says, tucking into her fry-up. 'I need to be with the girls and well away from home right now. I go to sex parties, have the Big O every time I go to the gym, including this morning, but that's nothing compared to what happened last night.'

'You have an orgasm when you go to the gym?' D asks, open-mouthed.

'Yes. Three times this morning: on the ball, doing the plank swipes and leg stretches – they all delivered whopping Big Os.'

'Amazing.' Miss D is wide-eyed at the thought.

'Coregasms, they call it. My hero Alfred Kinsey cracked that in 1953 and was crucified for it. You lucky girl!' Trolley Dolly sighs. Her eyes are glittering with excitement at the thought. 'But what happened last night?'

'My husband and I were having a duvet night on the sofa with our children.'

'Sounds very cosy,' I say.

Mrs takes a sip of my frothy cappuccino before she goes on. 'The first film was fine. The second was a disaster. My kids accidentally put on a porn film we made.'

'Oh no,' I say.

'Oh yes! I've got no hang-ups about my sexuality, but I don't know how to handle this one. I had to get out of the house this morning and let hubby deal with why his hands were in Mummy's bits.'

'I think we should go across to the wine bar and order a bottle as soon as it opens,' I say.

'I'm up for that,' Mrs says. She manages a smile when two mutual girlfriends, and KK regulars, turn up. 'I hope you don't mind us joining, ladies,' they chorus. 'Her hubby told us she could do with some girl time.'

'Of course not.' I know them both well. Emerald Isle joined KK after her university friends bought her membership for her twenty-first birthday, although her rules of engagement differ from those of most Kittens. A Catholic, she's only ever had sex once, when she was 18, and has no desire to repeat the experience until she finds 'the one'. Despite her ravishing good looks, she's not swayed by the many compliments thrown her way about the purity of her skin, the rich abundance of her long black hair or the mysteries of those alluring green eyes. She could lead any man or woman astray but for her, playing involves simply watching or hanging out with me at the bar. Her tall, curvaceous friend, Pearl, is a different story. She is a dedicated Kitten who always joins in with enthusiasm.

'So good to see you, Ems,' Pearl says as she kisses me on both cheeks. 'It's been a while.'

'Good to see you.' I smile at her. 'Where have you been hiding?'

She sighs a little ruefully. 'I've had to stop going to sex parties.'

'Really?' I ask, surprised.

'My new boyfriend doesn't approve!'

'Ah, I see.' Single Kittens often stop coming if they get into a relationship with a guy who doesn't share their predilection for my parties. They often pop up again a few months later. 'That's a shame – you'll be missed. Who's the lucky guy?'

She smiles happily. 'He's great. Handsome, sexy and very rich. I'm going to try to be faithful now we're exclusive.'

'As long as you're happy.'

'I am. He says I'm the one. But I am not happy about how much time he spends at work. I've barely seen him.'

'I know that feeling,' I reply. I might as well be single myself considering how often I see my boyfriend.

'I had a right go at him last Saturday. He had to go to Switzerland on business and it was hard to get hold of him most of the time. He even had to sneak out of a business meeting to talk to me.'

I frown, remembering Mr B's odd revelation over dinner about a woman who stopped going to my parties as she had begun dating a friend of his. My stomach lurches. Surely he's not playing me? 'Switzerland? Last Saturday? That's weird. It wasn't Davos by any chance, was it?'

'Yeah, that's right. He has a chalet there. He's going to take me. He says we can make love in front of the fire.' She smiles at me. 'That sounds romantic, doesn't it? And when he got back from his business weekend, he sent me a huge bunch of roses to make up for being away. I actually prefer lilies, but apparently his PA fucked up.'

I say slowly, 'Your boyfriend isn't ... Mr Black, is he?'

As soon as I say it, I know it's true. Even though I can hardly believe it, it explains everything: the scurrying to the office, being glued to his phone over our trip, the wrong flowers. He's been two-timing me with this woman. The Kitten looks surprised. 'Yes, it's Mr Black. How do you know?'

'The fucking two-faced cheating prick!' barks Miss D, who's been listening in, fury growing on her face.

'He's dead meat,' I snarl.

Trolley Dolly says, 'Wait, ladies! This is not looking good, but we need facts first before we strap him into the electric chair.'

'I know it's true,' I say. Anger is boiling up inside me. I've been cheated on. I look at the Kitten. 'I am afraid that we've both been played.'

'What?' Her face crumbles and she stares at me in horror.

Miss Emerald Isle's shoulders slump. 'I just don't trust

men. They spread diseases, get women pregnant and cheat. That's what makes a man!'

'Don't be so ridiculous!' Miss D says, rolling her eyes. 'You need a damn good shag!'

'Enough!' I'm incandescent with rage.

'How long have you been dating?' asks Trolley Dolly, beginning her cross-examination.

'Six weeks,' Pearl gulps.

'How did you meet?'

'He chased me.'

'He chased you. When and how?'

'I was out having dinner with friends. He sent a bottle of bubbly over to our table with a note saying that I was a real darling.'

'When did you start sleeping with him?'

'A couple of weeks later.'

'Where?'

'At his place.'

I don't need to hear another word. 'D, settle the bill. We're heading across the road. I've got an idea.'

The five of us cross the road and head into the wine bar. I take out my mobile and call Mr Black. He answers and I click on the speakerphone.

'Hello, darling,' he says.

'Hi!' I say in a cooing tone.

'It's so lovely to hear your voice. I've missed you.'

'How sweet.'

'Shall I send my driver to come and pick you up? I'd love to see you.'

His other girlfriend narrows her eyes, anger sparking there. She was stunned a few minutes ago. Now his arrogant selfishness is enraging her.

I grin, putting my finger to my lips to remind her to keep quiet. 'Why don't you come join me at my sex party tonight?'

'Really?' he says excitedly. 'Oh darling, I knew you'd come to your senses. Does this mean you're on for a threesome?'

'There will be a lot of threesomes going on!' I declare. Beside me, Mrs and Trolley Dolly are stifling giggles and egging me on.

'Oh darling, I'm there with you. I can't wait to share this with you – you'll always be my number one, though. Always. What's the address?'

He's walked into my trap. 'I have a beautiful woman who'll join us. Her name is Pearl. She's wearing a pearl thong.'

'How could I possibly say no to that?' he purrs.

I'm ready to pull the trigger. 'And here's a funny thing, she tells me you've been in her too.'

'What?' He sounds innocent, but I know it's just a trick.

'Let me put it bluntly to you: you've been fucking her. So why don't we all get together right now before you take her to Switzerland?'

There's a deathly silence.

'You fucking bastard!' Pearl's voice is hoarse and emotional. 'You stopped me going to the sex parties because you wanted to go yourself with Emma.'

I cannot contain my anger. 'Don't ever fucking call me again. And the same goes for your PA. Fuck off!' I hang up.

'Job well done, Emma!' Trolley Dolly says. 'I wished I'd never introduced you to him.'

'He's a fucking prick!' I say vehemently.

We all look at each other and my anger turns to amusement at the crazy situation. Trolley Dolly orders a bottle of wine and we start to laugh at the fact that my boyfriend is a two-timing bastard.

My life is mad.

And I guess I'm a single woman again now.

Chapter Ten

'Mostly it is loss which teaches us about
the worth of things.'
Arthur Schopenhauer

I wake late the next afternoon to my phone ringing and I pick it up blearily, not even looking at the incoming number. I didn't get home until the very early hours and now I'm in a state of sleepy confusion, half expecting it to be Mr Black on the end of the line, either furious or begging me to take him back.

'Hello,' I sigh.

'Emma, it's Pa.' Colonel's voice is barely a whisper. He sounds nervous.

'Hi. Are you all right? You sound funny. Do you have a cold?' I yawn widely as I start to come out of my dozy state.

'No, it's not that.' His voice still sounds weird.

'Is something wrong?' I ask.

'Yes. It's Ma.'

'What about her? Is she OK?' My heart is racing. There's a long pause that only makes me feel worse. At last he says: 'She's not sick. But you'd better go and see her right now. She needs your support.'

'I don't understand. What's wrong? Tell me!'

'Just go to her.'

* * *

My heart is pumping when I arrive with my sister and brother at our family home in Buckinghamshire. I called them as soon as Pa hung up after he refused to elaborate any further. I called Ma too, but she didn't answer the phone, which only served to heighten my anxiety. Georgie and Jonny agreed to come as soon as they heard the worry in my voice, and I picked them up along the way before we all sped down the motorway together, fearful of what we might find.

I knock on the door, not wanting to use my keys unless there's no answer. I don't need them: Ma opens the door. I stare at her, frightened. My usually soignée, elegant mother looks haggard and broken. The pained look on her face causes a big knot of fear to build in my stomach. All I can think is that Ma has been diagnosed with a terminal illness.

I hug her, the others waiting their turn to embrace her. They both have frightened expressions; I can tell we're all thinking the same thing. 'What's wrong?' I ask her, releasing her to Georgie's hug.

'Are you OK, Ma?' asks Jonny anxiously.

Mothership stares at us with deadened eyes and then says in a flat voice, 'It's Pa.'

I'm astonished. 'What, is *he* sick?'

'Yes, he's sick in the head. Pa has left me.'

There's a shocked silence. All thoughts of Mr Black's infidelity pale in comparison. 'What?' is all I can say.

'Are you joking?' asks Georgie, disbelief all over her face. I can tell that she's thinking the same as I am. Colonel has left Mothership? It can't be possible. They're an unbreakable partnership, the rock of our lives. It can't be true, can it? But my mother's awful expression of hopeless pain tells us that it is.

'He's met someone else,' she says in the same dreadful tone, and I feel a shudder of horror pass over me.

'No!' I cry.

Ma turns and walks into the drawing room and we follow her. She picks up a full glass of Pinot Noir that's waiting for her there and takes a big gulp. I see now that her eyes are swollen and reddened and that she's trying not to cry as we all sit down with her, trying not to look at the family photographs placed all around the room.

I take her hand. 'Ma.' I want to tell her that we love her, but I can hardly speak. I'm still trying to take it in.

'How did it happen?' asks Georgie, sinking down on the sofa next to my mother. 'Did you have any idea?'

Jonny seems too anguished to speak and is instead standing silently by the fireplace, his hands balled into fists and stuffed in his pockets.

Mothership shakes her head. 'Not a clue,' she says, her voice weighed down with sadness. 'He asked me to the pub for a late lunch. He said he had something to tell me. I thought he was going to say that he'd gone bankrupt, or been to a brothel – something like that, something we could have dealt with together.' Her hands are shaking, her lips trembling. 'But it wasn't that. As soon as I walked into the pub, I could see by his face that it was something much worse than that.'

'Go on, Ma, tell us. Tell us *everything*.' I head to the drinks cabinet, find the biggest glasses there and start pouring wine. I hand the glasses around.

'He told me he was having an affair. She's in her thirties, Polish and a massage therapist. I asked your pa if he loved her. He said yes.'

My head is spinning. I am struggling to compose myself. 'Pa doesn't even like massages,' I mutter, confused. An avalanche of pain is beginning to hit me. The ground no longer feels solid. Instead, it is giving way beneath my feet and I feel as though I'm in a horrible, stomach-churning fall. I clutch at what seems like the best outcome. 'It may just be a silly fling. Pa is having some kind of midlife crisis. He's 60 years old!'

'That might have something to do with it, but you'd better believe he's deadly serious. It's all been going on for some time and he's determined to start a new life with her. It's not just a romantic thing either. Your pa told me she's his soul mate. And he's going to make her his business partner.'

We all gasp. This is terrible. This is more than just an old man getting infatuated with a younger woman. He obviously means to destroy his old life entirely. I can hardly take it in. I'm so used to this being home, to Colonel and Mothership being like one – or at least, two sides of the same coin. I need them both to balance out my life and give me a sense of security and a firm foundation. Is that all really about to end, just like that?

'What did you say?' whispers Georgie, her eyes full of tears.

'I thanked him for telling me, stood up and walked out of the pub.'

'This is madness. It can't be true!' I gaze at her, confused, shaking my head.

Ma's face is taut with sadness. 'I'm afraid it is true. After 30 years of marriage, raising a family, supporting my husband's career and keeping a comfortable home for him, I've been dumped for a younger model.'

It's almost more than I can stand. Georgie bursts into tears, while Jonny goes to stare out of the window. I clasp my mother's hand and feel helpless to comfort her as she stands in the wreckage of her life.

Ten-star hangover.

The sunlight is peeking through the window, so morning must be well advanced. I don't know where I am until I realize that I'm in my old bedroom at home and everything comes back to me in a rush. How we drank wine and talked until late in the night, discussing my father and the awful blow he has dealt us all. I can't even remember rolling into bed, but here I am.

I half crack open my eyes, wanting to get out of bed but feeling like I have morphed overnight into the fat version of Rosemary, star of the Hollywood film *Shallow Hal*. The extra weight is pinning me down, holding me back. I can't move at all. It feels like I've been here an eternity, marinating in a stew of toxins, as I finally fully open my eyes to my stonking hangover. Red wine always does this to me, which is why I hardly ever drink it. Not by the bucket load, anyway. But I guess the knowledge that your family life has been destroyed can warp your judgement. I drank myself into total oblivion last night.

My legs feel like lead as I eventually manage to manoeuvre myself out of bed, catching sight of my reflection in the mirror. My eyeliner is smudged and my hair looks worse than a bird's nest. I sigh as I try, but fail, to run my hands through it. Then it hits me again and I shudder.

My father has walked out on my mother for a woman young enough to be my sister!

Tears prick my eyes; the last time I felt this type of betrayal was just days earlier with Mr B. Now my rose-tinted glasses have been ripped off me again and it turns out

my larger-than-life father, previously the fount of all knowledge and wisdom, doesn't have a big plan after all. He's no
hero, just human and a cheating *liar*. I want to call him, ask
him why, but I can't; I'm too hurt. My words would run
wild.

Silence is golden, Ems!

I stumble like a zombie downstairs, dying of thirst. If I
don't get some fluids down me, this hangover is the one that
could kill me. The others are in the kitchen, Georgie sitting
at the table looking as fresh as a daisy. She is perfectly put
together in an effortless way – her long brown hair tumbling
down her back, her complexion pretty much flawless. But I
can see that she's angry. Ma is on the phone ordering a skip.
I get myself a large glass of water and gulp it back with
some painkillers. I need my brain back to get through today,
of all days.

'I'd like the skip as soon as possible,' Ma says, her voice
cold.

I crash on the couch next to Jonny and rest my head on
his shoulders. My brother is tall and powerfully built with
blond hair, a strong jawline and deep-blue eyes like mine.
We get them from our mother. He squeezes my hand and
embraces me. I bury myself in his chest and, for a fleeting
moment, feel safe.

'All right. First thing tomorrow,' Ma says. 'I'll be ready.'
From the look on her face, I can tell that Mothership has
decided to use her anger and devastation to stop herself
going to pieces. Instead, she'll become stronger and braver.
I'm lost in admiration for her spirit. Twenty hours ago, her
life was safe and secure. Now she's betrayed and alone, but
she's not going to let it break her. Mothership puts the
phone down and gazes at me appraisingly, taking in my

dishevelled state. 'You look dreadful, Emma. Let me make you some scrambled eggs.'

'I'm fine,' I lie, although actually scrambled eggs are exactly what I need.

'You don't look it,' she says gently. 'Has Georgie told you the latest?'

'No.'

'I'll let her tell you.' She makes her way to the fridge and takes out the eggs, milk and butter. Her back is turned as she starts cracking eggs on the rim of a mixing bowl. I suspect she's shedding a tear.

'Ma has been on the phone to the bank,' Georgie says softly.

'Go on.' The knot in my stomach is back.

She pauses and looks at me. 'There's hardly any money left in their joint account.'

I gasp. I didn't think this could get much worse. 'How much is in the account?'

'There's just £1,000 left.'

I'm horrified. 'What? How ... *How?*'

'It looks like Pa has blown a fortune on that woman: clothes, hair, dinners ... Fortnum's, Harrods, Harvey Nicks. Ma got them to read out the last few statements. It's all there. Thousands have been spent.'

'No. I don't believe this!' I take a deep breath. Georgie looks ashen. Jonny looks like he's ready to wage war. He's clenching his fists to the point that his knuckles are turning red.

Georgie goes on, 'He's even set her up with a flat of her own and bought her everything ...'

'I don't fucking believe this!' My body is shaking with rage. 'I hope you've frozen the account. He's a silly fool. He'll only go and blow every last penny on the floozy.'

Ma has the scrambled eggs ready for me. She beckons me to the table to eat, dashing a tear from her face. 'I did it first thing this morning. It had *never* crossed my mind to check up on him. That's not what loving someone is about.' She closes her eyes as if trying to contain her pain. When she opens them, she says dully, 'It all makes perfect sense now. Pa has been going to London most weekends for work. I told him last weekend I'd had enough of his seven-day weeks. I never got to see him. Your pa said to me, "I haven't got time to talk to you now. Maybe we can do supper?" It was a strange thing for a husband to say to his wife.'

I pick at my eggs. I feel sick. Colonel is not only leaving Ma, his family, but also the whole deal: friendship, trust, companionship, deep love, everything. A life.

I wish I could understand it. But I can't.

They say all is fair in love and war. They also say hell hath no fury like a woman scorned. In my opinion, hell also hath no fury like a father's children scorned. We begin to get things ready for the skip's arrival. Jonny finds Pa's digital camera, full of cheesy photographs of the two lovebirds holding hands and kissing all over London. I feel sick as I look at it. This was no young love affair filled with passion and promise. Pa looks ridiculous and floozy ordinary, which makes us feel just slightly better. I look at her face with a mixture of revulsion and horror, wondering how she can walk in and break up a family like this, but then I look away. I don't want to see her; it's too painful.

But our feelings pale into insignificance compared to what Ma feels at Pa's betrayal. We whirl around the house, picking up his possessions and tossing them into bin bags. We collect all the things that have irritated us for years;

anything tacky, from lumpy old family heirlooms to annoying light fittings. We smash things to smithereens. A Buddha statue he bought us at a market during his travels is the first to be split in two and then chucked into a bin bag, followed by a grotesque glass bowl his Annoying Distant Relative bought us. Good riddance.

Ma is throwing one shoe from every pair he owns into a bin liner. She's in overdrive, trying to sort out herself and her life, while mourning her loss and trying to come to terms with the facts as she now knows them.

Hurt and anger cross her face depending on her feelings, and she walks about venting them loudly. 'I feel so bloody stupid! It's like I have "expired" stamped across my forehead. I gave him my best years, my youth! And now he thinks I'm past it. It's unbelievable.'

'He's the fucking idiot!' Jonny shouts. He's laden with a pile of Pa's boxer shorts, which he's cramming into a bag.

'We didn't have a dead marriage, which is why his leaving is such a shock.' Her brow furrows again with confusion. 'We had a love life.'

Jonny looks uncomfortable as he glances at Pa's boxers, then at Mothership. 'Do I have to hear this?'

'Let her get it off her chest, Jonny,' Georgie urges.

Ma goes on as if Jonny hasn't spoken. 'I don't doubt your pa loved me once, but in some ways, I was a trophy. When I met him, I was the catch. He was a quiet academic at the start of an army career. I was a boisterous, headstrong, tall, leggy blonde. He was very proud of me; he showed me off. He used to say: "I'd like you to say this to that person, and if this person asks you x, then you answer y. If the ambassador asks where you'd like to go next, charm him with this answer."'

'He's a fool!' shouts Georgie, going red in the face with a fresh wave of anger. She's pulling a bag of stuff towards the back door.

'I think where it started to go wrong was when I got a good job after years of waiting to settle in England. I went from a "wife of" to *me*, which must have been threatening for him.'

As she hurls one of his favourite brown loafers towards the back door, I'm chilled to the bone to see Mothership tossing more than 30 years of marriage away. I'm suddenly determined that we won't let her lie down and take this. We can't leave her alone with her sadness. I can't abandon her to the silent emptiness of a dying family home.

I go and take her hand. 'Ma, I want you to come and stay with me for a while.'

She shakes her head slowly. 'No, Emma. That's a lovely idea but, really, I'll be OK. You don't have to look after me. You have your own life to lead.'

'It can just be for a little while. You can come back home whenever you want. Please, Ma. I insist.' I give her the determined look she's known since my childhood, the one that says I'm going to get my own way.

'I think it's a good idea, Ma,' pipes up Georgie. 'And Jonny and I are close by too – we can pop in and see you.'

'Go on,' Jonny urges her. 'Let's show the old bastard a united front. We'll all drive back to London after we're done with the skip tomorrow. He'll know he's going to have to take us all on.'

Ma's lips start trembling. I can tell she's moved by our show of loyalty. Her eyes well up and she says in a shaky voice, 'Maybe it's not such a bad idea.'

'That's decided then,' I say firmly. 'You need to pack some

things. And the first thing we are doing when we get to London is buying you something you would never, ever buy for yourself from the £1,000. Something FU.'

'FU?'

'Fuck you. Every time you have a wobbly moment, you wear the FU – be it a dress, lingerie, shoes, whatever it is you choose. It'll inspire confidence in you.'

I don't think she's convinced, but at least she's not going to be left here on her own. It looks like I've got a new flatmate.

After dropping Jonny off home the next morning, my Jaeger-MaxMara-Gucci-scarf-wearing Ma totters into LK Bennett with her girls and buys a pair of pink FU shoes. According to Pa, pink doesn't suit Ma – it makes her look slutty. Her style has always been conservative, simple – nothing flashy or overly fashionable – but we think she looks fantastic in them.

'Wow,' says Georgie, smiling. 'They are FU, Ma!'

Mothership smiles too, but it doesn't last long, and as she gazes at her reflection in the pink platform stilettos, she bites her bottom lip again, having a wobbly moment.

'If your Pa was here, he'd probably say I have enough shoes to last for the rest of my life.' She looks pained again.

'But he's not here,' I say soothingly. 'Fuck him. FU shoes *will* get you through the wobbles – even when you are having a really shit day. Keep them on.'

She regards them thoughtfully. 'They do make me feel feminine, younger, more confident.'

'Good. My point exactly. Then we're taking them. Get out that credit card, Ma. It's time a little of that money came your way instead of to Dad's mistress.'

Ma says unhappily, 'I suppose I'll have to face him again at some point.' She looks at me miserably. 'I just don't know how I'm going to manage it.'

'Don't worry about that now,' I say stoutly, squeezing her arm. 'For now, we're both young, free and single and we're going to have some fun.'

My phone rings several times that week and the name displayed is my father's. I don't answer. Instead, I press end to shut off his attempt to communicate with me. I don't think I could speak without crying, anyway. I'm too angry and churned up and appalled at what's happened to speak to him. I glance back at my phone when it starts ringing again. It's Pa. My mind drifts back to when I was five. I took my wheelie case everywhere, ready to leave whenever Colonel or Mothership annoyed me. Many times, I told Colonel to stop the car, because I was bored. He always smiled at Mothership before opening the door and warning me it was a long road ahead. He was right. I always changed my mind, pleading: 'Wait for me, Colonel! Come back, please!' Colonel was still smiling when I clambered back into the car with my case. A tiny smile tugs at my lips at the memory, but all that is gone now.

Instead, I work at supporting my broken mother. I hate to see her looking so unhappy and so defeated. I want her to realize how much life she has to live, and what her newfound freedom can mean to her.

One evening I bring home a pair of trainers and an iPod with a playlist crammed with Dolly Parton being sassy and up-and-at-'em music.

'What are these for?' my mother asks, looking at them, bemused.

'For you, of course. Once you get moving, you'll feel loads better. Imagine you're pounding over his face while you're running. Sing, scream, cry – do what you like, just run it all out.'

She looks doubtful. 'I don't think I can.'

'Of course you can. I'm going down to the river to train tomorrow. You can come too, and run along the bank while we're rowing.'

'Of course.' She perks up for a moment. 'The Sisterhood challenge, I'd forgotten about it. How's it going?'

'Really well. Lots of corporate types are interested in sponsoring us. I've got well over 50 grand already in sponsorship alone, before the girls have raised anything privately.'

'Emma, that's amazing!' She jumps up and hugs me. 'You're inspiring me not to sit around moping. You're right, I will go out for a run tomorrow. I'm sure it will make me feel better and I'd love to see the girls in action.'

'Kate Middleton's joining us,' I say casually.

'Is she?' My mother looks surprised, then knowing. She nods. 'The broken heart thing.'

'Yeah, I guess so. Nothing like a bit of physical exertion to help take your mind off the grimness of being dumped.'

Mothership takes my hand. 'How about you, Emma? You haven't told me about any boyfriends lately.'

I shrug and give her a wan smile. 'Not much going on there at the moment.'

'I don't understand,' she says softly. 'You're a beautiful, clever girl. I know I'm your mother and I'm biased, but you are. I wish you could find someone who truly values you.'

'You and me both.' I think of Mr Black and his shoddy two-timing ways.

'Have you heard from Aidan recently?'

I give her a look. Ma always liked Aidan. I know she wishes he hadn't moved to Australia. 'No, not for a while.'

'Ah.' She doesn't say anything else.

'Single women of the world unite!' I say heartily. 'So you'll come to the river tomorrow?'

'You bet. I'm looking forward to it.'

Chapter Eleven

'You are not meant for crawling, so don't. You have
wings. Learn to use them and fly.'

Rumi

It's a glorious spring morning. The banks of the River
Thames look beautiful as the sun's rays peek through the
trees that are just coming into leaf. From my vantage point
in the rear of the dragon boat, I can see people walking
their dogs on the riverbank, or jogging along it for their
early-morning exercise. In front of me are the backs of my
18-strong crew, working hard to keep their oars in sync as
we paddle vigorously down the river. We sit in pairs in the
long, shallow boat, and our short-handled paddles hit the
water according to the pace set by the stroke pair in the
front. We need a minimum of 50 strokes a minute, preferably more, to reach anything like a decent speed. It's
tough: very soon the repetitive movement of paddling
starts to make the muscles sing and then burn with the
effort. I'm breathless with the exertion, gulping in lung-
fuls of the morning air as we strive to get our paddles
moving in perfect harmony, training ourselves to endure
long hours of this hard work. When we cross the Channel,
we could be going continuously for up to seven hours or
more, depending on how the crossing goes. The last record
was set by an all-male crew, who crossed in seven hours and

45 minutes, but I hope we'll be over in a lot less than that. I know our rivals, the Brotherhood, intend to smash that record by a considerable margin, so we need to train very hard indeed to be in with a hope of beating them over to France.

Behind me, standing at the helm and guiding our craft through the tranquil waters of the Thames is Kate Middleton. In the era of the 24-hour all-consuming media, we've miraculously managed to keep it a secret that one of the world's most photographed women has been training hard with us three times a week for the past three weeks. Kate was very down when she first joined, but our clandestine morning training sessions quickly became her therapy. Once she stepped onto the dragon boat, she left her stresses behind, like we all did. She told us that she'd always put William first and the race was a chance to do something for herself, during a delicate time. She felt safe in our company and she flourished with us, enjoying the liberation of training in peace and quiet, away from the world's prying eyes. My coach and I were so impressed with her commitment and enthusiasm that I decided to share the helm with her.

This morning, she's doing a great job of negotiating the currents of the Thames, but the Channel will be a much greater challenge. For one thing, there's the considerable danger of shipping and the strong wash that comes in the wake of large vessels. The skipper will need a cool head and a calm heart to avoid our being capsized and to know when to pick up the pace or let it drop.

Kate fits perfectly into the crew, some of whom are her old friends. We're all fit, confident women in search of challenges that can help us do some good in the world, and we are fiercely protective of each other.

We paddle on, training hard, the rhythmic breeze through the trees helping us pick up pace on these tranquil waters. But our peace and quiet doesn't last long.

I don't spot them at first, but they are there. One breaks cover, and then the next, and suddenly they're everywhere. Some are on bridges as we pass underneath. Others are on bicycles and scooters, keeping pace with us as we glide through the water. Some are lurking in the undergrowth and a few have trespassed onto the private property of the boat club. They all have long lenses and are interested in just one thing.

'Kate!'

'Kate, over here, Kate!'

'Look this way, Kate! Kate!'

My heart sinks. Our secret's out. The world's paparazzi, with the dedication of stalkers, have finally caught up with us. Despite our furtiveness, we all knew, deep down, this day would come and that it was only a matter of time before they eventually tracked Kate down. But now they've found us, the flashing and clicking takes us completely by surprise. The quiet riverbank suddenly has a Wild West feel to it, as the photographers race along it, trying to get a picture of their prey, knocking startled bystanders out of their way with abandon as they pursue their shot. It's horrible and disturbing. Even the water fowl are affected by it: the ducks begin honking and quacking, and I spot a distressed swan in the distance twisting its long neck, squawking and flapping its wings, unsure of how to fight off this pack of intruders. Two men, one with a giant lens, sprint alongside us. One is shouting: 'Come on, you fucker! Give us the shot!'

'Fuck me!' I pant. 'This is a nightmare! The gorillas have found us. Try to ignore them, everyone!'

The 19 other women aboard with me are incredibly impressive. They're calm and composed and continue to paddle hard. In a way, it's an excellent test of our ability to rely on each other in a crisis, but the constant flashbulbs are hard to block out and I worry for the safety of my crew. We're not yet that experienced, and this training session could easily end in our boat capsizing if we lose our rhythm or get seriously spooked.

Behind me, the target of the pap's onslaught continues her job as if they were not there. She's utterly unflappable, refusing to react or respond no matter what they shout at her. She's going to steer this boat, dammit, and she's going to do it to the best of her ability. I'm impressed by the way she delivers effortlessly despite being under great stress. The girl has serious courage. What an addition to the Sisterhood.

Nevertheless, I can't let this go on. The activity on the riverbank is crazy and upsetting for everyone and it has to stop.

'Training is over, girls!' I shout. 'This is just too risky. We'll come up with another plan – train earlier if we have to. Or maybe all wear identical wigs, sunglasses and outfits so they don't know which of us is which. But we can't have this – it's not safe.'

We head back to our boathouse, but they've worked out where we're going and by the time we're at the riverside, they're there, besieging us as we lug our 400-pound boat and equipment. They carry on bombarding us with camera flashes and a merciless torrent of shouts, trying to upset Kate while pursuing her for that money shot.

'Hey, ladies! Smile for us. Come on, just a smile, Kate!'

'Kate, this way, look over here!'

'How does it feel to be single again, Kate?'

'Give us a smile, eh, show William what he's missing!'

'Come on, ladies. Come on, Kate! Just smile!' They sound like a broken record.

We make it into the boathouse and I take great satisfaction in slamming the door on the photographers outside. We all breathe out, relieved to be out of the storm for a while. We crowd round Kate, offering her support. She's amazing in her stoical acceptance and refusal to be cowed. Instead, she apologizes to us all for the disturbance and makes her exit without fuss, running the gauntlet of the press as she does so. I'm impressed with her commitment. She's down-to-earth, physically very fit and mentally strong – which is just what we need for the gruelling race.

My BlackBerry rings. It's Ma.

'Hi, darling, I've got Georgie with me and we've finished our run – but it's utter mayhem out here! We can't get near the boathouse. How are we going to meet you?'

'Kate's just gone, so they're probably all chasing her or giving up. I'm planning to sneak out the back, so I'll see you just down from the boathouse in about 10 minutes.'

'OK, sounds like a plan,' says Mothership. 'I really want you girls with me. I'll explain why when I see you.'

I congratulate the remaining crew on their cool heads and we agree that we'll start training earlier from now on, in a bid to outwit the paps. Then I slip out the back of the boathouse, only to run straight into one of the most unattractive men I've seen for ages. He's fat and grey-skinned, a picture of bad health; the kind of man who gorges on greasy burgers in his car and never gets enough sleep. He's standing in my way and trying to push something into my hand. I realize it's a business card.

'Take it!' he says, his voice insistent. 'I'm not a pap, if that's what you're thinking. I'm a specialist photographer, the best, and a newsmaker too.'

I want to tell him he's actually a sneak photographer who deals in gossip, but resist the temptation. 'Sorry, but I really don't want your card.'

'But I can make you famous!' He begins to wave his card at me, thrusting it into my face. 'You'll be a star. You've got the body for it. I can enhance you. We can work together as a team on this. You let me know the days, times and locations you're training, and I'll make the paps go away. What do you say?'

'That's very kind of you,' I reply, my tone sardonic. 'But I've got no interest in colluding with you, or selling out my friends. It's just not my style.'

He blinks at me, astonished at my resistance to his offer. 'But I can take pictures of you ladies in the most flattering light possible … I'm the best at my game.'

I push down my disdain for him. After all, I know he's trying to make a living like the rest of us. But I don't intend to cooperate and I have to make that plain. 'I appreciate the offer, but I really don't need any assistance when it comes to enhancing myself.'

His expression changes. 'You're making a big mistake, lady,' he says icily.

'I'm sorry if you're disappointed, but that's the way it is. Now, can you please get out of my way? My family are waiting for me.' I smile sweetly.

He turns and walks off, muttering, his expression dark. I'm hit with the unnerving thought that I've made a mistake in getting on his bad side. He's pushy and wants to get that exclusive shot by any means necessary. I can picture him hiring a boat and putting my crew at risk. Will he start stalking me? Possibilities run through my mind as I spot Mothership and Georgie waiting for me further down the riverbank. I wave and as I approach, Mothership fishes a camera out of her bag.

'You're not joining the paparazzi, are you?' I call as I get near. 'Put that away! I've seen enough cameras today to last me a lifetime!'

'So have I, Emma.' Mothership raises her eyebrows at me. 'What a fiasco out there! I was quite worried. I can assure you that taking photographs is the last thing on my mind after just watching Piccadilly Circus break out on the River Thames.'

Now I'm confused. 'So what's with the camera then?'

'It's Pa's,' pipes up Georgie. 'Remember – it's the one we found when we were clearing out his things.'

I look at it, recalling how we found those pictures of Pa and his Polish masseuse, the ones that made me feel ill. Sadness sweeps over me. I've still not spoken to my father. He hasn't tried to call me recently. Perhaps he's given up on me – on all of us – for good.

'Don't look so miserable,' Ma says gently. 'I don't want this awful thing any more, not now I know what it's been used for. I've downloaded all the photographs onto a memory stick and posted it to his office. He can have the pictures if he wants but I'm going to get rid of this.'

Before we can say anything, Mothership hurls the camera into the river. Georgie and I gasp, and then laugh, as it disappears with a loud plop, leaving barely a ripple on the surface.

Mothership looks at us both, her face very solemn. 'I want you and Georgie to witness something else. Your father has asked me for a divorce and I've said yes. There's no going back now. I'm going to let go of the past and move on.'

She pulls off her wedding ring. I take a deep breath and reach for Georgie's hand.

'Are you sure about this?' My voice feels tight in my throat and my eyes are stinging.

'Absolutely.'

Georgie wipes away a tear.

Mothership smiles. 'Don't worry, girls. Like I said, I have to get rid of anything tacky.' She lifts her hand and flings the ring as far as she can. It curves in a graceful arc over the dark water, catching the light with a glint on its golden surface before it vanishes into the water forever.

She turns to us with a smile. 'There. That's over with. Now, let's go home, get changed and celebrate.'

A few hours later, I'm opening an ice-cold bottle of Pinot Grigio for our very liquid lunch. We've had barely anything to eat, but this is our second bottle in less than an hour. It slips down very easily as we sit in the tiny garden of my flat, warmed by the spring sunshine.

'Another glass, Ma?' I ask, smiling. I feel almost light-hearted after the sombre moment by the river, but I know that a sadness has settled deep in my heart. I don't want to think about that now. 'It's a problem solver and stress buster all in just one glass!'

'Yes, please, darling.' She shoots me a return smile. The wine is evidently relaxing her, helping her grief and worry disappear, if only for a little while.

'Cheers, Ma!'

Georgie, Mothership and I clink glasses for yet another toast.

Ma sips her wine and then says, 'One good thing about no longer having a husband is that I can come and go as I like now.'

'Yes!' says Georgie eagerly. 'No husband and no kids means you can do exactly what you want. You don't have to answer to anyone.'

'Top me up some more,' Ma replies cheekily. 'I'm definitely getting used to this!'

'Sure,' says Georgie and refills Ma's wine glass. 'But this liquid lunch is a one-off. We can't have a bottle of wine accompanying you everywhere instead of a husband.'

'Don't worry, it won't become a habit,' says Ma, looking at Georgie fondly. My little sister has always been so grown up and sensible.

We munch on some odds and ends I've managed to rustle up, drink more wine and discuss what Mothership's life will be like now. It's a curious feeling when we talk about my father. He has disappeared so thoroughly, it's almost as though he's been abducted from our lives.

I notice that Mothership is wobbling as she reaches for the wine bottle again. She's obviously quite drunk, furtively grabbing the table for support, but still keen to keep on drinking.

Georgie and I swap looks, and Georgie says, 'I think that's enough, Ma.'

'Come on! I've only had a few glasses.' She's speaking in her wine voice, pronouncing every word slowly and trying to convince us she is sober.

'You mean a few too many,' Georgie replies. 'You've had more than a bottle.'

'How could two glasses turn into a bottle?' She looks confused and takes a good gulp from her glass. 'It can't be that much.'

'It's definitely that much. You'll be pickled from the inside if you continue at this rate,' I say. 'Sorry, Ma. The bar is officially closed now.'

She giggles like a naughty girl. I'm glad to see her happy drunk. Having her here, without Pa by her side, is a constant reminder of the tsunami that's hit us, destroying the life we knew and leaving everything in ruins. It feels as though Pa fled to the hills as fast as his legs could carry him, leaving us to deal with the devastation. Ma tries to cope and she tries to hide her hurt from us – I'm in awe of her determination to carry on and live life as fully as she can – but today she needs to be put to bed, kissed goodnight, mothered. And grounded for a week.

'Just one more glass!' she suggests, slurring more than a little.

'I don't think so. I think you'd be better off in bed.'

She consults her watch, squinting at it until she can focus, and then says indignantly, 'It's only four o'clock!'

'I know. But you need to sleep some of this off. You'll feel better for it. And Georgie and I are grounding you for a week too!'

'What?'

'You heard. Early nights for you until we say otherwise.'

She's secretly enjoying the fuss. 'OK. I'll do as I'm told. Just this once. Perhaps it is a good idea to have a nap.' Ma gets up and wobbles inside. Before she closes the door behind her, she looks back at Georgie and me with a fond expression on her face and says, 'I loooove you, girls! I really love you.'

Georgie gets up, smiling. 'We love you too, Ma. I'll help you get to bed, OK?'

I watch them go inside, feeling both deeply sad and very comforted at the same time. I switch on my BlackBerry and listen to dozens of voice messages from media organizations asking me for a comment on my new crew member. I can't face it today, so switch it off before it can start ringing again.

When the effects of the wine I've drunk have worn off and Georgie's gone back to her place, I sit down to catch up on a bit of work while Mothership slumbers. I'm arranging a party in a country hotel and need to make sure I've ordered the hundreds of condoms necessary to replenish my stock. I'm also in the middle of arranging a dream-come-true scenario for a Killing Kitten member. She's a powerful CEO who fantasizes about dominating her male colleague. Her PA has sent me a photograph of her young crush. I've found a handsome escort in his late twenties who resembles him and is the man she craves. She needs him to be respectful, but willing to learn new skills and appreciate her experience. She wants to seduce him, to be the object of a young man's lust. I'm sure she's going to have a fantastic time when she makes her move over lunch in a Mayfair hotel and invites him upstairs to her room.

I'm just sorting out the last details, when an email pings into my inbox. I open it up.

Dear Emma,
I am writing on behalf of Miss CEO. Could you include
handcuffs, a flogger and a blindfold in her bedroom hamper?

I enclose a photograph of another colleague she's also got her eye on. Could you sort this one out for the following week?

Please let me know at your earliest convenience.

With kind regards,

Mrs PA

I'm just about to reply with an obliging yes when I hear a loud knocking on my front door and go to answer it.

It's Plaything and his friend Mr Safe. I've known Mr Safe for ages, as he often hangs out with Plaything after their personal-training sessions. He's a handsome, quiet, intelligent banker.

'Hi!' says Plaything, cheerful and good-humoured as usual. 'We were just passing and thought we'd drop in. Are you busy?'

'Nothing that can't wait.' I stand back to let them enter. 'Come in.'

Plaything looks like he's won the lottery. He's wearing black Versace jeans, a V-neck cashmere jumper and Prada shoes. His hair has been cut. His face is gleaming and it looks like he's had his teeth whitened too. But he's got a neck brace on again.

'Been having slightly too athletic sex again, Plaything?' I ask as we go through to my little sitting room. 'Your neck is like a barometer of your sex life. The worse it is, the more thoroughly you've been laid.'

Plaything gives me a kiss and grins. 'You'd better believe it.'

Mr Safe kisses me on each cheek and smiles at me. 'Hi, Emma. You look lovely as ever.' He squeezes my hand. 'Sorry to hear about your pa. Plaything told me.'

'Thanks,' I say. 'That's nice of you.' I lean in to hug him and as our bodies meet, I feel a strange sensation surge through me. I've always felt at ease with Mr Safe, but right now I'm drawing great comfort from him and a deep, warm affection for him rises up in me.

'How are you?' he asks. His eyes are a warm hazel with a blue line around the iris and as he looks at me, I have the most intense feeling that he knows me intimately, and cares for me too.

'I'm fine,' I say, hiding the odd feelings I'm experiencing. 'How are you?'

'Good. Working hard. I've been reading about you in the *Evening Standard* – I'm very impressed at what the Sisterhood is setting out to do. But it looks like you're being given a hard time by the paparazzi.'

'Gosh, the paps don't waste any time selling their photos, do they?'

'No, they don't. I just saw a photographer loitering outside actually – I told him to piss off.'

I'm filled with another surge of affection for him as I smile wryly. 'Thanks. I appreciate it. The press are in over-drive now that they know who's in my crew. I've been inun-dated with requests for interviews – they all want to talk about Kate, of course, but I will make sure I only discuss the Sisterhood and our challenge.'

'Won't they leap big time on the Killing Kittens connection?' Plaything asks, sitting down delicately, keep-ing his neck straight. 'I'm no newspaper editor, but I can already see the headlines about Kate and the sex entrepreneur.'

'Of course.' I make a face. 'What can I do about that? The story's too good not to use it. I'd do the same if I were working on it. I'm happy to get my business out there – I'm just not going to discuss the private life of one of my friends. They all know that.'

I glance over at Mr Safe, who has settled down in an armchair and is regarding me with those warm eyes of his, and I wonder what he knows about my work. I don't keep it a secret and I'm sure Plaything would have told him everything. But what exact impression has he formed of me? Does he – like so many others – assume I'm a raving nymphomaniac who strips off at my own parties and can't wait to join the fun? Or does he understand that I'm primarily a businesswoman on a mission to make women's sexuality as mainstream and accepted as men's?

I turn to Plaything as we all sit down. 'So, who is she this time?'

Plaything begins to tell us about the woman he met at the Killing Kittens Valentine's party. They had a wild time there and swapped numbers. It turns out not only is this lady the director of a multi-national company, she also lives in Norway, and when Plaything told her he was too busy with his work to visit her there, she flew to London for a marathon sex session with him at the Mandarin Oriental Hotel in Knightsbridge – handy for her favourite beauty spa in Harrods. She and Plaything spent some very happy hours getting laid and causing not inconsiderable damage to the fixtures and fittings of the hotel room.

'Sex and Viagra,' declares Plaything, touching his neck tenderly but smiling broadly. 'Does it every time. I have to suffer for my art. But it was the best sex I've had to date.'

I laugh. 'I actually saw you guys at it in the Japanese bath at the KK party – and walked out.'

'You should have come and said hello! Three is not a crowd as far as I am concerned, Emma.' Plaything grins mischievously.

'Um, no thanks!' I know he's not serious. There's never been anything like that between us. I feel a hot blush creeping up my cheek anyway and realize it's because I don't want Mr Safe to think that Plaything and I are fuck buddies. 'So, is it serious? Are you dating her? Two sexual encounters with the same woman is practically like getting engaged for you.'

Plaything looks mortified by the idea. 'Dating? Hell, no! I'm only 28. She's in her mid-thirties.'

'So? There's nothing wrong with dating. Maybe it would be nice to get to know her better.'

'Hmm. I'm not sure.' Plaything shoots me a piercing look. 'What about you? Are you dating?'

'Not right now,' I say breezily. 'Too busy.'

I'm suddenly hyper-aware of Mr Safe, sitting across from me, regarding me intently. He's so different to Mr Black and to my father – there isn't that air of control freakery, or the desire to dominate me. Mr Safe is kind, I can feel that. His presence is comforting. He's also very attractive. I don't know why I haven't noticed it before.

'Too busy to go out for a drink some time?' Mr Safe says casually. 'I hardly ever see you these days. It would be great to catch up properly.'

There's a loaded pause before Plaything says, 'You should do, Emma. You two look pretty cosy together – you'd make a good couple.'

'Er – it's just a drink!' I say jokily.

'So you'd like to?' asks Mr Safe. He's smiling in a sweet way that draws me to him more strongly than ever.

I gaze back at him. I know this man. There are no nasty surprises, I need a bit of that right now. I've been caught off-guard, but the idea of a date with Mr Safe is suddenly the most appealing idea I can think of.

I smile at him. 'Why the hell not? I'd love to.'

Chapter Twelve

'Those who do not move,
do not notice their chains.'
Rosa Luxemburg

I'm sipping a Martini in the living room of Trolley Dolly's spacious three-bedroom flat in leafy Hampstead Village, North London, and looking out at her beautifully manicured garden: it's emerald green and looks like it has been trimmed by Edward Scissorhands. The Martini and the gentle play of the fountain outside are both very relaxing. Inside it's light and airy, with white oak flooring and white walls. There are shelves of legal reference books in the lounge. Taking centre stage on the bookshelf is a framed graduation photograph. Trolley Dolly looks the quintessential English rose, smiling innocently and clutching a rolled certificate of her first-class law degree from Oxford University. On either side of her stand her prim-and-proper parents, beaming with pride. She looks like butter wouldn't melt.

Today the two of us are celebrating the completion of the sleek built-in bar in her lounge. It's stunning, with white marble countertops and glass cabinets. Trolley Dolly is making another round of drinks while dressed in just her underwear.

'Aren't I just the best cocktail maker?' she teases, giving a cheeky twirl. She pours out some fresh Martinis and hands one to me.

'I think we should have another toast,' I say, raising my glass. 'Here's to baptizing your bar!'

'A woman after my own heart!' Work has been keeping Trolley Dolly tied to her desk till midnight every night for the last week, and tonight she's on a mission to unwind with alcohol and sex.

In the middle of her living room is a huge suitcase stuffed with stockings, sexy lingerie, whips, vibrators, glittering eye masks, nipple clamps and bondage gear. Trolley Dolly is doing some serious plucking and preening for the Killing Kittens party later this evening.

'Pull out the teeny-weeny Victoria's Secret lace-trimmed black knickers and bra, and the cropped sleeveless black leather jacket,' she demands, coming over from the bar. 'I'm adding a bit of bondage to my vampire look.'

'You'll be the vampire vixen with added bite.' I hold up the garment for our inspection. 'As usual.'

My horror-themed party is taking place at a hotel in the country, one that specializes in sex parties. I'm looking forward to escaping from the city. The last few weeks have been frantic, with intense juggling going on. I've been hard at work on Killing Kittens, sorting out the next few months' parties and getting new members vetted and approved. As well as keeping Mothership on track and making sure she stays positive, I'm deep into the final arrangements for the Sisterhood challenge too, which is a much bigger undertaking than I'd ever imagined. Sorting out the training schedules, the practicalities of our crossing, the details of sponsorship and getting publicity for our challenge while keeping a crew of 20 united and focused is not easy. In fact, it's incredibly time-consuming. And that's without battling the world's press, who are ringing my BlackBerry off the hook and ambushing me and the crew at every opportunity for photographs and interviews. I pride myself on my high energy levels, but I'm beginning to feel exhausted.

The truth is that our training sessions on the Thames have become a media circus. We started training earlier, at 5.30 a.m., to avoid the paparazzi, but it's been totally pointless. They have trebled in number and so too have the column inches in the national newspapers, with headlines about Kate Middleton and her sex-entrepreneur rowing partner. The story has gone global, with TV stations from Australia, New York, Los Angeles and South Africa calling me. I've even left my flat temporarily, and for the past few days Trolley Dolly's place has been the perfect escape from the photographers who are now camped on my doorstep, when they're not stalking me on the riverbank.

'You could do with kicking back tonight, Emma,' Trolley Dolly says, fixing me with a knowing look. 'You're more stressed out than I've ever seen you. Even with your dates with Mr Safe. Is he coming tonight?'

I shake my head. 'No. It's going really well – he's very romantic – but he isn't interested in my work. He doesn't even like to talk about it.'

Trolley Dolly gives me a meaningful glance. 'Oh.'

We both know that it isn't a great sign, but I'm still holding onto the fact that, so far, Mr Safe and I are having a lovely time. He's taken me out on three dinner dates so far, each one textbook romantic: the flowers, the candlelit table, the delicious food and wine, the kiss at the end of the night. The only thing is that, while I feel cherished and comforted after an evening with him, I'm not filled with wild passion. And while he wants to know about my home life, my family and what makes me tick, he doesn't want to discuss Killing Kittens or my work. I can't help finding that odd. It's a vital part of who I am – you can't have one without the other.

And we're not yet leaping into bed with one another, even though I like kissing him a lot. When it came to escaping from the press, it didn't occur to me to stay with him. But then, he has flatmates, and the last thing I need is more scrutiny from strangers.

'You're under a lot of pressure, Ems,' Trolley Dolly says, sitting down opposite me. 'Now is not the time to make big relationship decisions. Just relax and enjoy it.' She picks up the paper that's lying on the coffee table. 'Have you seen this piece today?'

I lean forward to look. 'No. What does it say?'

'It says some of the crew have been moaning that Kate wears push-up bras and immaculate make-up and makes the rest of you look like Lithuanian lesbians.'

I roll my eyes. 'And what's wrong with looking like a Lithuanian lesbian?'

We both giggle.

Trolley Dolly says, 'They seriously need to get their eyes tested.' She tosses the newspaper into the bin just as there's a buzz from the intercom.

'There's Emerald Isle,' says Trolley Dolly, and she heads down the hallway and presses the button to open the front door. As Miss D is away on business with her wedding-planner boss in New York, we're in need of a sober driver and Emerald Isle has volunteered for the role. She comes in a moment later, clutching a bag and two bottles of sparkling water.

'What's in there?' demands Trolley Dolly, kissing her hello.

'My costume for tonight. I'm going to be an Egyptian mummy. But I can't wear it while I'm driving, so I'm going to put it on when we get there.'

'A mummy?' I say, laughing. 'It's not exactly a sexy look, is it? Wrapped in bandages?'

'My take is very sexy,' shoots back Emerald Isle. 'And when the bandages are gauze, it takes on a whole new aspect, believe me.'

'Does this mean you're going to rise from the dead and finally have some sex tonight?' asks Trolley Dolly, with a mischievous glint in her eye.

Emerald Isle blushes as she dumps the bottles of sparkling water on the table. 'Of course I'm not!'

'Let's hope you finally get round to it before you're dead for real,' Trolley Dolly retorts.

'I'll do it when I'm happily married,' says Emerald Isle. 'Some of us can control ourselves, you know. Watching is enough while I wait for the right one.' She gives Trolley Dolly an apprehensive look, as though worried her friend has given up on meaningful relationships altogether in favour of a busy career and sex parties. 'Don't you want to get married some day and have children?'

Trolley Dolly takes another gulp of her Martini. 'Of course I bloody do! My parents have been married for 25 years. But I haven't met Mr Right yet, so I make do with Mr Right Now whenever I fancy it! Just because I don't have a boyfriend doesn't mean I have to forfeit sex.'

Emerald Isle shrugs her shoulders. 'But you're not going to meet Mr Right at a sex party, are you?'

'Stranger things could happen,' Trolley Dolly returns. She smiles. 'When you let go of that Catholic guilt, Emerald Isle, you'll realize it's OK to have a sex life, married or not.'

'All right, ladies,' I say, putting out my hand in a calm-down gesture. 'Let's stop the heated discussions and enjoy getting ready for the party tonight. Each to her own, remember? No judgements allowed in Killing Kittens, just fun.'

A couple of hours later, we whizz along the motorway in Trolley Dolly's Porsche with Emerald Isle at the wheel, arriving at the sex hotel in record-breaking time. I'm wearing my raven-beauty costume, a black corset with a jagged-cut miniskirt, and I've painted two red puncture marks on my neck. I'm carrying a big brown box full of condoms.

The manager greets us with a friendly smile and directs us to where Kitty Kat is finishing up the preparations for tonight. He doesn't turn a hair when I ask if he'd mind carrying 500 condoms to the first floor of his hotel. The truth is, he's used to it. Sex hotels exist up and down the country, and you'll find them if you open your eyes and look. There's no need to jump on a plane and head to the middle of the Nevada desert or the beaches of Ibiza. They are everywhere. This place is tucked away in an historic English town in Surrey and it has a solid reputation as a place where people can sneak off to be naughty or relieve the frustrations of everyday life. Even if they aren't attending as part of a larger party, couples in the know only have to look under the bed to find a box containing a love swing designed to bring a little sparkle to the eye and a flush to the cheek. On the ceiling is a hook where it can be attached. My plan is that, in a couple of hours, my Kittens will literally be swinging from the rooftops and having the time of their lives.

I've booked out the entire hotel and Kitty Kat has already been at work. The reception looks beautiful, with candles flickering everywhere. I leave Trolley Dolly with Emerald Isle and head upstairs to find Kitty Kat assembling the love swing in the Parisian suite. She looks sensational in a black fishnet dress, a headband with furry cat ears, a cat-collar choker and a tail that emerges from the back of her dress.

'Hi, Emma!' she says, as she attaches the swing to the ceiling hook. It doesn't look like much at the moment, just an assemblage of straps hanging off a sturdy central one, but I know that once those straps have been put in the right places, a lot of fun can be had. A sex swing frees up hands and legs, and lets gravity and momentum do a lot of the work. Some ladies find the heightened sensation it brings utterly irresistible. Whatever happens, a love swing certainly adds to the general enjoyment.

'Hi, Kitty. Do you need a hand?'

She leaps down from the bed, satisfied that the swing is safely attached. 'No. I'm going to put some candles in the bathrooms now. Have you seen the bath? It can fit four easily.'

'Good. Just the thing.'

'Did you bring the condoms?'

'Yup, downstairs.' I reply. 'The manager will bring them up.'

Kitty looks around the room appraisingly. 'This is a terrific venue. The soundproofing is excellent here. I know most Kittens won't be bothered when they get started, but they won't hear a peep from their neighbours next door.'

'Great.'

She looks at me with a worried frown. 'Is Miss D here? I will seriously kick her butt if I find her getting up to no good again.'

'You don't have to worry, she's overseas. But I'm sure you'll claw anyone who misbehaves tonight. Your tail looks pretty lethal too.'

'Thanks. I love your outfit as well,' she says, grinning. 'You look stunning.' She consults her watch. 'It's almost party time. I'd better check the champagne is chilled. Oh, and Jupiter's arrived. He'll be on patrol all evening.'

The crowd attending tonight includes a lot of married couples, most in their mid-thirties to forties. For some reason, the out-of-town hotel parties seem to attract that crowd. Some are bored with their sex lives and need them spicing up, while others are keen to push their partners out of their comfort zones, challenging them to try something new. I've invited some of my most enthusiastic Killing Kittens members to really liven things up. There's Plaything, of course, but also a friend of his called McDreamy (because of his very handsome looks). I've known him for years; he was the first to call me up and congratulate me when I formed Killing Kittens – and then asked if I would make him a member. Since then he's come to lots of parties, ostensibly to see me rather than join the fun, but I only have to turn my back for a moment to find that he's disappeared into the mêlée. His good looks mean that he has no trouble getting offers from Kittens wanting a bit of his handsome body – he's a fitness fanatic and ex rugby player, which seems to go down very well indeed with the Kittens. I'm fond of McDreamy, but I've never wanted to date him, as I happen to know he's a serial monogamist who doesn't stay long with any girl.

There's also Rock, a beautiful wannabe actress and sexaholic whose oral skills are legendary. I'm told that her mouth has reduced some to actual tears of joy.

The first guest to arrive is my latest recruit, a pretty and funny blonde from the Northwest of England. She called me personally regarding membership of Killing Kittens. I told her all you need to join is the right mind-set. Jordie immediately put in her application and I took great pleasure in fast-tracking her into the club. She looks like she'll fit in perfectly, in a black leather cat suit with a sexy ring-pull zipper front.

'So lovely to meet you, Jordie!' I exclaim.

'You too,' she gushes, kissing me on both cheeks. 'It's the northern invasion. I'm going to get everyone from my hood to join Killing Kittens. You wait and see.'

'The more the merrier,' I reply.

I introduce her to Trolley Dolly and Emerald Isle, and it feels like we've known this charming creature for years. Jordie tells us that she almost gave up on sex parties following a disastrous experience in the Northwest of England. The house was palatial and they mingled with some famous faces but it all went drastically downhill when Jordie stumbled into the cellar and discovered a woman with both her arms and legs chained, her nipples clamped and hordes of men having sex with her. The men were controlling her, treating her like a piece of meat. Jordie quickly scarpered when two men asked if she wanted to be chained up alongside her and gangbanged.

She looks disturbed as she tells us about it, her brow furrowing at the memory. 'I mean, I love my sex, but *those* men scared the fuck out of me. It turned me off instead of on. I thought that sex parties weren't going to be for me after all. But then I read about your parties in the newspapers and thought they sounded like a different cup of tea altogether. So I got in touch and here I am.'

'Yes, this is completely different!' I exclaim. 'Nothing like that would ever happen here, I can guarantee it. *You* are in control here – not the men. They can't approach you unless *you* say so.'

'I know.' She grins. 'And thank goodness for that!' She looks at her boyfriend. 'We're looking forward to it.'

He nods in agreement and I smile, glad to have found more people who share my vision for how happy sex parties, free of coercion and unpleasantness, can work successfully.

More guests arrive. The drinks are being handed out. A buzz of chatter is growing in the bar. As the champagne flows, couples begin to exchange polite, even nervous, niceties. A few seem uncertain about whether to commit to a conversation with their new friends in case they are contracting themselves to something more intimate that they are not quite ready for. I've seen this many times. A few more glasses of champagne will relax them and when the party eventually gets started, so will they. It just takes a bit more time for some.

'So what is your favourite vampire film?' one man nervously asks the woman in another couple.

She darts an anxious look at her husband and says, 'Bram Stoker's *Dracula*, isn't it, darling? The one with Sadie Frost in it. Gary Oldman. You know.'

'Yes,' says her husband gruffly and takes a big gulp of his drink.

The other wife looks relieved, relaxing a little. 'Oh, wonderful! That's ours too. But did you see *Interview with the Vampire*? I loved it.'

I smile. Give them a couple of hours and they'll be sucking on each other like vampires.

A wealthy New York socialite is already struggling to contain the arousal growing in his trousers. His eyes are glued to an incredibly sexy, tanned woman dressed in a skimpy black leather bikini and eye mask. Her ample bosoms are bursting out of her bikini top. She's smiling at him, teasing him, biding her time before she strikes.

It's now 11.30 p.m. and the low-key vibe is picking up. There's a bit more flirtatious dancing and banter. Then Rock sashays in with her handsome new boyfriend and, all of a sudden, the atmosphere changes.

Finally. Action time!

Rock is beautiful to the point of hypnotic. She has a 1950s look about her, with a classic hourglass figure, perfectly coiffed jet-black hair tumbling around her shoulders and scarlet lips. She walks slowly to the bar, wiggling her hips, and gets a drink for herself and Mr Rock. The air is full of sex, I can feel it shimmering through the room, setting everyone alight. It won't be long now.

Plaything and McDreamy arrive just as the vibe gets sexy. I'm standing near the bar watching things take off, and they come right over.

'You look magnificent, Ems,' Plaything says, greeting me with a kiss. 'Love your costume.'

'Thanks. How's the neck?'

'In great shape for a sexy lady vampire to take advantage of it,' he says with a smile.

McDreamy says hello and looks about with interest. 'I've just come to see you, Emma,' he says with complete sincerity.

'Really? So you won't be sneaking off in five minutes to find someone who wants to invite you to join in?'

'Of course not!' McDreamy looks shocked at the very idea, and I laugh.

Emerald Isle comes up to us. 'Wow, look at Rock! She looks amazing!'

We all look over to where Rock is standing with her boyfriend. She's wearing a long fur coat and sipping champagne. As we watch, she drops the coat to the floor and reveals she is entirely naked underneath. A strange kind of quiver goes through the room, as though Rock has just fired a silent starting pistol. She sits down, pulling Mr Rock down next to her, then leans into him and begins to roll her tongue over his earlobe. Everyone is watching as her hands quickly wander down south to his groin. When she discovers he's wide awake, she slides off her seat, drops to her knees in front of him, unzips his trousers and pulls out his now huge erection.

'Oh goodness,' whispers Emerald Isle breathlessly. 'That is the biggest snake I have seen for a while. It must be at least 10 inches.'

Plaything shakes his head, his eyes gleaming with lust as he observes Rock's powers. 'She's amazing at this. I've gotta see it.'

Rock's tongue snakes out and attacks the tip of her lover's penis. When she's tormented him for a while, she locks her plump red lips around the head. We can't see what she's doing inside her mouth but there's no doubt that her man is utterly at the mercy of this woman's lethal tongue.

'Ooooohhhh yesssss!' he groans. His eyes are glassy and his breathing is coming rapidly. He's evidently experiencing some incredible sensations. Rock loves performing her oral magic, especially with an audience. She opens her mouth wider, takes him further in and begins to suck harder and deeper. Soon she is taking all 10 inches of hard, hot flesh into her mouth. Mr Rock's breath is rasping as he slides faster into her throat.

'She just loves sucking a man's penis!' whispers Emerald Isle.

'Deep throat is her speciality,' I reply. Rock has told me how much she loves it, what pleasure it gives her. I know she's enjoying herself immensely.

She takes him in again, engulfing him all the way to the root while she tickles his balls. His body is twitching and he is on the brink of coming. But she doesn't take her mouth away – she wants every last drop.

'Oh God!' groans Mr Rock and climaxes hard into her mouth. She carries on sucking until his cock has stopped throbbing and he's collapsed back in his chair. 'You are fucking good,' he adds.

Rock doesn't release him until he finally begins to soften. Licking her lips as she pulls away, she smiles and says, 'That was just the beginning. I'm going upstairs.'

I look around and realize that the playing has properly started now: mouths are touching; hands are exploring bodies. A prom-queen zombie sits at the bar in a short bloodstained dress, with a 'Miss Living Dead' sash and crown. She smiles when her zombie policeman handcuffs her and they head upstairs. A blonde woman wearing a black minidress adorned with glow-in-the-dark skeleton bones finds her match – a man in a skeleton jumpsuit – and beckons him over with an inviting look. A handsome devil in a smart dinner jacket, bow tie and horns is sucking a Halloween bride's breasts. In another corner a zombie priest looks like he's in heaven as a fallen angel ministers to his needs.

Emerald Isle is totally fixated on the action unfolding before her eyes. Trolley Dolly has already sneaked upstairs with a young marine, followed by Plaything, who I suspect is on the hunt for Rock and her magnificent mouth. McDreamy is chatting to Kitty, but I have a feeling it won't be long before he disappears too. So much for just wanting to see me, I chuckle to myself. Jupiter is prowling with his usual attention to the underlying vibe, making sure everyone is happy and the mood is good.

I turn to Emerald Isle. 'I'm going to check the bedrooms. Why don't you pop up with me?'

She replies by giving me an apprehensive look. 'Really?'

'It's cool,' I say. 'I'm not getting involved. Not everyone is having sex. You have been to these parties before.'

'I know,' she replies. 'I just haven't had enough booze yet. Being sober makes me feel so nervous!'

She accepts my hand and we head upstairs together. In one room, we find that the bikini girl is no longer flirting with New York socialite. She is naked and riding the sex swing. The straps support her back and bottom and legs, and she is riding hard on his throbbing penis, the swing pushing her deep onto him. She's high on the excitement she's experiencing and the pleasure the swing brings her.

'Oh yes!' she cries.

I spot Rock on the bed. She has her mouth full, her hands gripping the base of a penis as she slides it down her throat. Who is the lucky guy this time?

It's Plaything!

He's clearly ecstatic, groaning loudly as Rock takes his length into her mouth. Emerald Isle and I make a sharp exit. I know my inhibition level is pretty low these days, but I'm still not enamoured of seeing my oldest friends at their most intimate activities. I don't need a picture of Plaything's cock in my mind, or the image of his panting, lust-glazed face. I'd rather not go there.

We head to another suite where I'm happy to see Jordie is having a splendid time. A pneumatic blonde is pulling down her sexy ring-pull zipper as Mr Jordie watches, waiting for his turn. I don't want to spoil their fun.

There are threesomes, foursomes and fivesomes all in the throes of various intimate acts in the other rooms. Some are having full-blown sex, either oblivious to or turned on by the audience piling in to watch. A few women on the sidelines begin to slide into the pile. In one room, Trolley Dolly is hard at work with her marine, bouncing up and down on his penis. In another, Mr Rock has found his mojo again and is playing with two ladies, a zombie maid and a witch, who are taking it in turns to have his magical fingers play with them. He inserts a finger into the pretty zombie maid and begins stroking backwards and forwards, finding her G-spot. He's driving her wild as he picks up momentum and sticks his middle finger in. He presses down on her swollen clitoris with the palm of his hand as he moves his fingers in and out. It's not long before she tenses, her head threshing, as she judders on the brink of orgasm.

'Ahhhh!' she moans as she surrenders to a fierce climax. 'Oh my God!'

'That's it. Gooood girl!' Rock murmurs as she comes all over his hand.

The witch looks like she's about to explode at any moment, and he hasn't even touched her yet.

I glance at Emerald Isle's face. By turns, I see desire, longing and guilt. When she sees me looking at her, she turns bright red. 'I'm very hot – I need some fresh air.'

'So do I. Let's go out.'

We head downstairs. Outside, the rain is spilling from the heavens, pelting our faces. Emerald Isle scurries inside and returns with a golf umbrella. I'm already soaking, turning my face to the downpour.

'Are you crazy?' she asks, trying to cover me with the umbrella.

'What are you so scared about?' I ask. 'It's only a bit of rain!'

Kitty Kat comes out, dry beneath her own umbrella. 'Are you all right, ladies?'

'Just getting some air,' I reply. 'How's it all going?'

'It's a great party,' Kitty says. 'Everyone is just going for it. Is it the swings, do you think? Or being so far from home?'

'It's just one of those weird things, you can't manufacture it. You can just be glad when it happens,' I say.

Just then, I hear a scream. It's faint, but it comes to us on the wind, a kind of howling sob. 'Did you hear that?' I ask, alert.

We all listen and hear another of the strange cries.

'Could it be a fox?' asks Emerald Isle.

'I'm not sure.'

'I'll take a look,' Kitty says and darts off to investigate. I watch for an anxious minute, then, just as I'm about to run inside and find Jupiter, I see Kitty coming back. She's shielding her umbrella over a teenage girl I've never seen before. The girl is sobbing and shivering, and is dressed in just a T-shirt and trainers.

I gaze at her, horrified. It's obvious she's been attacked.

'What shall we do, Emma?' Kitty says as she reaches us. 'I think something awful has happened.'

'I'm c-c-cold,' sobs the girl, clinging onto Kitty.

'It's OK,' I say as calmly and reassuringly as I can, even though I'm shocked and frightened by the state of her. 'You're safe here, we're going to look after you. Come inside.'

We lead the sobbing girl into the warm hotel. Luckily, the downstairs is deserted. Kitty sprints upstairs to tell the Kittens to stay where they are for now and returns with a blanket. Emerald Isle is making tea behind the bar. I help the girl take off her drenched trainers and start rubbing her feet and hands, trying to warm her up. She's cold as ice.

'What happened?' I ask gently.

'I can't remember.'

'OK, don't worry. It's all right. But I think we need to call the police.'

'But I can't remember anything, I can't!' Her face is white and her eyes panicked. Her hair hangs in wet tendrils and she looks terribly young and vulnerable.

'It's all right,' I soothe, my heart going out to her.

'But where are my jeans? Where are they?'

'We'll find them. Don't worry, you're safe now.'

'But my jeans ...' She sobs again.

'Don't worry,' I say again. 'We've got you now.'

Kitty helps me tuck the blanket around her and says quietly that she'll call the police. Jupiter is staying upstairs – I don't think this girl should see a man right now.

'Do you remember if you were with friends tonight?' I ask gently.

She frowns, trying to recall through a haze of shock. 'Yeah, that's right. I was out in town having drinks with friends. But I can't remember anything else.'

'Do you think someone bought you a drink?'

'I can't remember!' Her voice rises in panic again.

I realize I can't go on questioning her. She's in no state. 'It's OK, you're safe. You relax now.'

Kitty Kat comes back from making her call and sits next to the girl. She says softly, 'You told me when I found you that a taxi wouldn't pick you up because you didn't have enough money.'

This seems to help her remember something. She grips my hand. 'Yes, I started crying and screaming because I didn't know how I was going to get home.'

I smile, trying to reassure her, even though I'm furious at the idea of a taxi driver leaving a girl on her own in this condition. 'The police are coming, so try not to worry. Can we call your parents?'

She looks distraught. 'I don't want my dad to see me like this! Where are my jeans?'

We sit with her as she calms down and we wait for the police. Inside, I'm only too aware of the irony. She's safer in here than she is outside. This is supposedly a den of vice, and yet no woman would be treated like this poor girl under my roof. In a supposedly respectable bar or club, a woman is not really safe from having her drink spiked, or being followed home, or being targeted by ruthless strangers. I feel speechless with rage and horror when I think about the way women are treated and what happens to them when they're subjected to abuse and rape – not just the violence to their bodies, but to their minds and their own sexuality.

The vileness of it strikes me anew. The selfishness of the act of rape is so deeply disgusting. I only have to look at the poor girl in front of me and I start trembling with emotion.

I'm sad, angry, appalled for women of the world who have been violated in the most intrusive way possible. The girl looks at me, calmer now. She's still white and shaken, but she's come to herself. 'Thank you,' she says in a small voice. 'You saved me. Others drove past in the rain but you didn't – you looked for me. You found me and took me in. Thank you.'

I glance at Emerald Isle and Kitty Kat. All our expressions speak of the same sense of outrage and sorrow.

I put my arm around the girl's shoulders. 'That's all right,' I say. 'You need to be strong, but you can do it. You're a fighter. Don't let whoever did this break your spirit. You're better than that.'

She rests her head against my arm, and we wait for the police to arrive.

In the end, she leaves in the company of three police officers – one of whom is a woman with experience in sexual attacks – and her ashen-faced father, who is clearly distraught at the state of his daughter, though he tries to hold it together for her sake. I give the police my number in case they ever need to contact me, but all I can do is just hope they catch whoever did it.

Chapter Thirteen

'Opinion has caused more trouble on this little
earth than plagues or earthquakes.'
Voltaire

It's 7.30 a.m. and we are stuck in the rat race, chugging along with hordes of drivers in London's rush hour. Mr Safe is slowly ferrying me in his big Audi to London Television Centre, but there is an added difficulty in the form of the trailer we're towing behind us. My dragon boat is on it, and we're taking it with us for the big Sisterhood interview on ITV's breakfast show, *This Morning*.

The other drivers don't seem to appreciate the opportunity to see a dragon boat close up. Instead, they're honking and muttering. One hard-faced driver leans out of his window, delivers the one-finger salute and shouts: 'Why don't you get on your slow boat to China and get the fuck out of my way?!'

'Charming!' I say, trying to contain my anger. I want to roll down my window and scream at the top of my lungs, but I flash him a smile instead. 'Love you too, sweetie!'

He manoeuvres round us and roars away as far as the next traffic lights.

'This is why I got out of the rat race,' I say. 'It's brutal, everyone racing against each other, doing something they couldn't care less about, and ending up achieving nothing meaningful.'

Mr Safe looks cross and I remember that, after he's dropped me off, he'll be going to work in a big, black glossy corporate cube in the City.

Plaything is sitting in the back. He's come to help me lug my boat into the television studio. With my Sisterhood crew under the media microscope, we've decided to give an interview to the man most women in Great Britain love waking up with in the morning, Eamonn Holmes.

Plaything says, 'That guy's problem is that he's not getting enough sex.'

'Sex is your answer to everything,' I chide. 'You're sad? You are not having enough sex. You're tired? You are having too much sex. You're suicidal? Have sex!'

Mr Safe rolls his eyes. 'Can you both stop with the sex talk, seriously? You guys never stop.'

I give him a sideways glance. His irritation is plain to see. I know he's stressed by this early-morning drive, but even so. I've stopped feeling quite so comfortable around him. I get the distinct feeling that he would prefer me to be someone else. A thought pops into my head.

We don't share the same sense of humour. We don't laugh at the same things. Our outlooks are worlds apart.

Just then, my BlackBerry beeps and I read the text that's just arrived from one of my crew.

Kate can't get the time off work so won't be coming. You'll have to cover for her. She says you'll be fine.

My heart sinks. Oh great. Now I have to be Kate Middleton's mouthpiece live on national television. The producers are going to be disappointed that Kate's a no-show – but I don't care. As long as they do the item on the Sisterhood and help us raise money, I'll be happy.

My stress levels move up several notches nonetheless, and my inner tension is not helped when I see that Mr Safe is suddenly looking concerned, his eyes narrowing on the road.

'Is everything OK?' I ask.

'I think the trailer might be slightly loose.'

'What! Are you serious?' Panic rises in my voice.

'I am deadly serious.' He slows the car so we're crawling along. 'Don't worry. We secured the boat well before we left.'

I am not convinced. 'Shit!' I cry. 'My boat *can't* fall off. It can't be damaged now, there isn't time to fix it.'

I can tell Mr Safe is more worried about the jam we could cause if we lose the trailer.

I bob around with anxiety, twisting in my seat to see if the trailer is still attached. 'Besides, Eamonn Holmes and Ruth Langsford are expecting us to do our TV interview *in* it!'

'The boat is fine,' Mr Safe says. 'We used the best lashing straps. It's the trailer I'm worried about.' He stops the car. 'Plaything, go and have a look.'

My wingman jumps out and, cool as a cucumber, reattaches the hitch of the trailer to the car. He ignores the evil stares and beeps from other cars, and a moment later he is back in the Audi and we're good to go. I breathe out. *And ... relaaax.*

Mr Safe can't wait to drop us off. He has a busy day ahead, full of PowerPoint presentations and strategy meetings.

We draw to a halt outside the centre. My old friends the paps are there, waiting to see Kate arrive. I get out and they start flashing away as Plaything goes to unhook the trailer.

Mr Safe leans over the passenger seat to talk to me through the window. 'I'll see you for dinner tonight. Good luck.'

The trailer now free of his car, he speeds off, obviously happy to be away from this mêlée.

Now the press begin shouting at me as I help Plaything undo the boat and keep an eye out for the rest of the girls. They're all arriving separately and should be here any minute.

'Smile, Emma!' shouts a photographer. 'Where's Kate?'

They all begin to clamour for her. *Kate, Kate, Kate, Kate, Kate ...*

It must be so weird to have the world hungry for a glimpse of you. It must be so suffocating, so relentless, so exhausting. I know this woman. She's a wonderful girl, but she's human like everyone else. What's the fascination?

I say loudly, 'Don't worry, guys, she'll be here soon!'

'When exactly?' demands one.

'I reckon five minutes.' I smile and make my way inside the television studio as Plaything entrusts the boat to the TV-centre staff.

Back from the ad break and ... Three. Two. One.

We are live on national television.

My crew and I are in our kit, sitting in our dragon boat facing the glassy eyes of the cameras, while Eamonn Holmes and Ruth Langsford, the presenters, move about and interview us. Eamonn's in fine form, teasing us. He asks where Kate Middleton is and whether anyone has read about her mother, whom he fancies. Finally, he calls out my name. A furry microphone is shoved in front of me and they both start firing questions, a lot about 'the gorgeous' Kate. 'Show us what Kate does,' says Eamonn. 'Is Kate sporty?' asks Ruth with cheeky eyes. 'Did she have to do an audition?'

'Will you be getting a royal send-off?' 'Is *he* coming?' I smile when I'm given a break and a crewmember is asked if we're worried about safety on race day with all the press attention because of Kate. They're doing their job and a brilliant one.

Once my charities are mentioned, I feel I can relax. Our job is done. We manage the rest of the interview in fine style and I think I coped all right with the questions about Kate. I didn't say anything that might get her or me into trouble. Eamonn and Ruth ask us a few more questions about the 30-kilometre challenge, then they wind it up.

'Thank you, girls,' says Eamonn, when the show has gone to the break and we're scrambling to get off the set. 'And good luck! Send our best to Kate.'

Later that evening, I'm at Zuma in Knightsbridge with Trolley Dolly and Mr Safe. They're toasting my performance on live television that morning.

'You were great. You didn't put a foot wrong,' says Trolley Dolly proudly. 'And I must admit I was worried about you swearing.'

'I thought you might be giving me shit because I didn't smile enough,' I joke.

'It was very good,' Mr Safe says with a smile. He likes my work with the Sisterhood and wants to follow in the safety boat that will tail us across the Channel, but I haven't decided on that yet. 'Well done, Emma.' He leans over and kisses me.

Trolley Dolly raises her eyebrows at me. She knows I'm not feeling secure about Mr Safe. We've been sleeping together now and then, but the whole experience has left me a bit underwhelmed and I can't seem to muster that wonderful surge of emotion I felt that day in my flat. He's kind, he's nice and he's sensible – but I don't feel connected to him. I've convinced myself to keep trying. We may not be lighting any fireworks of love, but when I wake sad and lonely in the night, thinking about the fact that my father still hasn't been in touch with me after all these weeks, Mr Safe's arms around me are a comfort.

'Is Mr Player on his way?' I ask, looking at my watch. We're waiting for Trolley Dolly's former colleague to join us. Mr Player is an eligible bachelor in his mid-thirties, self-assured and opinionated. He's in a long-term relation-ship, but according to Trolley Dolly will bed any beautiful woman that comes his way. He's currently conducting a passionate affair with his 20-something PA.

Trolley Dolly checks her phone. 'Five minutes, he says.'

'Before he gets here – have you slept with him?' I ask.

'Of course not!' She looks scandalized, as though she's not that type of girl, which makes me laugh.

'That makes a change!' I say and sip at my wine.

'I never mix business with pleasure. Besides, he can be a bit of an arrogant prick sometimes. And as I'm 34, I'm a fossil in his eyes.'

'A fossil?' I echo. 'You are just about to reach your sexual peak.'

She shakes her head. 'I've seen how he treats older women in their mid-thirties. He always runs a mile from them. He says they have that tick-tock look in their eyes.'

'Urgh! You mean he automatically thinks every woman wants to marry him and have his babies. What a prick!'

'Emma …' says Trolley Dolly, suddenly going still, her eyes fixed on a figure approaching our table. 'Speaking of pricks, there's an even bigger one coming our way.'

I look in the direction she's indicating and see Mr Black walking towards me, looking good in a very sharp suit. I draw in a shocked breath but instantly control myself.

I'm not going to let him floor me. Two can play this game. Act surprised. Be fabulous, Emma!

He reaches our table, a smooth smile on his tanned face, and leans in to kiss me. 'Hi, Emma. What a lovely surprise.'

'Fancy bumping into you here,' I reply casually, offering one cheek for him to pay homage to.

'You know sushi is my favourite,' he says with a leer. 'How are you, darling?' He's molesting me with his creepy eyes. He looks so arrogant.

I'm going to wipe that smirk off your face!

'I'm great!' I reach for Mr Safe's hand and turn to him. 'Mr Safe, this is my ex, Mr Black. I had to let him go, sadly, as he was fucking a friend of mine. Mr Black, this is Mr Safe, my very young, very fit lover.'

Mr Black has the wind taken right out of his sails. He wants to whip back some kind of witty riposte, but the words won't come out. I've touched his tender spot.

'Well, it's really nice seeing you,' I say, smiling. 'Enjoy your sushi.'

Mr Black turns and slopes back to his table, where, I notice, he's dining alone. Good.

'Well done, Ems!' says Trolley Dolly. 'That's the way to do it.' She hasn't forgotten the day I discovered Mr Black was two-timing me. Another little victory over him pleases her almost as much as it does me.

'You dated him?' Mr Safe asks, raising an eyebrow. 'He's old enough to be your dad.'

'We all make mistakes.'

'Hmm.' Mr Safe frowns.

I stare at him, and I suddenly realize what's wrong. I don't fit into Mr Safe's template of an ideal woman. I may look and sound like her, but I keep, very irritatingly, doing things that jar with Mr Safe's conception of who I should be. I have a feeling this could be a big problem.

When am I going to find a man who likes me for who I am? For myself?

Just then, Mr Player turns up. His timing is good, as his arrival thaws the frosty atmosphere brewing between me and Mr Safe. The boys start chatting while Trolley Dolly and I catch up on other news.

Then I hear Mr Player ask Mr Safe what I do for a living.

'Emma runs a charity and she's doing a dragon boat race across the English Channel,' replies Mr Safe.

Mr Player looks impressed. 'Goodness me. That's very noble.' He shoots me a look as if to say that I don't seem the type to be a living saint but that perhaps appearances can be deceptive.

I don't like this at all. I break off what I'm saying to Trolley Dolly, lean towards Mr Safe and say in a sweet voice, 'You forgot to mention that I also run sex parties.'

An embarrassed look crosses his face. 'But that's just a hobby, isn't it? I mean, you'll give all that up at some point, won't you?'

'What?' I ask, exasperated. 'Of course not. It's my business. And a good one too.' I anaesthetize my anger by gulping down wine.

Mr Player's expression has changed. He looks judgemental, and when he speaks, his voice is full of scorn. 'You run sex parties?'

'Yes, I do. Do you have a problem with that?'

'Parties where people buy sex toys? Or where they actually have sex?'

'Oh, they have sex. Lots. With lots of people. If that's what they want.'

Mr Player doesn't mince his words. 'Then, yes, I do have a problem with it. The sex industry is revolting and your business is a shameful, sleazy and downright disgusting one.'

Trolley Dolly leaps to my defence. 'That's ridiculous. Orgies have been going on for centuries,' she says hotly. 'It's not unlawful sex, it's consensual group sex.'

'I beg to differ,' says Mr Player. 'It's just morally wrong.'

Mr Safe sits in silence.

I'm full of anger at Mr Player's hypocrisy, which seems to me like the world's hypocrisy. All of them look down their noses at what I do, but tolerate much, much worse every single day. I say very clearly, 'When it comes to relationships with men, friends or family, the values I hold dear are respect, loyalty and trust. Everything else is peripheral. When I look around my parties, I see a large amount of respect, loyalty and trust within couples. That's what it's all about.'

Mr Player scoffs. 'Don't be so absurd. It's cheap and nasty.' He lifts his chin. He's sneering down at me. 'These couples you're talking about have lost their moral compass. So have you.'

'Rubbish,' I declare. 'Take nightclubs. They may be socially acceptable and respected establishments, but inside all morals go out the window. You get groups of lecherous guys cheating on their partners left, right and centre, even if they've got wedding rings on. The last time I went to a nightclub I couldn't get across the dance floor without six pairs of male hands groping my arse as I walked past, totally against my wishes. I find it disgusting that *that* kind of sleazy behaviour is considered acceptable. And people like you judge couples as sinners when they're honest with each other and come to my parties to have sex with others quite openly. Nothing is hidden, there are no lies.'

I've had enough criticism for the night. I don't want to spend a minute longer with either of my male companions. I stand up.

'Well, it's been a pleasure. Now, I'm afraid that my compass is taking me home to organize an orgy I'm hosting.'

'When? Where?' asks Mr Safe, frowning.

My heart is pounding. 'Please don't speak to me. I don't want to hear another word.' His refusal to acknowledge my career, to understand me or to defend me to Mr Player has hurt. I can hardly bring myself to look at him.

I kiss Trolley Dolly goodnight. 'Sorry to leave you before we've eaten, but I'm afraid I have a bad taste in my mouth. I've been served enough shit tonight.' I turn to Mr Player and look him in the eye. 'Your double standards make me sick. I know you cheat on your girlfriend, and lie to her about it. So before you judge people who are honest and open, why don't you tell the world that you fuck your PA and then go home to your poor, ignorant partner?'

Mr Player has turned very red and is stuttering. People on neighbouring tables have turned to look, and Trolley Dolly is hiding a smirk behind her hand.

'You're the sleazy one around here,' I say. 'But you can't admit it, even to yourself. Goodnight.'

I turn and march out of the restaurant. I have no idea if I want to see Mr Safe again, and at this moment, I don't care.

Chapter Fourteen

'A lie can travel halfway around the world while
the truth is still putting on its shoes.'
Mark Twain

'It's like the London Underground in here,' says Mothership, inspecting my kitchen cupboards.

'What do you mean?' I ask, foraging in the bread bin for something to toast.

'Sardines, sardines and more sardines. I'm going to have to do a proper shop. Is this really all you live off? For breakfast, lunch and dinner?'

'What's not to love about the humble yet helpful sardine? Pass me a tin, will you?'

Mothership fixes me with a gimlet gaze. 'Are you going to tell me what's wrong? I know something's up. You're cracking open cans of your smelly sardines and it's not even 8 a.m.'

Ever since boarding school, sardines have got me through exams, break-ups or any crisis. It's a habit I can't break. I got off the phone to Kate Middleton about two minutes ago and the first thing I thought of were sardines.

I sigh. I can't hide things from Mothership. 'I've just talked to Kate. She's pulling out of the race.'

Ma's face falls. 'Oh no! Why?'

'It's not her fault. She's really upset, but it's all to do with security issues. Clarence House has told her it's for the best.'

I sigh, depressed. I feel sorry for Kate, and upset for the crew who will hate to lose her. But Kate told me she is fighting to be a private person and, all of a sudden, she is on the front page of every newspaper and magazine across the world because of our dragon boat challenge. That aside, she's also worried her presence will jeopardize the safety of my crew with all the paparazzi attention. Clarence House feared the race could end in disaster and our boat capsizing on race day in just two weeks' time.

'I'm sorry, Emma,' says Mothership sympathetically. 'What a great shame.'

'Kate's gutted,' I reply. 'I'm sure the rest of the crew will be too, when I break the news to them. Kate was totally committed to the race, and she's got a real feisty side too. She really, *really* wanted to beat the boys. That's why I decided to share the helm with her.'

'I know,' says Mothership soothingly. 'But it was getting ridiculous on the river with all the paps on your backs. Can you imagine what it would be like on race day? I think this may be the best decision all round, even though it's a disappointment. The safety of you girls is paramount.'

'True.' I pop a slice of bread into the toaster. 'I guess the one good thing is that they'll all go away now.'

'Speaking of headlines, have I told you I am about to make a little splash of my own?'

'Really?' I'm intrigued. 'Spill.'

'The *Sunday Times Style* magazine wants to interview me about my pink shoes.'

'You mean your Fuck You shoes?'

'Yes. The piece is about how I was dumped for a younger model and saved by my FU shoes.'

I laugh. 'That's great.' I'm delighted to see that Mothership is getting some of her zest for life back. 'Go for it, but how did it come about?'

'Oh, you know. Little birdies. A friend told a friend who happens to be a journalist about how a middle-aged woman survived her marriage break-up thanks to a beautiful pair of FU shoes.'

'That's awesome, Ma,' I giggle. 'I bet the journalist loved it. You'll be an inspiration to others going through divorce.'

'A little silver lining to the great big cloud,' smiles Mothership and heads off to work.

After my sardine snack-attack, I'm ready to face the other prickly issue of the day.

Mr Safe and I are over, that much is clear. We've only been dating a short while, but I've sensed almost from the beginning that we weren't exactly soul mates. And now, after what happened last night, the haze of love has burned off entirely. It's obvious that Mr Safe dislikes my work and has issues with it. Fine. But my work is part of the package. I don't have any hang-ups about Killing Kittens or think my business is wrong. I haven't got time to hang around with someone who finds it all too much of a challenge. Mr Safe has been sweet and kind in other respects, and he's comforted me when I felt low, but after he let me down so badly last night, I can't continue it. Having a man on my arm is nice, but by no means a necessity for me.

I call him. He picks up right away.

'Hello, Emma.' His tone is friendly, but guarded.

'Hello back.'

'I'm sorry about last night.'

'I know you are.' I take a deep breath. I want this to be as simple and straightforward as possible. 'I'm sorry, but I'm not ready for a relationship, and certainly not with someone as nice as you.'

'Are you dumping me?'

He knows the answer. I count to 10 to let it sink in, then say, 'I'm so sorry.'

'Is it because I upset you last night? I've said I'm sorry for that.'

'I know you are.'

'So can't we try again, give it another go?'

My mind is made up. 'No,' I say, gently but firmly. The truth is, Killing Kittens will always be an issue, so this has to be the end of the road for us, but I'm keen to spare his feelings, so I bite my tongue and add, 'It's just not the right time, with my parents, my work, the race. I'm not ready.'

He sighs and there's a long pause before he says quietly, 'OK. Guess I'll see you around.'

Then he hangs up.

I put my phone down with a sense of relief tempered by sadness. Another one bites the dust. When will a man come along who doesn't end up letting me down?

I put that out of my mind. I've got a record to break.

Chapter Fifteen

'Love will find a way through paths
where wolves fear to prey.'
Lord Byron

The Sisterhood takes on the challenge at last!

Despite no Kate, one broken collarbone and being inside the world's busiest shipping lane, we smashed the previous record for crossing the English Channel in a dragon boat and raised £100,000 for children's charities. Our boat was little more than an oversized canoe, but we succeeded in completing the perilous 21-mile journey, even with the 700 ships and ferries that cross it each day.

We may not have got off to the best of starts. Controlling my crew was like herding a bunch of wild cats and nerves were running high, especially as the boys were gung-ho and super-confident, but we were determined to do our best to beat them. Finally, the girls were all aboard and ready. The conditions were near perfect as we set off from Shakespeare Beach in Dover at the same time as the Brotherhood, with flapjacks, biltong and cheese to sustain us during the hard hours to come.

We set off at a brilliant pace and managed to maintain a speed of between 5.5 and 6.5 knots all the way across. The boys pulled ahead, but they didn't have the advantage we did – namely that Debra, our navigator, had plotted a brilliant course. As they hadn't, they were well on the way to Portugal at some points. It was hairy at times, with tankers and ferries coming close and at times giving us a hell of a ride over the waves of their wash, but we stayed firm. As we spotted the coast of France and entered the last six miles, it looked like we might be in with a chance. The Brotherhood were ahead but still off course.

'With a little cool and a lot of graft, anything is possible, girls!' I screamed.

We forgot about our aching arms and exhausted bodies and raced our hearts out, singing 'The Raiders March' theme tune from the *Indiana Jones* films. We pulled with all our might and for five painful miles we went for it, but the boys reached the beach just one mile ahead of us. We made it soon afterwards, though, landing with lots of laughter, hugs and tears of joy and achievement.

Being second to the Brotherhood did not spoil our triumph. Simply reaching France gave us girls an entry in the record books – no other female dragon-boat team had achieved it before. We crossed the Channel in three hours, 45 minutes and 26 seconds, smashing the original record set by a male crew by a full four hours.

And Jordie and I both made £400 each from the bookies too. We bet that the Sisterhood would be the first female dragon-boat team to reach France.

Not bad for a bunch of girls. Who said Girl Power was dead?

One week on, my body is still broken. I'm curled up on the sofa, checking the names of guests attending tomorrow night's Killing Kittens party. The blisters on my thumbs have healed, but I'm exhausted. My muscles ache and I've been advised to put my feet up and rest, otherwise I face suffering from overtraining symptoms. I don't even have Mothership to look after me, since she's finally returned home, feeling able at last to face the house without my father there.

Ow, ow, ow! Why did I do this?

I know why we did it. I'm so proud of my girls and what we achieved. We raised a massive amount for charity. And after all that suffering, the Sisterhood are now clamouring at me to set them another challenge. I have a feeling this is just the start of the story.

My BlackBerry starts trilling and I pick it up. My father's name is on the screen. Panic grips me. I've been eaten up with misery at being abandoned by him, but I've still not been able to answer when he's rung me in the past, and lately he seems to have stopped trying. I know that he's in touch with Mothership through their lawyers as the horrible legal process of dissolving our family begins. But I thought he'd given up on me.

Bolts of pain shoot through me and I know that this time it's nothing to do with my exertions last week.

Damn you, fucking phone! Why do you keep ringing? I'm going to have to decide what to do.

I stare at it, wanting to turn him off as I have before, but somehow this time is different. With a shaking hand, I connect and lift the handset to my ear.

'Hello, Pa,' I say in a neutral tone. Emotions rush through me: anger, sadness, shock, confusion, love and hate. But I sound almost normal. At least, I think I do.

'Hello, Emma.'

My heart sinks at his tone. I'd hoped he might be conciliatory, loving, apologetic. But he sounds self-righteous, and

I recognize the tone from my childhood. He's trying to force me into the role of obedient, awe-struck, doting daughter.

I don't say anything. I don't trust myself to speak. A surge of emotion rushes through me.

'Emma,' he says. He sounds so formal. 'There's something I need to talk to you about.'

'What do you want to talk about?' *Is he going to congratulate me on completing my dragon-boating challenge? Or is he going to bring up the divorce? Surely not …*

'There's a question I've got to ask.'

'Fire away,' I reply. I may sound calm, but I feel lost. This is our first conversation since he walked out and there's no 'how are you?', no 'are you OK?' and no 'congratulations on the race'.

'You did it, didn't you?' he says, suddenly sounding angry.

'Did what?' I'm stunned by his sudden attack.

'*You* wrote *that* article.'

'What article?'

'Your mother's article in the *Sunday Times* magazine. "Dumped for a Younger Model".' His voice is extraordinarily loud now. 'She wasn't named, but I know it was about her. The diplomat's wife! And I know *you* wrote it.'

So that's what it's about. His hurt pride. So much for the loving father. Does he actually give a shit about me at all?

I keep my cool despite the hurt welling up inside me. 'Pa, you're wrong. I didn't write any article.'

'Apparently you threw my belongings into a skip.' His voice explodes down the line. It's so powerful I could do with earplugs. I don't just hear it; I feel it, in my head, in my heart.

'Pa, I'm shocked you say that,' I reply. 'It wasn't just me who chucked your stuff away, it was all of us.

I'd count yourself lucky that you still have any possessions left.'

'What?' he yells.

'You heard me,' I say coolly. 'We could have destroyed everything – just like you've destroyed your family.'

There's a deathly silence. When he speaks again, that self-righteous tone is back, along with a helping of disdain.

'What about those ridiculous *pink* shoes?'

'You are unbelievable,' I reply, shocked. This is just childish. 'Are you blaming me for the FU shoes too?'

'Your mother doesn't wear pink.'

'She does now,' I retort. 'She picked them and bought them herself.'

'She's never worn pink. *Ever.*'

'Perhaps that's because you wouldn't let her,' I bark back.

He's not sorry. He's not even acknowledged my pain. Why do controlling people assume they have all the rights? When are my feelings going to be valid in his eyes? I muster every ounce of strength and courage to take a stand against my father – the man still wants to control us, despite walking out. 'You're living in cloud cuckoo land.'

'What?'

My beloved father may have fed and clothed me, educated and loved me, but right now I can't bear to hear his self-centred voice.

'You heard me,' I reply through gritted teeth. 'Pick up any newspaper or magazine anywhere in the world and I guarantee you that there will be some article about women and divorce. They asked Ma and she said yes. Not me. You can't control what *you* left.'

Pa has nothing to say to me. He just hangs up.

* * *

I sit still and wait, clutching my BlackBerry for dear life, hoping, wishing and praying he'll ring me again.

He will call back. He will say sorry. He's my father!

I wait and wait and wait. Five minutes pass, another 10 and then an hour. But the phone stays silent. I can't believe he's not going to call. A black despair engulfs me and I find tears blurring my vision. I feel shaky and suffocated, and jumbled thoughts run through my head as I realize that he's not going to call and comfort me. I'm struggling with my anger when I start to think of how he's abandoned us all for that woman. I feel like I'm being ripped apart like a finished jigsaw puzzle and broken into hundreds of pieces. My new reality is that life as I knew it is over – no more family Sunday roasts, no more Ma and Pa waving me goodbye, no more family home to escape to. My pa is now just another midlife crisis statistic, a randy old trout who's waved good-bye to growing old gracefully and instead become like a testosterone-fuelled teenager. I cringe to think of him and his floozy hitting the bars and my pa dancing his arse off with a bottle of alcopop in a club on Saturday nights. Am I going to bump into him in one of these joints? Perish the thought! Is he going to start splurging on a new wardrobe, flash cars and Botox and now consider himself too young to watch *Newsnight*?

I don't know how long I lie on the sofa, shivering and thinking about the destruction of my family, but I'm brought back to the present by a loud knocking on my front door. I struggle to my feet, battling my aching muscles as I head off to answer it, my blanket still wrapped round me.

It must be Pa. He listened! He didn't call back because he wanted to come round and see me instead.

I trip over my blanket, tangled in it as I hurry to the door. I open it and gasp as I see who's standing there. It's not Pa after all.

'Hello, Emma. Surprise.'

I gape at him. He's smiling at me with that familiar, gorgeous, heart-breaking smile and those eyes full of affection. He knows me so well. We've shared so much together over the years.

'But ...' I gasp. 'What are you doing here?'

'I should have called first, but I hinted in my Valentine's card that there was a surprise coming your way.'

'Aidan!' I rush into his arms and he hugs me to him. It feels so good. I laugh and realize I'm crying at the same time. 'I'm so happy to see you!'

He pulls away and looks at me. 'You look terrible,' he says in a wondering tone. 'What's happened?'

Where do I start?

'Never mind that. You look great,' I say with a broken laugh, and I mean it. It's wonderful to see him, the man I fell in love with at university. Our love affair may have been punctuated with frequent splits, but it also came with a condition that a break-up never really meant 'it's over'. 'I can't believe you're here. Why aren't you in Australia?'

'I'm here on work. And I wanted to see you.'

I'm filled with longing for him. I need him; it's a deep, elemental, physical need. I crave him and the love I know he has for me. I don't want to talk, I don't want a drink; I don't want a paracetamol to kill my throbbing headache. I want the best natural painkiller there is: sex.

I drop my BlackBerry and my blanket to the floor as I let him in. He closes the door behind him and as soon it's shut, we're both possessed by desire for one another. We kiss passionately and the moment our mouths meet, it's like a touch paper has been lit. We devour each other as we start tearing our clothes off, leaving them where they fall as we stumble, locked together, towards my bedroom.

'You'll have to be gentle,' I murmur between kisses.

'Gentle? You've changed,' he laughs, dropping kisses on my neck, cheek and lips.

'Because I've just rowed to France!'

'Why does that not surprise me?' he murmurs back. 'You always were my Supergirl.'

We find the bedroom and then the bed.

Oh, Aidan, I've never needed you like I need you today.

Soon, we forget everything but the pleasure of our bodies being joined again. We've always had this connection: both of us desiring the other with that elemental force. Every time I'm in his arms, it feels like our first time. I revel in the beauty of Aidan's body, his strong arms and thighs, the broad shoulders, a ripped six-pack and those intense blue eyes. We hold each other, skin to skin, our kisses becoming deeper and more passionate. I close my eyes to concentrate on the touch of his fingers weaving through my hair, the touch of his lips, the warmth of his mouth against mine and his extraordinary ability to make love to me. His arousal intensifies mine as his hands tighten their grip on my body. Having sex with Aidan has always been exquisite. I breathe him in. His smell is intoxicating, just as I remember it. We fit perfectly together. The intensity surges as we pant, moan and eventually break out in cries of mutual pleasure as we collapse in a wonderful burst of delight and then sink back into contentment.

* * *

I love hearing the downpour of rain hitting the windows while I'm tucked up in a warm bed with this man. At this very moment, life is just perfect. I'm happy and complete. The empty space in my heart is gone.

I'm lying on my back, and Aidan is propped up on his side, staring at me while running his fingers through my hair. It's like we've never been apart. We are so alike in so many ways, and I realized a long time ago that we're made for each other. He caresses me gently, as he's always enjoyed doing after our lovemaking.

'How long are you staying?' I ask.

'Only two days. Business, I'm afraid.'

My heart sinks. 'Great,' I reply, trying not to sound too disappointed. I'm stone still.

He's staring at me, smiling tenderly 'It's crazy, isn't it? If what I feel right now is not the basis for a lifelong relationship, then I don't know what is.'

I say impulsively, 'Why don't you move back to England? It's your home. You grew up here.'

'Can you hear that outside?'

The heavy rain is now pelting against the windows. It's torrential and sounds like it's going to fall all night.

Aidan says, 'I grew up in the thick rain, the fog, the damp and the cold. It's the worst weather in the world.'

'I know! That's why I always try to get away as often as I can during winter. You could too.'

'I'm not sure, Ems. My family is in Australia now that my father's retired there. I can't leave him. I love the weather. Australia is right for my lifestyle. You'd love it too – you love the outdoors as much as I do. Why don't you come to me instead?'

I shake my head slowly. 'I can't. England is home.'

We gaze at each other, both baffled by the impossibility of making something we both want happen.

'At some point we're going to have to make a decision,' I say softly.

He smiles at me. 'Maybe, when we get to 40, we'll have to toss a coin to decide where we live.'

'Ah,' I say giggling. 'Our old pact. So you think I'll still be single at 40, do you?'

'OK, maybe not. But *if* we're both single at 40, that's how we'll decide.'

'I guess,' I reply, sighing.

'When did life become so complicated, hey?'

'Maybe it was when you left,' I say, putting my hand gently over his. He takes my fingers and wraps them firmly under his hand.

'I've come back to you, as I always do. I'm here right now, aren't I?'

'Yes. And I'm really glad.' I smile. 'But you look tired, jet-lagged. You need sleep.'

'Sleep is overrated when I'm with you,' he replies, with a mischievous twinkle in his eye. 'I love you, Saylo,' he whispers, pulling me to him, and he begins to gently kiss me all over again, just the way I like.

Chapter Sixteen

'The madness of love is the greatest
of heaven's blessings.'
Plato

'You've been with Sir Lancelot!' exclaims Miss D, her voice accusing. 'I know it. You've got *that* look in your eyes.'

I haven't even made it through the doors of the venue for tonight's Killing Kittens soirée before Miss D has unearthed my secret. Sir Lancelot was my name for Aidan – the knight who rides to my rescue when things are bad, the one who truly loves me.

'What look in my eyes?' I say evasively. 'I don't know what you're talking about.'

Miss D and Kitty Kat are standing outside the ex-embassy in the heart of London, my favourite venue for our parties. They both scrutinize me carefully. I blush; I can't help myself.

'It's true, isn't it?' Miss D says triumphantly. 'Aidan's back! I can read it in your eyes. You always look different when you've seen him. Your eyes are bluer, your skin glows … and you're walking like you've been shagging for a week!' She turns to Kitty for support. 'You saw how she was moving those hips, didn't you?'

Kitty's eyes narrow as she gazes at me. 'Hmm, I think you're right. There's definitely been some action of the carnal variety in the very recent past.'

I laugh, but my stomach clenches in a very pleasant knot at the memory of last night. Aidan had me crawling the walls. My knees shook, my mouth watered, my entire body exploded all night. I want to do it again …

'Tell, tell, tell!' they chant, grinning at me.

'Guys, can you let me get through the doors?' I ask. 'This is not a coffee meeting. I am hosting a sex party tonight, remember?'

Miss D steps aside. 'Of course we will. You can tell us everything once we're inside.'

I shoot her a look, but I can tell she's not going to let me get away with anything. 'All right.'

We go inside. I've walked into this place many times, but I'm still hit by the splendour of my surroundings as I come in. I take in the magnificent marble-floored hall and the grand staircase. This gem of a house may be falling apart at the seams – I spot chipped cornices and peeling wallpaper – but it's still perfect as far as I'm concerned. It's one of London's hidden secrets, a delightful place to host my soirées.

Kitty Kat is determined not to let the subject drop. 'Come on, Emma, we're inside now. We haven't got all day. I've got to do a condom count and I'm still waiting for the blue silk rose petals to arrive.'

I shrug. 'I'm not sure if I should. After all, a lady never kisses and tells.'

'Come on, you promised!' cries Miss D, and when she sees the smile playing on my lips, she exclaims, 'I knew it!'

'OK!' I hold out my hands in a gesture of surrender. 'You win! Yes, I did see Aidan last night.'

Kitty Kat says thoughtfully, 'Well, whatever flame it is you've rekindled, it seems to suit you. Who is this guy?'

Miss D says excitedly, 'He's Emma's FWB! Her Friend with Benefits.'

I turn to Kitty. 'Aidan's an old boyfriend. I enjoy his company and we sleep together whenever he's in the country. Is there anything wrong with that?'

Miss D says sincerely, 'There's absolutely *nothing* wrong with FWB. I have an army of yummy FWBs in my little black book. But it's more than that, isn't it, Ems? You're the LOHL.'

Kitty looks mystified. 'The what?'

Miss D relishes explaining everything to Kitty. 'When Emma and Aidan were going out with each other at university, they made a pact. If they were both single at 40, they'd get married. I don't know why they're going to wait until then, considering they're made for each other. She's the LOHL and he's hers. Love of his life, that is.'

'Ah – that's nice!' Kitty looks a little misty-eyed with the romance of it. 'That's lovely, Emma. The last man I was keen on promised me the world, then dumped me as soon as we'd slept together.'

'She is lucky,' declares Miss D. 'He's gorgeous, single and he loves her. So why are you wasting time, Emma?'

I give her a look. We've talked about this before. 'There's no rush – I've got more than a decade on the clock before I hit the big 4–0.'

'But I don't understand why you date these totally unsuitable guys who just want to use you, or aren't good enough for you, when all the time Mr Right is under your nose!'

Kitty looks at me, her eyes shining. She obviously thinks I've found the perfect solution to my love-life conundrum.

I throw a gimlet-eyed look at Miss D. 'You know perfectly well why. How do you propose this relationship – let alone a marriage – would work with Aidan living in Australia and me here in England? Now, if the Spanish Inquisition is over for today–'

'Emigrate. I'm deadly serious,' Miss D replies. 'Or you could end up losing him. How would you feel about that? What if one day he calls you up and says that he's married someone else?'

I don't even want to acknowledge that eventuality and put on my blue sparkling eye mask to hide the burst of unexpected panic I feel at the thought. 'I spent enough time moving from country to country as a child, D. London's my home and my business is here. I'm not about to abandon it now, just as it's really taking off.' I try to lighten it all with a joke. 'Besides, who'd keep an eye on you?'

'You could set up Killing Kittens Down Under?' Miss D suggests.

'I don't think so. I'm happy where I am, the arrangement suits me fine. Now, I'm going to check out the house, OK? You can close down the interrogation room for a bit.'

I march off and leave them both staring after me.

The mansion looks heavenly. Candles flicker in the ballroom, where four huge beds have been pushed together to form one underneath a vast chandelier. The theme tonight is politics, and the beds are covered in satin sheets of various hues to represent the political parties of the nation: blue for Conservative, red for Labour, yellow for the Lib Dems and green for – you've guessed it – the Greens.

Tonight I'm expecting 200 guests, some flying in especially for the party. There are models, lawyers, aristocrats, civil servants, bankers, a scientist and an Olympic athlete. We even have a politician, which is fitting.

I take a sip of champagne and remind myself to have a look at which colour bed he decides to frolic on. It could be interesting.

By 9.30 p.m., my gorgeous waiters are serving the masked guests oysters and vintage champagne in the ground-floor rooms. Even though it's early, a dark and dashing gentleman in a blue mask is already undressing a beautiful brunette. She doesn't bat an eyelid when he unhooks her yellow halter-neck dress to reveal her large breasts. It's almost surreal to hear them chat about the weather as he begins caressing them, smoothing his hands across her tanned skin and tweaking her nipples lightly.

Glad to see that things are already warming up, I head to the bar and check that the drinks are arranged neatly on the counter. Miss Emerald Isle is there, looking like a green goddess in a floaty kaftan dress.

'You're wearing green!' I say, kissing her on both cheeks. 'What a surprise.'

'Of course,' she replies. She takes a sip of champagne, looking miserable.

'Emerald, tell me why your Irish eyes are crying.'

'Oh, Ems. I've already made a right eejit of myself.'

'What did you do?'

'I saw an Olympic athlete, one I've got a massive crush on.'

'Yes, I know who you mean. We call him Muscleman here. And I have to agree, he's hot.'

'He's even more beautiful in the flesh. I was overcome with all sorts of naughty imaginings when I laid eyes on him.'

'Really?' I ask, intrigued. This is an unusual admission for Emerald. 'Do you want to have sex with him?'

'I don't know,' she says, biting her bottom lip. 'I mean, no! Of course not.'

'You seem unsure.' I touch her hand, which is shaking slightly.

'I don't know what came over me. But I went up and spoke to him, and the first thing I said was: "I recognize you, you're ..." And he just said, "No, I'm not," and walked off.'

I give her a sympathetic look but say firmly, 'You know the rules, Emerald. Identities are protected here. All Killing Kittens are sworn to secrecy. Muscleman's very famous, but he knows he's safe once he's inside these doors. Everyone's treated the same here. No one cares who you are. It's all about being able to let yourself go completely without worrying who's watching.'

'I know,' she replies. 'He probably thinks I'm some nutty celebrity stalker and he'll run a mile if he bumps into me.'

'I'm sure it'll be fine. If you see him, just smile and act normally. He'll forget what happened.'

She manages a small smile. 'OK. Thanks.'

Trolley Dolly comes up to us, arm in arm with Mr and Mrs. She looks sensational in a tight-fitting blue dress with a sexy slash above her bust. Mrs is glamorous in a tight, short print dress in shades of yellow and blue.

'Hi, everyone!' Trolley Dolly looks like she's ready to play even though she's barely through the door. 'So, tonight is just the night for some really *scandalous* sex – the kind the papers would love to hear that cabinet ministers get up to.'

I laugh. 'Can we at least have a drink and a chat before you all go off to play? You vanished into thin air at the hotel party.'

'Sure.' Trolley Dolly beckons for drinks and then hands out the glasses of fizz. We start talking as more guests arrive. While Mr and Mrs are talking to Emerald Isle, Trolley Dolly says to me, 'We're planning a foursome tonight, Ems.'

Par for the course. 'Who's the lucky fourth?'

'It's our good friend, McDreamy.'

Now I'm surprised. 'Really? I didn't think you and he had ever hooked up. You've never seemed interested in each other. Although now I think of it, you'd go quite well together.'

'Yeah.' Trolley Dolly smiles. 'We got talking at the hotel party, and we've stayed in touch. He's had a crap week on the trading floor and I've had a crap week in court. So I suggested we have a date with Mr and Mrs to see if we can enjoy a bit of respite from work.' She gulps down her glass of champagne, then smooths down her dress and puts on her sexiest smile. 'So, shall we head downstairs? I'm in the mood for some Jacuzzi action.'

Mrs drains her glass and looks about expectantly. 'What about your date? Shouldn't we wait for him?'

'He'll find us,' Trolley Dolly says, and takes Mr's arm. 'Come on. You can squire us both for now. I don't want to start on the main course, but I'm definitely ready for some hors d'oeuvres.'

The three of them head off downstairs. Others are already making their way upstairs to the bedrooms. It's time for a walk around to see how things are shaping up, so I leave Emerald at the bar and find Kitty on the stairs, doing the rounds with Jupiter.

'Everything all right?' I ask.

Kitty grins. 'It is now. I've just had to turn Rhys Ifans away.'

'Rhys Ifans wanted to come in?' I laugh. 'On his own? We can't have that, even if he is a celeb. Shame – I've heard he's the life and soul of the party.'

'I know. But the rule applies to everyone, right? No single males allowed. And even if he'd had a girl with him, I don't know that I'd have let him in. You should have seen the state of him.'

I guess it was pretty bad, judging by the contemptuous look on Kitty's face. 'Tell me.'

Kitty wrinkles her nose in disgust. 'He may be the big Hollywood star, but he certainly wasn't dressed like one. He was wearing battered jeans and weeks of stubble. His hair hadn't seen a comb for at least a week. And he looked and smelled like he'd fallen headfirst into a pint of beer. But he was cool about it. Took it nicely and was very sweet, even though people on the street could see him being turned away.'

'Good work, Kitty,' I say approvingly. I know Kitty can't be swayed by fame. It's one of the reasons I trust her absolutely.

'Just doing my job.'

'And a bloody good one too! Catch you later.'

I continue on my way and check out what's happening in the upstairs rooms. The bedrooms are already hives of activity, crammed with people, some taking part and others just going from room to room, observing the action and seeing what new permutations are taking place. In one room, around 20 people in various states of undress are playing together by candlelight in twos, threes and fours. I notice an impressive physique by the window illuminated by the lights from the street below and realize I'm looking at one hell of a man. Then it comes to me.

It's Muscleman.

He's naked, unashamed of his fantastic form. No wonder he makes women go weak at the knees. This body has featured on hundreds of magazine covers, and here it is, in all its magnificence, the real thing in full view, ready to play with the beautiful blonde standing beside him. His cock stands rigid and proud, a truly glorious specimen.

He doesn't speak to the blonde but watches intently as she strips off her dress to stand naked beside him, then turns her back to him, looking back over her shoulder provocatively as she leans onto the windowsill. Then she stares out of the window. She might look as though she's watching the traffic snaking past in the street below, but I know she's totally alert to him. He moves closer to her and begins to stroke her body, taking his time as he smooths his huge hands over her back, her breasts and her bottom. He's adoring her gorgeous feminine shape while she stretches and moves under his caress. He spends a while stroking her, then gradually pushes his erection closer to her until she can feel it pressing hard into the small of her back. She leans forward on the windowsill and moves her legs apart so that he can see her in all her glory, juicy and inviting, ready for him. His huge cock rears up even stiffer at the sight, its thick girth almost pulsing as it swells. She wants him now, and he's ready for it too.

He grips his shaft with one hand and moves it to her entrance, letting it play there for a while, teasing her with the tiny prodding movements that seem to promise that he'll soon push inside and take possession of her. She gasps and moans with desire, evidently wanting him badly.

At last, he relents and pushes inside her, his length disappearing slowly but smoothly into her. She stretches to engulf him, crying out a little at the exquisite sensation as he fills her up. Muscleman starts moving in and out, withdrawing his cock very slowly and then thrusting back in again. His huge thighs meet her slender ones as he bangs against her buttocks. They fuck slowly for a while, and then he begins to pick up pace. The two of them look so beautiful, standing there in the half-light, their naked bodies so perfectly matched. They could be painted by an artist, they look so amazing. I've seen a lot of copulating in my time, but this is something different, and I'm engrossed by the sight as they fuck on in splendid rhythm, each taking great pleasure from the other. I wonder what Muscleman's huge strength and massive form feels like, what it would be like to fuck him …

Then I remember Aidan and the beautiful experience I had last night. Muscleman might be a perfect physical specimen, but it is the thought of Aidan that makes my stomach twist with painful yet pleasurable longing.

'Enjoying yourself, Emma?'

I turn to find Kitty Kat standing next to me. 'I'm just watching Muscleman in action. He's something else.'

Kitty Kat looks over and says, 'Wow! I see what you mean.' Then she turns back to me. 'However, I'm afraid we've got a situation downstairs and you're needed.'

'Rhys Ifans hasn't turned up again, has he?' I joke. We start to head for the door.

'I wish. I'm afraid it's worse. We have some old bloke from Westminster Council outside and he's got his knickers in a right twist.'

'The council? What the hell are they doing here?' I sigh with annoyance. I'm not breaking any law. My club operates legally, as money is paid for membership only and all activity inside is fully consensual. The authorities can only get involved if there are complaints about noise or anti-social behaviour. So the council don't have a problem with me. It's 'Fast Eddie' Davenport, the notorious owner, they've got their eye on. It's his private residence, but they suspect he's hiring it out for commercial and non-residential purposes without having a licence. They're desperate to catch him out. I've no intention of getting involved or telling council chappie that, KK aside, Eddie's hired it out for photoshoots and filming. I told Eddie if the council are granted an injunction to stop him from using it for non-residential purposes – as I suspect will happen someday – I'd no longer use it. I'm not in the mood for this, so I decide to have a bit of fun with Mr Westminster Council. 'Don't you worry, Kitty. Leave him to me.'

I hurry downstairs to find an anxious-looking man in glasses holding a clipboard and standing in the hall, peering about him. I put on my best smile and say politely, 'Good evening. How can I help?'

'Yes, hello.' He coughs and looks embarrassed. 'I'm from Westminster Council. I'm afraid we know there's a sex party going on in these premises.'

'I'm so sorry,' I say mischievously. 'Did you say a sex party?'

He consults his clipboard and says, 'Yes. We believe a Killing Kittens sex party is taking place at one of Mr Davenport's properties this evening.'

'This is my own private party. In fact, we're discussing politics. Have a look if you don't believe me.' I lead him to the ground-floor drawing room we use as a bar and fling open the door. There are all the guests who are not playing, looking quite calm and composed. 'You see? That's why some of them are dressed in red, yellow, blue and some even in green tonight. Party political colours.'

Emerald Isle waves, looking delightfully innocent.

The council man looks about, clutching his clipboard to his chest, and frowns as he sees a group of clothed guests drinking wine together with no sign of hanky-panky. 'I see,' he says, evidently confused. 'I must say, it all looks very civilized.'

'Well, there you are. I did hear a rumour about a sex party, but apparently it's taking place around the corner in Cavendish Square. Everyone's talking about it.'

Out comes the council man's pen and he begins to scribble furiously on the clipboard. 'Westminster Council don't have an issue with adult parties, as long as the owner of the property has the appropriate licence. Do you know what number in Cavendish Square?'

'I'm afraid I don't know the exact address.'

'Leave it with me. I might go and check it out,' he replies, looking much happier now. 'Sorry to trouble you. You enjoy your party now.'

'Thanks.' I show him to the door. 'We certainly will.' I close the door behind him.

'Good job, Emma!' says Kitty, chortling. She came out just in time to see me sweet-talk him off the premises.

'Thanks. I hope he doesn't follow my wild goose chase!' We both laugh, glad to have solved the situation. 'I need a drink. Come on, let's go to the bar.'

'You go. I'm going to keep on the lookout with Jupiter, just in case that guy comes back.'

'OK.' I'm in need of some serious fortification after my brush with the council and so I join a group of sassy Russian models at the bar.

'Welcome!' says one leggy brunette with an almost perfect English accent. 'Please join us. You know, vodka is the only drink worth having. You can drink so much of it without being as hungover as you would be with a bottle of wine.'

'I agree,' I reply. 'Let's get the Stolichnaya open!'

I've enjoyed more than a few shots when Kitty comes running in, looking worried.

'Oh God, what now?' I ask. The world is distinctly hazy and I'm beginning to experience a vodka high.

'Trouble, Emma, come quickly.' Kitty beckons me back to the hall. I stumble after her, finding my balance on my stilettos with some difficulty. In the hall, Jupiter is restraining someone even taller and meatier than he is. The giant is irate and shouting, 'Emma Sayle! Where is she?' He looks like he might be a bouncer.

The vodka has given me courage, or else made me foolhardy, because I totter towards him smiling and say, 'Hello there! Would you like a glass of champagne?'

He ignores my suggestion, glares angrily and stabs a finger at me over Jupiter's broad shoulder. 'You sent the council round to us! They've just raided our party!'

'I most certainly did not,' I say with as much dignity as I can muster. My fun with Mr Westminster Council has backfired massively. 'They were round here earlier. But I've no idea where you're from, so how could I send them to you? They must be on some kind of tour of the area, that's all.'

'You don't expect me to believe that, do you?' the giant bouncer snarls. His little eyes look piggy and furious.

'Well, it's true,' I say, still trying to disarm him with sweetness. 'I'm not on their side. Why would I be? I've got my own business to run and I've got no interest in messing up other people's. Now, why don't you have a drink and relax? Follow me and we can have a nice conversation in peace and quiet upstairs.'

The giant seems mollified for the moment, and Jupiter carefully lets him go, checking with a look that I'm happy to have the guy on the loose. But I think he looks calmer so I give the nod.

'Come on,' I say, turning towards the staircase while gesturing to Kitty to bring out a glass of champagne for our guest. 'Follow me.'

He takes the drink and obeys, and I lead him up the grand staircase, with Jupiter close behind in case he decides to turn nasty again. We're just walking past one of the bedrooms when we hear cries of ecstasy emerging from it. The giant bouncer stops, frowning, and turns to see where the noise is coming from.

'You're not allowed in the bedrooms, I'm afraid, as you're not a member,' I say, recognizing the high-pitched moans coming from inside the room.

It's Miss D, who loves having strangers watch her have sex.

'Ems, let him come watch!' she calls. 'You're the boss – you can vet him right now. My friend says it's fine. We insist.'

'My lady's wish is my command,' her companion pipes up. 'Come inside.' His voice is deep yet musical.

Miss D can be a liability, but tonight she's a saviour. 'Let's see what's happening then,' I say and open the door.

As we look inside the dimly lit room, I have to suppress the urge to giggle. There on the bed is the politician. I can just about make out his face in the glowing candlelight, but the giant bouncer barely notices him. He's more interested in the beautiful companion he's rolling around in bed with. Miss D's never voted in her life, but tonight she seems to be converted to the political cause, judging by the way she's responding to him.

The giant bouncer watches, stunned, as the action unfolds.

The MP presses two fingers deep into Miss D as they kiss passionately. When her mouth is free, she moans for more, rubbing her hands over her chest and tweaking at her nipples. He obliges and eases three fingers into her, working away hard as she writhes and shudders with delight. She begins to beg him to fuck her. He smiles at her evident desire to have him inside her but doesn't give in quite yet. He seems to be enjoying driving her crazy by holding back and only using his hand for her pleasure.

The scary ogre is now a gentle giant as we watch the two frolic on the bed. At last, the naked and very upstanding politician rolls on a condom and gives Miss D what she's longing for. As they start to pound away, they moan, gasp and shriek, their eyes wild.

They clearly do like an audience. They pick up the pace and give us a grand finale: Miss D grips the politician's thighs with hers, claims his mouth and moans as he pumps into her. At last, they reach their climax with bucking and shrieking, and then he collapses on top of her like an exhausted animal.

'You were the best, darling!' she says, looking at him adoringly.

'No – you were!' he pants, happy he's won her vote.

'Fuck the council,' says the giant bouncer suddenly. 'Do you mind if I stay here a bit longer? I've never been to an orgy.'

I hesitate. It's against club rules, after all. 'Oh please let him stay, Ems,' begs Miss D breathlessly. 'I can think of plenty of good uses for him,' she adds wickedly, beckoning him towards her.

I can't help smiling. 'OK,' I relent, 'just this once, for you.'

The now-gentle giant lumbers into the room with a dazed look on his face, where Miss D awaits him on the bed, her hand outstretched to welcome him into their little private party. I leave Miss D and her playmates to it, while Jupiter stands guard to make sure the bouncer really has become gentle now. As I head for the stairs, I bump into a man, fully clothed and wearing a full-face mask.

'Sorry,' I say, trying to pass him so that I can go back downstairs. I feel the need for more vodka.

'I've been watching you,' murmurs the stranger. I stop and frown at him. 'What? Why? What do you mean, watching me?'

'Just that. I've been most impressed by the way you've handled things tonight.'

I know that voice. A huge smile crosses my face and I pull the mask from his head. Aidan's grinning face emerges. 'What the hell are you doing here?' I demand. 'You said you couldn't come out!'

'I know. But my meeting was cancelled.' His eyes turn tender and he takes my hand. 'I wanted to see you. I'm leaving tomorrow.'

'I know.' A stab of despair pierces me. I've been trying to forget it and put it out of my mind. I only want to remember the good times.

'Do you know why I'm so turned on?' he asks in a low voice.

'Er …' I gesture around me with a laugh. 'Because of this? I mean, how else are you supposed to be at an orgy?'

'No.' He takes my hand and kisses my neck gently. The touch of his lips is delicious. 'What turns me on is seeing you charm your way out of a sticky situation with a man from the council. I like seeing you down shots of vodka with Russian models before going out to face an irate bouncer who looks like he wants to tear your head off for sending the council to his joint. That's what turns me on. That's why I want you right now.'

'Oh …' I sigh. Aidan knows exactly how to melt my heart. He always has.

'So shall we go? After all, we don't have much time. My flight is tomorrow, early.'

'Yes, please. I might go crazy if we don't.'

He reaches for my hand and smiles. 'Then I'm taking you home this minute.'

Chapter Seventeen

'Nothing ever becomes real till
it is experienced.'
John Keats

I sit in bed, laptop on my knees, and wonder if I should press 'send'. It looks strange now that it's all there in black and white. But it's what I feel in my heart.

Aidan has just left, getting out of our cosy bed with reluctance and a few last kisses so he could make his early-morning flight.

'You should do it,' he said gently, when I showed him the email I'd drafted. 'I think it would be a brave thing to do, Emma. The one who makes the first move to reconciliation is always the real hero.'

God, I'm missing him already. He convinced me to come clean to my pa about my true feelings, yet I never made it crystal clear how I really feel about him. I hate the image of him on that plane, heading back halfway across the earth. He couldn't be further away from me.

I put that out of my mind and read my email back, feeling slightly shaky.

Pa,

You have to understand that you've blown up our family in my face and I'm desperately hurt. If you want to make amends, then I need you to read what I've set out below and try to understand.

Just because I'm grown up, it doesn't mean I can take all this on the chin. I may be independent, but your departure has left a massive hole in my life and shattered my faith in things. I feel as though I don't know what is real any more. Please understand how much I'm hurting and how confused I feel.

Just because you're wrapped up in a new life and enjoying yourself, it doesn't mean you can stop making an effort. I'm still your daughter and I need you too. In case you've forgotten, you have two daughters and a son. So please call me and ask me how I am, because I need you to stay involved in my life. I don't want to lose my father! I need you and always will.

This is a very important point. Please, I beg you, don't use me or Georgie or Jonny as pawns in your battle with Ma. Communicate directly with her. Don't ask me to send any messages back and forth. You created this mess, so you fix it.

Please, if you talk about Ma to me (or Georgie and Jonnie), say positive things. (That goes for anything pink too!) If you can't, do me a favour and don't bother saying anything. We don't want to hear it. Really. It hurts us more than you know.

I would like you to start building bridges with us. I know you have a new interest in your life, but I think we still have the right to be treated with love and respect too.

Speak soon,

Em xx

I haven't even mentioned how I feel about the way he's treated Ma, or his running off with that woman. I can't go there right now, or maybe even ever. I need to concentrate on my relationship with him. Until that's mended, there's hardly any point in bothering about the rest; we'll just be too angry to hear what we're saying to one another.

My finger hovers over the keyboard, and then I do it. The message disappears and I hear the whooshing sound that means it's gone.

I wonder where I got the strength to do this and remember the talk I had with Aidan and the comfort of his presence; I felt so secure with him. I miss him so much already. But he told me to try to connect with Pa if I can, and that's what I've done.

It's strange, but I feel better already.

'Houston, we have a problem!'

I clamber into the front seat of the van parked not exactly legally on a yellow line in a busy Chelsea street, but Kitty's waiting in the passenger seat, ready to warn me if a traffic warden should come along. As I get in I exclaim, 'How the hell am I going to find the right girl when they all look like clones around here?'

'Don't panic,' replies Kitty Kat. She passes me a photograph. 'We'll find her.'

'No, seriously! This is a total nightmare. What if we end up abducting the wrong one?' I sit down beside her and study the photograph of Sophia, the young woman we're here to kidnap. She and her boyfriend, O, look like love's young dream as they gaze out of the photograph. They look as though they couldn't be happier or more perfectly suited, but the reality is that their three-year romance is on the rocks because their sex life is less than satisfactory. I've come across many couples in the same boat: outwardly they look like the ideal match, but in private things are disintegrating because they're failing to connect sexually. Without that all-important physical relationship, the romance is beginning to wither. Sophia and O tried their best to reignite their passion with all the usual tactics, like date nights, candles and bubble baths, but eventually resorted to a sex therapist. She talked to them about what turned them on and the fantasies they dared not discuss with each other. After those revelations, they decided to come to me for some practical help.

My job today is to make them remember just how much they've been missing sex and how much they desire each other. The idea is that they'll reignite their passion, learn more about how to please one another, and should they ever hit these troubled waters again, they can look back on this day and remember it. Just thinking about it should make them want to dive into bed with each other immediately.

That's the idea, but it's not going to happen if I abduct the wrong woman!

I look in the rear-view mirror and see Plaything sitting happily in the back, gawping at the coiffed and perfectly made-up women swinging their designer handbags as they sashay down the street. I feel like a mess compared to them. I'm in a onesie and a pair of sunglasses, but it was all I could muster in the wake of Aidan's departure. The women walking past look as though they've stepped from the pages of a fashion magazine. My parents told me how they used to hang out here in the Sixties and spot the famous faces of the day: Mick Jagger, Twiggy, Terence Stamp and Michael Caine. But these days it's posh Chelsea girls who own the

King's Road. It's Miss D's ambition to move back here, where her family used to have a house before they went bust, as soon as she hooks up with someone rich enough to support her.

'Take your time, Ems,' says Plaything as he adjusts his loincloth.

'Enjoying the view, are we, Tarzan?'

He grins. 'I most certainly am. They say that the most beautiful girls in London are on the King's Road, and they're not wrong. It's got me thinking ...'

'Don't tell me. Your new project is to find a rich young woman who's bored of her floppy-haired posh boyfriend.'

'My thoughts exactly!'

'But you have a girlfriend,' I tease. 'Hasn't Miss Norwegian Wood been dashing over to see you? That's what I've heard. And rumour has it that you two managed to run up a bill for five grand after breaking a lamp in the Mandarin Oriental! No wonder you keep doing your neck in. Isn't your girlfriend just as rich and fabulous as these fine specimens?'

His expression changes from cheerful to morose in an instant. 'I've changed her name to Miss Psycho,' he says moodily.

'Miss Psycho? That doesn't sound like true love to me.'

'She's delusional.'

'Really?' I give him a surprised look in the mirror. 'Miss Norwegian Wood has always been naughty but never psycho at my parties.'

'That's different. The fact is, we've only had sex a few times and we're not dating – but she's already talking about moving in. I mean, we're not even a couple!' Plaything looks agonized.

I'm secretly amused. I think it might do Plaything good to experience something a little more complicated than all the no-strings playtime he likes so much. 'Ah, I see. Well, you'd better make it clear to her then: playing only, no heavy stuff.'

'But she's stalking me on Facebook. Every time I post a new photo or status update, she's texting me from Norway, asking for an explanation.'

He has a point. 'OK, that's worrying.'

'Be careful,' puts in Kitty. 'De-friend her, that's my advice. And be completely straight with her about how it is.'

'What am I supposed to do when she never listens?' asks Plaything plaintively.

I suddenly see Sophia coming along the street and immediately Plaything's problems vanish from my mind. 'There she is! At last!'

'Where?' asks Plaything, craning to look out of the window.

'There!' I point to a pretty blonde wandering along the street with a friend, gazing in the shop windows. She looks thoroughly Chelsea, dressed in a safari-print playsuit with a slashed low V-neck and high boots. A designer bag is slung over one shoulder and her hair falls in tumbling blow-dried waves over her shoulders.

Plaything looks at her appreciatively. 'I'm glad I'm helping you on this one.' He begins to adjust the tiny gold swimming trunks underneath his loincloth.

I shoot him a stern look. 'She's off limits, Tarzan! I know you love swinging from the trees, but Sophia has a boyfriend. We don't want anything happening that would require hospitalization, arrest or lawsuits. Got it?'

He turns his eyes up. 'Message received loud and clear.'

I switch on the engine and watch as Sophia comes into range. 'Kitty, you've got O's mission cards, right?'

'Yes, in the glove box.'

'Good. You know the drill. Go and warn passers-by discreetly that this isn't a real kidnap and there's no need to call the cops.'

'Sure thing.' She jumps out and starts work.

Sophia is aware that she faces an 'attack' today, but she has no idea when or exactly what is going to happen. A moment later, Kitty gives me the all-clear sign.

'Go, go, go, Tarzan! Go swing for her. It's now or never.'

As soon as she sees Plaything jump out of the van, Kitty Kat runs over, grabs Sophia from behind and puts her hand over her mouth. 'Don't make a sound,' she orders. I see Sophia's eyes widen with shock. This must feel so weird and real.

In the blink of an eye, Tarzan has raced up to her and hurled her over his shoulder. Her long limbs dangle as he dashes back and bundles her into the van, where he flings her onto a waiting inflatable mattress. It all happens so quickly that nobody bats an eyelid. Kitty Kat quickly takes her friend to one side and explains the situation. It's obvious that Sophia must have warned her, as she stays calm, nodding, and doesn't do anything rash.

In the back, as Plaything slams the doors shut, Sophia looks dumbstruck, confused and frightened.

She was expecting this, right? I hope this is Sophia! I often have this nagging doubt when someone who knows they're going to be kidnapped seems so shocked, but it's quite normal. Soon her reaction will change as she realizes her fantasy is underway, and she can start to enjoy it, even while feeling the fear that comes from being out of control.

She yelps when Tarzan ties up her wrists and ankles.

'Keep quiet. Don't bother shouting. Nobody can hear you,' he says roughly. He calls to us, 'We should double the ransom money! She's beautiful. Fuck £10,000. Let's ask for a million – she's worth it.'

Kitty twists round in her seat to stare at Sophia cowering in the back. Her gaze falls on the cascade of loose curls. 'Maybe we could cut off a lock of her hair and give it to O,' she snarls. 'So he knows we mean business.'

'Please, don't touch my hair!' Sophia cries, looking mortified.

'The boss said no touching!' I bark to Plaything. 'Shut up, Tarzan, and that goes for you, too, Miss Prisoner. Otherwise I'll lock you in Cell Block H for eternity.'

Kitty cackles. 'You're toast anyway, if your man doesn't solve the riddles or pay our ransom.'

Sophia goes quiet, and we set off on the next stage of the mission, a coffee shop where I've arranged a rendezvous with O. I spot him straight away sitting at a table, looking nervous and jumping every time a phone rings or someone walks through the door. I decide to let him sweat a little more, head to the counter and take my time ordering a skinny cappuccino before I casually flop down in a chair beside him.

'You have got every reason to be scared,' I say in a low, menacing voice.

O shoots me a terrified look and starts shaking. I dig an envelope out from my bag. O is now trembling so much that his iced coffee flies out of his hand. He groans as he sits there, a giant brown coffee stain on his trousers and a puddle forming round his feet. I try not to laugh.

'You have to solve a riddle before I give you this,' I say firmly.

He looks over at me fearfully. 'What?'

'You heard me.'

'OK.'

'What is short, but gets longer as you pull it, pass it between your breasts and put it into a small hole?' I stare at him. 'Well?'

'That's pretty obvious,' he says, looking relieved.

'Think carefully,' I warn, giving him a serious look. 'If you get it wrong, you *won't* see Sophia again. Ever.'

'It's a—'

'Put your filthy mind away,' I warn. 'It's not what you think it is.'

O looks at his feet and fiddles nervously.

'I don't have all day. My watch is ticking.'

'It's a seatbelt,' he whispers.

I stand up with my skinny cappuccino and fling the envelope at him. 'Correct, smarty-pants. Now open and read.'

'Out loud?'

'Yes, do as I say. Read!'

He opens it. 'Drive to the Welcome Break services on the M40. You must leave your car there. Pink Lady will be waiting for you outside Krispy Kreme and will ask you for the codename: it is Operation Wetballs. You will receive further instructions when you fulfil these orders.'

'Goodbye,' I say, heading for the door.

'But how am I going to find her if I have to leave my car at the services?'

'You figure it out.'

With that, I run back to the van, smiling. What O doesn't know is that we've arranged for him to rescue Sophia in style. An Aston Martin sports car awaits him at the Welcome Break service station. Pink Lady will give him clues to find it and the key. A note hidden inside will tell him where his love is being held hostage.

We head out of London and bomb up the motorway towards the venue for Sophia's rescue. A castle owner who's fallen on hard times has rented me his pile for two days. It also comes complete with a large vaulted dungeon, which I've used before for those who enjoy dungeon breaks. Inside is a fully furnished playground with shackles, stretching racks, whipping posts and appendage clamps. We won't be using the dungeon for Sophia and O, as I've rigged out the master suite for them. An enormous four-poster bed awaits them, along with lacy La Perla lingerie and a hamper of sex toys. In the past, the castle owner and I have conducted upstairs/downstairs soirées when he has rented the castle to a wedding party at the same time as secretly hiring the dungeon out to me. Thanks to the thick, soundproof stone walls, plenty of action can go on in the dungeon while a wedding takes place serenely upstairs, with the bride and groom none the wiser.

We finally reach the estate and head to the parkland. When I've brought the van to a halt, Plaything gently blindfolds Sophia. She's not frightened in the least, knowing that the real fun will soon begin. We get her out of the van and lead her over to a tree, where she's bound to the trunk with rope. All we have to do now is wait for O, who should have made his rendezvous at the Welcome Break services by now and be well on his way to rescue his ladylove, as long as he followed the instructions.

When we hear the roar of the Aston Martin's engine, we dart behind a nearby tree and watch as O screeches to a stop on the gravel and races across the grass to where Sophia awaits him. He whips off her blindfold and they kiss with incredible passion.

'I've got you, baby,' he says lovingly when they stop kissing for a moment. 'I've found you. I love you.'

Those are just the three words she needs to hear. Her eyes soften as she gazes at him with evident desire. They kiss again with even greater force, O's hands roaming over her body, his fingers plucking at her buttons and undoing them so that they can slide under her playsuit to the soft skin beneath.

'Oh, darling,' she gasps. 'I want you so much!'

'I want to fuck you right here,' O growls as he kisses her neck and collarbone.

I wonder for a moment if we're going to be stuck behind this tree for hours while they go at it. Can we sneak away without being seen? But then, to my relief, O says: 'But I want to take you to the bedroom. This castle is ours tonight. Our room awaits. And do you know what I'm doing to do to you there?'

'No,' she says, breathless with anticipation.

As he unties her bonds, he tells her what he intends to do to her once he has her upstairs where he wants her. From what I can hear, he's going to tether her to the four-poster and tease her with all the little bits and pieces we've thoughtfully supplied, from nipple clamps to pleasure beads. He tells her how he'll render her helpless before he drives her wild with physical sensations.

I can see that Sophia is flushed with arousal, ready to surrender to whatever O wants. Whatever the dynamic of their relationship in everyday life, today he is the master and she is his willing slave. I just know they're going to have a fabulous time. Amazing what a little dream-come-true action can achieve for a couple who thought their sex life was all but over.

'The lucky bastard!' whispers Plaything, watching as O takes Sophia by the hand and leads her towards the castle.

Kitty smiles at me. 'Some satisfied customers, Emma!'

'Not yet – but they soon will be.'

When the coast is clear, we retrieve the ropes and the blindfold and head into the castle to make sure that the rest of the arrangements for Sophia and O's stay are in place. They'll be served dinner later, and then have the whole night together to enjoy. Kitty and I are sitting down with a well-deserved cup of tea, discussing what time to head back to London, when my phone rings. I answer it and hear a familiar voice speaking in tremulous tones.

'Hello, Wonder Woman. I require your services today.'

Oh no. It's Mr Kidnap! His timing is rubbish as usual. Why does he always call me at the last minute? He's incapable of giving anyone any notice.

I say quickly, 'Wonder Woman hates to disappoint, but I'm afraid it's not possible today. I'm not in London.'

'But you're Wonder Woman. Anything is possible for you.'

'It's very short notice,' I reply sternly, looking at my watch. 'It's already four o' clock.'

'But this is an easy job. I don't need Marilyn or Anna Nicole Smith.'

'Really?' This is a first for Mr Kidnap. 'You don't need a woman? I find that hard to believe.'

'I have a woman who's kindly volunteered her services. You know her, as it happens. She's a good friend of yours.'

'Oh? Who?'

'Her name is Miss D. We got chatting today when I found her number in my wallet. It's actually all her idea.'

So Miss D's plan has come to fruition after all. She must have been delighted when Mr Kidnap finally got round to calling her. But what's her game?

'Why does that not surprise me?' I say drily.

'We need a dungeon. Urgently.' He drops his voice almost to a whisper. 'We don't need transportation. My driver will take us.'

'Oh!' I start to smile. What a lucky coincidence. I give a thumbs-up to Kitty, who's listening anxiously. 'As it happens, I do have a dungeon available. You can use it anytime today until tomorrow morning.'

'Oh, thank you, Wonder Woman, you're amazing! How would I survive without you?'

'I'll text you the address and make sure it's all rigged out for you.'

'You don't need to worry about equipment,' he adds. 'Doctor Sparky has got all the kit.'

'Who?'

'Your friend, Miss D. She told me to call her Doctor Sparky. She's bringing her X-Terminator kit along with her.'

I'm not in the slightest bit surprised by this revelation. Who knows what tricks Miss D has got up her sleeve now? I'm only worried that Mr Kidnap doesn't quite realize what he's getting into. Doctor Sparky might turn out to be a bit more of a live wire than he's expecting. 'Well, I'm sure this will be an encounter you'll never forget.'

As soon as I'm off the phone to Mr Kidnap, I call Miss D.

'Hello, Doctor Sparky,' I say brightly.

'Hi, Ems!'

'Can you please explain your X-Terminator kit? I hope you are not intending to kill my client. I'd like him to leave the dungeon intact, if that's OK. No Frankenstein experiments today, if you don't mind.'

'Very funny, Ems,' she retorts. 'It's no big deal. The kit contains some odds and ends – a pair of electro clamps, an ElectraLoop, which I'm going to put on the base of Mr Kidnap's penis, a super-slick electro dildo, an electric spiked wheel, an electric cock ring and a–'

'Stop! I've heard enough. Electricity in the hands of amateurs can be very dangerous. I hope you know what you're doing. I don't think Mr Kidnap is signing up for a dose of ECT, is he?'

Miss D's voice drops to a murmur. 'Once he's experienced the leather penis strap that delivers amazing electrical impulses to his cock and balls, he'll be putty in my hands. You wait and see. By the time I've finished with Mr Kidnap, I'm going to be moving out of the dungeon and straight into his house.' She sounds very excited. 'It's on the King's Road, Emma!'

I sigh, half laughing at the same time. 'So, basically, you're going to brainwash my client with your electric-shock treatment.'

'Whatever it takes. Chelsea, Ems! Chelsea …'

'OK, you have fun. I'll warn the owner you're arriving, but I don't think I can face watching Mr Kidnap walking to his doom with Doctor Sparky, so I'm going to head back to London. You'd better tell me all about it when it's over. Just don't kill him, OK?'

'Of course not, Ems!' she says indignantly. 'Doctor Sparky isn't like that! She's very loving. She uses her powers wisely.'

'I'm glad to hear it.' I click off the call, shaking my head, hoping this isn't the beginning of something disastrous.

Chapter Eighteen

'If you don't know where you are going
any road can take you there.'
Lewis Carroll, Alice in Wonderland

After all my hard work sorting out everybody else's fun, it's time to have a little of my own. I need to shake off some of the misery I've been feeling since Aidan left a week ago. And I haven't heard from my father yet either. I guess he's still absorbing the contents of my email. I have to give him time, that's all. And there's plenty to keep me busy in the meantime.

When Plaything invites me to a boat party that one of his clients is throwing on the Thames, I jump at the chance. It's good to go to a party where I can kick back and enjoy myself instead of being the host. As soon as I'm on board, I start to relax. The rippling water and evening sunshine is a welcome answer to all my recent frantic activity.

By the time night has fallen, I'm on the dance floor grooving to 'Boogie Nights' with a glass of champagne in my hand, but after a while I crave some fresh air and head out to the deck where it's quieter and much less crowded. In fact, it's almost deserted, as most party-goers are inside at the bar or on the dance floor. The only person I can see is a stranger standing at the railing, looking very smart in a black suit and matching tie. The odd thing is that as soon as

I see him, I feel the strongest compulsion to go to him. He pulls me to him like iron filings to a magnet. I can tell he's handsome even before I've reached him. When I do, I see that he's devastatingly attractive, and almost Bond-like in his smooth sophistication.

He smiles at me and says, 'Hello there. You're Emma, aren't you?'

'Yes.' I'm surprised. 'How do you know my name?'

'I've heard all about you.'

'You have? From Plaything, I assume.'

'Yes. I've been looking forward to meeting you. I knew our paths would cross eventually.'

'Really?' I'm smiling at him, but I'm confused. Nevertheless, there's a delicious excitement spreading in my belly. This man has something irresistible about him. 'That's kind of strange.'

'Or maybe it's fate.' He takes my hand in his. 'Just call me Mr Fox.'

Over the course of the evening, I feel I get to know Mr Fox very well. He has style and substance, and he's a man who doesn't suffer from a shortage of self-confidence. He's sexy, charismatic and smooth talking, and he knows how to make me feel like the centre of the universe. I can tell at once that he's an Alpha male, the kind of man who loves the good things in life and adores high-end toys. He's also a man who never quits, but assumes he can do anything he sets his mind to – he does what he wants, when he wants. Most of all, he's the kind of man who loves women. Just looking at Mr Fox, I can see that he's experienced and knowing in bed. Everything about him speaks of a man who revels in sensuality.

And he's just turned all the power of his charm on me. It's pretty overwhelming, but I'm enjoying it immensely. I haven't felt like this for a long time. Since Aidan left, I've been reconciling myself to going back to the single life. But maybe that's not to be after all.

So how do I handle this one? Am I just going to join a long list of girls in his already overcrowded little black book?

I don't want to play hard to get because I'm not interested in games, but nor do I want to make it easy. I'm not sure if Mr Fox is just on another hunting expedition for the hell of it. It's abundantly clear he loves the chase.

We're soon at a table far from the dance floor, talking over a bottle of champagne, utterly mesmerized by each other and unaware of anything else that's going on around us. The sparks are flying between us. I need to know more about this man.

'So,' I say, 'tell me what you do for a living.'

'I work with my hands,' he replies, with a teasing smile.

'Don't we all?'

'I'm very good with my hands. I do lots of things with these hands to make my money.'

'Such as what?'

He's reluctant to say more and instead changes the subject. 'Why don't you tell me a bit more about yourself? What does a sex entrepreneur actually do?'

I raise my eyebrows. 'You really do know all about me.'

'Of course. I told you that.'

I'm intrigued. 'But why? How did you know we'd meet?'

'I'm prepared for any eventuality,' he says huskily, looking at me meaningfully.

I repay the compliment with what I call my flirting triangle, glancing at his eyes, down to his mouth and back to his eyes again. 'OK. Well … Having sex is part of life. I just enable people to open up, let go and enjoy it much more.'

He smiles. 'Oh, do you now? Do you crack your whip?'

'Only if I have to.'

'But you don't get involved, do you?'

'Correct.' I sip my champagne, gazing at him from under my lashes. I'm enjoying the banter with this mysterious fox. I decide to see just how far Mr Fox will go if I ask him.

'I have a proposal for you,' I say, looking him straight in the eye.

'Is it like an Indecent Proposal?'

'No.' I smile. 'But it's a one-off. Take it or leave it.'

'I'll take it.'

'You don't know what it is yet.'

'All right. What is it?'

'I'm offering you a job.'

There's a pause and then he laughs heartily. 'You want me to work for you?'

I nod. 'Yes. If you're interested in my parties, come and see them for yourself and help out. Men do work for women these days, you know. Even for sex entrepreneurs.' I gaze at him, the challenge in my eyes. Can he do this or not?

'How could I say no?' His smile broadens.

'You will be paid to work, not play, because you're *not* a member.'

'Understood. How much will you pay me?'

'Ten pounds an hour.'

'To do what?'

'You said you were good with your hands. Let's see just how good you are when you work behind the bar at my next party.'

'Emma,' he says, leaning towards me. 'You're on.'

* * *

I'm awakened by my BlackBerry vibrating on my bedside cabinet, tearing me from a deep sleep. I grab it quickly. I know who it is. Mr Fox has already begun the chase. A text has arrived from him: *It was lovely meeting you. Fancy another boat ride? Let's drop anchor and have dinner tonight.*

I try to contain my excitement as I let my fingers slide over the keys. *Not tonight, I'm busy. Another time?*

The answer pings back. *When are you free?*

I write back: *I'm a busy girl. I'll let you know.*

His reply is almost instant: *You'd better. I don't intend to let you slip away. Besides, you're my boss now. You need to tell me when to report for duty.*

I fall back on my pillows, giggling. I feel a tingle of excitement all the way to my toes. Perhaps … just perhaps … Is Mr Fox the one I've been waiting for?

I'm standing at the doors of my favourite eighteenth-century mansion with a clipboard in my hand, ready to check off the guest list for tonight's party. A handsome man, immaculately dressed in a pinstripe suit, approaches me.

'Good evening.' His voice is deep and cultured.

'Good evening yourself,' I return with a smile.

'Are you hosting your party dressed like that?' he asks, and kisses me on both cheeks. He looks down admiringly at my legs, which are well and truly on display tonight. I'm dressed as Alice, in a short blue-and-white tutu, my hair held back by a band.

'I thought I was attending a sex party, not a Mad Hatter's tea party,' he whispers, breathing into my ear. He smells my neck. He's giving me goose bumps.

'You're 10 minutes late, Mr Fox,' I say. 'I like my staff to be on time. My guests will be arriving any minute.'

I lead him through the double doors into the marble-floored hall. Kitty saunters over, grinning more than usual. Tonight she's the Cheshire Cat, dressed in a pink minidress, soft furry ears and fur leg warmers. She looks fabulous.

'Welcome to Wonderland,' she says mischievously. 'It's a madhouse here.'

'Wonderland.' Mr Fox shoots me a look. 'Will it live up to its name?'

'It never disappoints,' I tell him. 'Let me show you the way.'

Kitty and I lead Mr Fox into the drawing room and show him the bar. The room looks stunning, lit by candles and hundreds of fairy lights suspended from the chandeliers. Throughout the house the huge fireplaces have been decorated with more lights, orchids, feather boas, chocolates and roses.

I show Mr Fox the array of glasses and bottles chilling in the fridge. 'Your job tonight is to serve the bubbly potions to my guests. Understood?'

'Yes, ma'am.' He twinkles his dark eyes at me.

'The flutes must be sparkling. And the champagne always chilled.'

'Of course, Alice.'

'The rules are simple in Wonderland. We're here to ensure our friends have the best time possible.'

'Yes indeed.' He looks cool as a cucumber. Utterly unfazed. I'm impressed. So many men are apprehensive or afraid, or else unpleasantly excited and leering, at the prospect of one of my parties. Mr Fox is calm and unruffled. We've been texting non-stop since we met last week on the boat, and I feel as though we know each other well.

I say, 'Time freezes the minute my guests step inside. We don't care what's going on outside. The tea party finishes around 3 a.m., then it's back to the real world. Now, you need to wear this.' I hand him a sparkling black eye mask.

'I think that's a good idea,' he says drily and puts it on. 'I'd like to preserve my anonymity if I can.'

'I understand. But you'll see that the rules of KK guarantee complete safety when it comes to identity. Now, I'm going to leave you to it. Kitty will help you if you need it. Enjoy your adventure tonight, and I'll see you later.'

'Be careful not to tumble down any holes,' he quips, smiling. 'There'll be a potion waiting for you when you come back.'

I leave Mr Fox and make my way back to the hall. Guests are already arriving, and they seem to have taken the *Alice in Wonderland* theme to heart. They look amazing, and are clearly determined to put the pressures of life behind them once they are in Wonderland. Kitty and I are soon busy at the door, ticking off names and making sure everyone is wearing masks as the party kicks off.

It's still early when a man rocks up to the door with several glamourpusses hanging off his arm and an air of incredible arrogance about him. I recognize him at once. He's a very famous footballer, but one of those responsible for giving footballers a bad name. And, I note, his girlfriend is not among the six girls he's with.

He tries to barge past us into the club, but Kitty steps up and stops him.

'Sorry,' she says. 'This is private and you're not a member.'

He swaggers there on the step and drawls, 'Don't you know who I am, love?'

I make a big show of checking the list. 'Yes. But I'm sorry, sir, your name isn't down here. So you can't come in.'

His eyes widen with surprise. He's obviously not used to this treatment. 'But you do know who I am, right?'

I frown. 'Yes. I think you may be a footballer.'

He takes off his mask, his expression cocky. 'One of the best in the world.'

I smile. His ego is a great deal bigger than his small head. 'You're a role model to millions.'

'You've got it. I'm glad to see it's finally sunk in. Now, if you don't mind–'

He tries to push past me again, but I stand firm. 'I do mind, I'm afraid.'

His expression darkens. He doesn't like being treated like this in front of his gaggle of girls, who watch with their glossy mouths hanging open and their huge lashes fluttering. 'You are in serious trouble if you don't let me in.'

I raise an eyebrow. 'Should I take that as a threat?'

He's inches away from my face now. 'Yes, you can take it as a threat. My agent will have fucking words with your boss and get your fucking ass fired.'

'That's never going to happen,' I say firmly.

He's exasperated. 'That's what you fucking think, blondie.'

I smile sweetly. 'No, I know so. I *am* the boss. I'm afraid you've lost this game and I'll call my security if you don't leave. Now.'

He opens his mouth as if to argue but then thinks better of it. He knows he's lost and he turns away sulkily, muttering obscenities under his breath as he takes his armful of girls elsewhere. He looks like a spoiled jerk. I make a note never to grant him membership.

I head back inside, where a man in a white-rabbit mask with whiskers is muttering to a sweet-faced Alice, 'Oh dear! Oh dear! We don't want to be late!' and they hurry up the staircase together, giggling.

In the bar, Mr and Mrs are holding court dressed as the King and Queen of Hearts.

'Perfect choice of costume!' I say, going up to them. Mr Fox is standing behind the bar pouring out drinks. He winks as I arrive and I flash him a smile back.

'There won't be any "Off with his head!" tonight,' Mrs replies, smiling. 'Not in that way, anyhow.'

I kiss her hello on both cheeks. 'It's nice to see you chatting for a change. You usually dive straight in.'

'I was just telling your charming new barman about our recent adventure in Italy. Honestly, Emma, you've never seen anything like it. The wedding was beautiful, but the reception!' She rolls her eyes in delight at the memory. 'We played strip poker in the bride and groom's suite, and let's just say it went from there. Lots of happy action, I can tell you.'

'Don't tell me their first time having sex as man and wife was with you?' I ask, flabbergasted.

'Well, we were all naked. I got Mr to give my nipple clamps to the newlyweds to use on me ...'

'Go on.'

Mrs looks angelic. 'I was tempted, but I did the decent thing and let the bride and groom get it on alone.' She smirks. 'But I was all fired up. I ran naked to our room, chased by my husband and a young Italian stud. I got on all fours and had my husband's wonderful penis in my mouth and a beautiful stranger servicing my bottom. It was magical. The other bloke said afterwards he'd never been with a woman who was so willing to have bum sex.'

Mr Fox is staring, open-mouthed.

'I'm glad you've been properly introduced to my friends,' I say, wanting to laugh.

Mrs gets up and grabs Mr's hand. 'Come on. Playtime!'

Mr's looking quite fired up himself after all the talk of that wedding reception. 'Anything you want, my love,' he says fondly. I love the way Mr and Mrs are so at ease with each other's needs. They've been married since they were teenagers, but a few years ago Mrs told her husband that she had to be allowed to sow the wild oats she'd never sown as a young woman, or their marriage could be in serious danger. The result was that they joined the club and have been even more in love ever since.

'I've never seen a tea party quite like this,' says Mr Fox.

'It hasn't even started yet. Just wait till it really kicks off,' I reply with a grin and head back upstairs.

The house looks like fairyland tonight, and all the guests are enjoying their adventures. People are living out their fantasies wherever I look: one woman beckons a man to peel off his clothes and join her on the bed, where they quickly indulge in a bout of fierce fucking. A man dressed as the Knave of Hearts comes to stand nearby and watch. It isn't long before he's invited to join in as well, and the woman is soon enjoying a glorious tryst, with one hard cock in her juicy depths and another ramming into her hungry mouth.

The action soon attracts a leggy brunette dressed in just fishnet stockings and heels. She's holding a flogger whip with a glittering handle decorated in Swarovski crystals.

And then there were four.

'Do you mind if I join in?' she asks the woman.

The other releases the cock she is sucking long enough to say, 'Be my guest.'

'My boyfriend has been very naughty. I caught him steal-ing again. Can I spank him while he pleasures you?' She turns to the man who's pounding in and out of the first woman. 'You're very naughty, sticking your lovely cock into someone else,' she chides.

'You said I could, darling,' he pants, ramming home as his girlfriend strokes the soft fronds of the flogger over her palm.

She simply smiles and says, 'I've changed my mind.'

I leave them as she begins to land the flogger lightly on her delighted boyfriend's backside, making him thrust even harder into the happy woman he's servicing. I know that it's going to end in a delicious climax for all of them.

In another bedroom, there's a gentleman sitting on a chaise longue chatting to two beautiful Russian women while his hands are getting rather busy with their breasts and down the front of their lacy knickers. Guilt-free sex with beautiful strangers may not be everyone's cup of tea, but it is under my roof. In the next room, there must be at least 20 people on the bed, all having a glorious time, strok-ing and sucking and penetrating. They are all beautiful – and I'm not just talking about their physical appearance, but their attitude to life, sex and letting go.

As I return to the staircase to go back to the bar, I see a familiar face.

'Hi, Ems!' squeals Miss D. She's dressed in a sexy Alice costume herself, but the version in which a grown-up Alice has forgotten everything except her underwear.

'Ah, Doctor Sparky. How are you?' I say solemnly. 'I take it Mr Kidnap survived your tender ministrations?'

'Stop being silly! Yes, of course. In fact, he's here.'

I look around. 'Where is he then?'

'He's busy screwing the living daylights out of a woman who looks like–'

'Let me guess ... Marilyn Monroe?'

'Yes.' She shrugs. 'No surprises there.'

'And you're fine with that?'

'Of course!'

'OK then. But you're still keen on Mr Kidnap?'

'My mind's made up,' Miss D says firmly. 'I'm moving back to the King's Road, even if it means Marilyn has to join us occasionally. Living in Chelsea means that three is not a crowd.' She looks about. 'Now, I want to have some fun too. Where shall I go?'

I gesture to the doors down the corridor. 'Take your pick, it's all happening. Wherever you go, you'll find an adventure. That's the beauty of Wonderland.'

I head back to the bar. Mr Fox looks relaxed and comfortable as he serves a handsome man who's dressed as a Mad Hatter. Three women wearing just PVC masks, stiletto heels and bright-red lipstick walk up and start talking to the Mad Hatter.

'Would you like to join us downstairs?' asks one.

'How could I possibly turn down such a wonderful invitation?' he replies.

'Or we could pop upstairs?'

'I'm happy to go wherever you three lovely ladies are comfortable.'

Mr Fox looks intrigued as the party wanders off. 'Hi, Emma,' he says as I reach the bar. 'It's got a lot quieter now. Everyone seems to be otherwise engaged.'

'What do you make of your first night on the job?' I ask, smiling.

'It's interesting.' He smiles back. 'I don't know what I expected. It seems people are having a lot of fun. I get it, I really do.'

I'm very happy to hear it. I'm tired of being judged. I just want someone who accepts what I do and understands why I do it.

'So, do you want to stay on?' I ask.

'As your permanent barman?' He leans towards me and I'm suddenly aware of his presence and the magnetic attraction he exerts over me. 'Let's say that I'd prefer to stay freelance. If that's OK with you.'

'Sure. An ad hoc basis,' I breathe back. The attraction crackles between us. He stares into my eyes and says in a low voice, 'If the playrooms are upstairs, what's downstairs?'

I give him a playful look. 'Do you want a peep through the kaleidoscope?'

'Is that a challenge, Miss Sayle?'

'Yes, you deserve to have a peep. Kitty will take over. Follow me.'

We head downstairs to the Clubroom. My Kittens are making good use of the large bubbly Jacuzzi. There are some couples locked in embraces and several women chattering and laughing while wriggling their splendid bodies around each other in the tub. One smiles at me. 'Want to come and join us?'

Mr Fox is staring, transfixed, as the girls start getting closer to one another.

'No, thanks,' I say with a smile. 'You enjoy yourselves, though.'

The girl who spoke to me turns to her beautiful companion and begins to caress her large, firm breasts and then kiss them.

'Your nipples are hard as rocks,' the girl murmurs. 'I love getting my hands on big bouncy breasts like yours.'

Within a few moments, their tongues begin to explore each other's mouths and their hands roam across slippery wet skin. The first girl plunges her hand into the water to her lover's nether regions as their breasts press against each other. They begin to moan with pleasure as they kiss. I know that under the water there is plenty of teasing and touching going on.

On the edge of the Jacuzzi, a curvaceous brunette puts her legs up over the shoulders of her lover as he thrusts into her.

'Oh, darling,' she gasps. 'You're awesome.'

Her partner cups her buttocks in his hands as he slides in and out of her.

'Damn it. That feels so good!' she cries.

Mr Fox has a glint in his eye and is running his hands through his hair. The erotic scenes before us are having an effect on him. He turns to me. 'This tea party is almost over. It's almost 3 a.m.'

'It may finish a little later than planned.'

'No. When the clock strikes three, we're out of here.'

'Are we now?' I raise my eyebrows at him.

'Yes, whether you like it or not. I'm going to kidnap you.' He slips his hand over mine and holds it tightly.

'That doesn't sound like the action of a law-abiding citizen,' I say, smiling.

His voice is firm but soft. His lips are close to my ear. 'I *am* a good citizen, Emma. But I'm definitely not boring. And nor are you.'

Chapter Nineteen

'The way you make love is the way
God will be with you.'
Rumi

Sex, I love it. Married or not, I *need* sex. Everybody does.
Since my *Alice in Wonderland* soirée three nights ago, Mr Fox
and I have really let rip. We've become great explorers. Last
night we ended up breaking into Hyde Park and swimming
in the Serpentine together, kissing and playing in the dark
water. Then we went back to his place for some extremely
naughty fun and games. We've barely slept.

I want to be in bed right now, enjoying another orgasm.

We're all living in the twenty-first century. The days of
guilt and shame for women who are sexually liberated
should be long gone. But they're still here. I'm constantly
pulled up to explain why my sex business doesn't contradict
my Christian faith, and this is the reason why I've agreed to
appear on the BBC's live religious radio show this morning.
I strongly suspect eyebrows will be flying skyward as people
tune in for their weekly dose of spirituality only to hear me
pronounce that the big sex-before-marriage debate has well
and truly reached its expiry date. I just hope some people
listen before rushing in to judge.

I join the BBC's Claire Catford for a debate with Calum
Macleod, a committed Christian and former leader of
marriage courses at Broadcasting House, which is just round

the corner from my main KK venue. Both have strong, authoritative voices. Calum doesn't agree with a word I say. The feeling is mutual. I stand my ground. In my opinion, sex doesn't equate to marriage, no one's getting hurt or cheating on anyone at my parties, and who am I, he or whoever to say they can't do it?

When he talks of the long-term effects my parties could have on girls and couples, I make the point that single girls aren't coming to my parties to find a boyfriend or potential husband. I point out to Claire that it doesn't once say in the Bible you can't have sex before marriage when she suggests that this sort of sexual freedom must sit uneasily with my faith.

At last, after what feels like an eternity of interrogation, it's a wrap. I'm free. I stumble out of the BBC's studios into the back seat of Kitty Kat's car. She's been waiting with Miss D to drive us up to a country estate, the venue for tonight's party.

Miss D turns round to eye me suspiciously. 'Where the fuck have you been the past few days? I've been calling and texting you and Mr Kidnap non-stop. You've both been off radar.'

Apart from texting Kitty to arrange this morning's pick-up, I've had no communication with the outside world since Mr Fox and I hooked up. I've just been too busy enjoying myself.

'I've not been with Mr Kidnap if that's what you're thinking. I've just been taking a break,' I say crossly.

'Oooh, you are moody! You've been with a man, though, haven't you?'

'I beg you for peace, D. My body and soul are very, very tired.'

'You've been having sex with that bartender. I know it!'

I close my eyes. 'Ssh! I'm just about alive. Just. I need you to zip up and navigate.' I fall asleep almost instantly.

Kitty Kat wakes me from a blissful slumber.

'Ems, we're here. You've been out for the count for about three hours. We didn't want to wake you.'

I groan and pull myself back to full wakefulness. Miss D opens the back door for me. She's in high spirits. Again. 'Where is he? Where is he?' she asks excitedly.

'Who?' I'm bemused.

'Kitty told me. Why did I have to hear it from her? So who and where is Gatsby? The person you're throwing this party for. I knew it wasn't a regular KK one so soon after the Wonderland one.'

'Gatsby? What are you talking about?'

'I am talking about Gatsby the billionaire! The one whose party this is! Don't pretend.'

I'm irritated with Miss D and her endless quest for money. It's beginning to annoy me a lot. All she needs to hear is *ker-ching!* and her sex drive races to full speed.

'There are actually two billionaires coming and neither is called Gatsby,' I say.

My revelation is sweet music to D's ears. 'Two?' she says, open-mouthed. 'Come on, let me help you out of the car, darling, so you can discreetly show me who they are.'

I climb out of the car. 'I most certainly will not. You'll have to figure that one out for yourself.'

'Why?'

'Just because money and sex are the currency of your relationships doesn't mean I have to present my guests on a platter to you. Anyway, what about Mr Kidnap?'

Miss D looks sulky. 'I told you, he's gone off radar. I don't think he's in the bag, despite my best efforts. So I need to find a back-up. I've simply got to get back to the King's Road, Emma, you know that. And luxury travel and Michelin-starred restaurants don't hurt either.'

'So I've heard,' I say wryly.

Tonight's party is being held in an exquisite country mansion surrounded by rolling parkland. With 50 bedrooms to choose from, most of the guests are staying for a sleepover. Some are KK members, and some are people whose names have been supplied to me by the host – the elusive billionaire. He spends most of his time abroad as a non-dom tax payer, but tonight he wants to celebrate and treat his friends to a very special party. Evenings like this don't come along all that often.

The theme our host chose for this evening is 1920s Gangster and Molls, so I expect to see flapper dresses, braces, pinstripe suits and spats. I like to think that it celebrates the arrival of a new breed of independent woman: the flapper girl. Flappers were the first women to vote. They smoked, drank and danced and took risks. They wore make-up, cut their hair and went to petting parties. They are the forebears of my own brave, fun-loving Kittens.

By seven o'clock, my tiredness is a thing of the past and I'm ready to party again. I wish Mr Fox were here to enjoy the night with me, but he's had to stay in London. In fact, work is going to keep us apart for at least several days. I wish it weren't the case; I'm enjoying the connection we share and the fun we're having together. Mr Fox has certainly lived up to all his promise when it comes to the bedroom. Just thinking about him sends a delicious shiver

down my spine. When I think about Aidan, I tell myself
that I have no choice. As long as he's in Australia, we can
never be together. I have to find someone else – and maybe
that someone is Mr Fox.

Masked guests are already drinking on the terrace, looking fantastic in their array of costumes. Waiters circulate
with trays of canapés and there's a fantastic buffet laid out
for later. There's also a special treat for the party-goers: an
oyster shucker will move among them, supplying fresh
oysters to whoever wants them. It's a nice touch, I think;
one that originated at sex parties in the underground S&M
scene in Amsterdam. I've booked the services of the Oyster
Meister, a man in great demand. He mingles with the guests
with a bucket of fresh oysters hanging from his waist and
shucks them on the spot. He's served up his aphrodisiacs to
the likes of London's Mayor Boris Johnson at The Masked
Ball (which was not a KK party) and at Earl Spencer's
wedding reception at Althorp House.

Kitty Kat and I are wearing matching black beaded flapper dresses, long pearl necklaces and claret-red lipstick. As
we wander about making sure that everything is running
smoothly, I spot Jordie with Emerald Isle, both in Twenties-
style flapper dresses, and we head over.

'Hi, girls,' I say, kissing them on the cheeks. 'You both
look incredible.'

'All right, Emma? You look great this evening,' says
Jordie.

'Thanks.'

She leans in confidingly. 'I've got to tell you that Miss D
is getting on my nerves already. Is she on something or
what?'

Uh oh. 'Why is that?'

'She's running around like a madwoman looking for a billionaire called Gatsby.'

'Oh dear. Just ignore her.'

Emerald Isle says, 'She's convinced that guy over there is the one she's after.'

She points to a distinguished-looking middle-aged gentleman who is sitting at a table in the corner with his partner, a lady in a red dress. He's immaculately dressed in a pinstripe suite, red cravat, matching handkerchief and the most outlandish and biggest gold mask I've seen to date. It boasts raised eyebrows, cheeks, nostrils, mouth creases and a big smile – the dramatic happy mask that signifies comedy but is always paired with the grief-stricken face of tragedy. I shake my head and laugh.

'She's told us to join us there after she's powdered her nose. She says he's Gatsby.'

I sigh. 'I'll keep an eye on her. Don't worry.'

It's a particularly sophisticated and cosmopolitan crowd tonight. The atmosphere is playful and gentle and the party takes a while to get going. Lots of guests prefer to sit out on the terrace enjoying the beautiful gardens or wander in the grand rooms on the ground floor. Kitty takes over and does the rounds with Jupiter and the extra bouncers I've brought in to cover such a large venue, while I get a bite to eat.

I spot Plaything sitting at a table with a pretty blonde who must be Miss Norwegian Wood. She looks fantastic in an intricately embroidered white beaded dress with a tasselled skirt, and she's gone to town with her headwear, sporting a white feather-plumed headband. She's holding Plaything's hand.

'Hi!' I say, going up to them. Plaything introduces us and we chat away while I inspect her for signs of being Miss

Psycho. She can't be that bad if Plaything's brought her here tonight. In fact, she seems quite normal, and I'm just thinking that he must have made up all that stuff about the texts when I notice that she's holding Plaything's hand with a super-glue grip.

'So I hear you never take part in your own parties, Emma,' says Miss Norwegian Wood in her charming accent.

'That's right.' I gaze at her innocently. 'But you're welcome to. Do you like sharing?'

'Yes!' she says quickly. 'Of course. We're all here to share each other's fantasies, aren't we?'

'That's good.' I smile at her. 'And what about sharing Plaything? Would you ever get jealous?'

She grips Plaything's hand tighter than ever. 'Of course I get bloody jealous sometimes!' she proclaims rather too loudly.

'Ow!' says Plaything, wincing under her iron grip.

'Well, hello! Anyone care for an oyster?' It's the Oyster Meister himself, attracted by Miss Norwegian Wood's loud voice.

'Yes, please!' says Miss Norwegian Wood, successfully diverted.

'Did you know the legendary Casanova was said to have devoured as many as 50 raw oysters a day to sustain his insatiable appetite for sex? Care for a condiment?' he says as he takes out an oyster shell from the bucket of ice at his waist, twists the stubby knife into the hinge and prises it open to reveal the moist, plump creature inside.

'Just pepper, thanks.'

'Good choice,' he says, whipping an electric pepper grinder from his belt. 'My wife thought this gadget was a vibrator I bought from a sex shop in Soho. She wouldn't let me back into our bed for a week.'

Miss Norwegian Wood giggles and swallows her oyster quickly. 'Mmm, delicious.'

I leave the table as Miss Norway insists Plaything tucks in too, and I head inside. It's warming up a little now and some guests are already sneaking off to the playrooms. I pass Miss D. She's sitting with the gold-mask man and his girl-friend, full of smiles as he explains in a plummy voice that he's never played and is happy to sit back and watch his girlfriend.

'Oh, you must try it with your lovely *girlfriend*,' she gushes. 'You are so missing out! I am happy to give you some encouragement, if you like.'

Gold-mask man's partner looks horrified by the suggestion.

Making a mental note to come back later and make sure Miss D hasn't caused any trouble, I head upstairs to the playrooms. I haven't seen Gatsby yet, the host of tonight's party, but the other billionaire is already in one of the royal suites with his beautiful Latino girlfriend. He's safe enough from Miss D's clutches in there, and I have a feeling his girl-friend is more than a match for her. I shan't be revealing his identity in any case.

In another suite, two women sitting on a sofa are watch-ing erotic events unfolding on the four-poster bed where a masked man is doing a sterling job of keeping three women happy at once. One rides him cowgirl-style while another is sitting on his face. The third kneels by his side and moans as he strokes and pinches her erect nipples.

I walk into another room where the occupants are all in the zone. Among the mound of writhing flesh, I see one woman who is deliriously happy with her lover. He's feasting on her soft breast, flicking the tip of his hungry tongue across her nipple before taking it into his mouth. He takes his time, sucking, licking and nipping on both of her buds until they are swollen and hard. Now she's ready for him, spreading her thighs wide apart. They start to fuck slowly and deliciously and then gather speed as he plunges into her with hard, fierce strokes.

I leave as they slam together hard and fast, groaning with the sensations they're experiencing. Outside in the hall, I see Plaything and Miss Norwegian Wood wandering hand in hand, taking in the action and letting the erotic scenarios work their magic. He seems to like her, no matter what he says.

In the next suite, I spot Jordie sitting on a sofa and go over to join her.

'Where's the gang?' I ask.

Jordie makes a face. 'Miss D's still pestering the fellow with the gold mask. I had to get away. She's driving me nuts.'

'She has that effect,' I say, smiling.

We are interrupted by a stunning brunette with a deep, dark tan. She's staring at Jordie, smiling, as she approaches and says, 'Hi. My husband and I have had our eye on you all evening.'

Jordie blinks at her. 'You have?'

'Yes. We were wondering if you'd like to have sex with me. In fact, we thought it might be rather nice if you joined us for the whole night. In our room. My husband loves watching me make love to a beautiful woman.'

The brunette reaches for Jordie's hand. Jordie gives it to her, smiling back. 'We'll have to find Mr Jordie. He likes to watch too.' She looks at me almost apologetically. 'Do you mind, Emma?'

'Of course I don't. You go and have a good time.'

Jordie goes off, her eyes bright with anticipation. I'm glad to see that she has something to take her mind off the way Miss D has been annoying her. I'm just observing three women taking it in turns to suck off a handsome man in a black mask when Jupiter comes up to me.

Just then, I see a man with a shock of bleached hair come walking through the front door. He's smart in a Savile Row suit and mysterious in a velvet mask. But I know exactly who he is.

Gatsby.

I head over. 'Good evening, sir. I'm very pleased you could make it.'

'Good evening, Emma. Lovely to see you, as ever. Anything interesting going on tonight?'

'Always,' I say. 'I hope you'll enjoy yourself.'

'I'm sure I will.'

'Can I just say one thing? If a slightly neurotic-seeming girl in a red dress and a black sequinned headband tries to approach you, can you take my advice and steer clear? She means well, but it's best not to get involved.'

He smiles. 'Certainly.' He looks me up and down and says, 'And you, Emma? Are you in the market for some fun tonight?'

'I'm afraid not, sir,' I say. 'But please – enjoy yourself and let me know if I can help in any way.' I smile. 'Except that way.'

'Thank you.' He drifts off to explore the party, and I head off towards the library. I just hope Miss D hasn't found a copy of *The Great Gatsby*.

Chapter Twenty

'That which does not kill us
makes us stronger.'
Friedrich Nietzsche

I'm lying in my bikini on a sun lounger in Monte Carlo and a handsome waiter is bringing me a cocktail. I close my eyes and count my blessings … *I'm one lucky girl.*

Even though it's already early evening, the sun is still strong, its rays doing a good job of kissing my skin. It feels wonderful as I stretch my limbs to soak up all the warmth.

The waiter places my drink on the table by my lounger. 'Here you are, madam.'

'Thank you.'

'Would you like anything else?'

'I think I have everything I need. Thank you.' I smile at him.

Twelve hours ago, I was at the beautiful country house surveying the detritus of the 1920s party. Now I'm in an expensive hotel, lying by a pool on a sun deck lined with palm trees before I catch my flight back to London.

Katie, an actress on the cusp of real fame, called me last week. Her hectic filming schedule has given her little time for fun and games lately. When her producer called to inform her that filming on her latest project had been pushed back by a couple of days, Katie was straight on the phone to me to arrange a fantasy break for herself and her boyfriend. I've arranged everything just as they want it.

Tonight, Katie and her man are going to be seduced in a bar by a beautiful woman. They've talked about it for ages and now they're ready to act out this fantasy. For them, it's about pushing themselves beyond their normal sexual experiences and reaching a new level of excitement together. Thanks to a very discreet personal agency, I'm making it a reality for them. Cynthia, drop-dead gorgeous and very experienced, will find them as they enjoy a cocktail in the hotel bar, the one next to the pool where I'm relaxing. They have no idea what Cynthia looks like, but Cynthia knows her targets – I've already emailed her a photograph of the happy couple.

I pick up my phone and make my last call to Cynthia.

'Hi, Emma,' she answers.

'Are you close?'

'I am very close. I'm in the ladies near the bar. I'll come past soon to find them. I'm just going to pop in my jiggle balls.'

Yikes!

Five minutes later, Cynthia is walking towards me. She is a knockout, tall with short blonde hair and dressed in a short black-and-nude lace dress. I give her a discreet smile as she walks past me. I'm not her target and she isn't going to talk to me. She has her eyes fixed firmly on the bar, where Katie and her man are already waiting, sipping their drinks and looking just a little nervous as well as excited.

Little do they know that their fantasy is about to walk through the door.

I leave them to it and go for a swim in the pool, doing 50 lengths before I get out, wrap myself in a fluffy white robe and wander over to the bar to see how things are going.

It's all warming up very nicely. The three of them are snuggled around a table. Katie is drinking champagne in a lazy, blissed-out way. I notice that, beneath the table, Cynthia's hand is stroking her thigh. Katie turns her head to Cynthia, and very lightly the other woman drops a kiss on her lips and says, 'Why don't we go upstairs and have a drink in private?'

In less than a moment, the three of them are on their feet, dropping money on the table for the champagne and making their way out of the bar to the lift. I smile. It's going exactly as I'd hoped.

I head back to my own room to shower and pack for the return trip. I'm going to catch the last plane back to London tonight.

The next morning, there's a text on my phone from Katie.

Amazing! Thank you! And the jiggle balls!!! Off to La La Land now. Would love you to throw a naughty party for a movie producer pal! Will be in touch. Xxx

Another satisfied customer.

I'm taken up with work for a few days and hardly notice that I've not heard from Mr Fox until a text message pops up on my phone. He wants to see me. Good. I've missed him. I text back that I'll meet him after the party later tonight, and he sends me the address of the place where he'll be.

This evening it's the Killing Kittens Burlesque Party, which takes place in a discreet basement nightclub. The walls are mirrored and the ceilings sparkling pink, and each table is equipped with a telephone that means Kittens can call each other to exchange sweet nothings or invite someone they like to join them. If they don't fancy talking, there's also a postcard system that's operated by Kitty Kat, who delivers the little notes between tables. Meanwhile, a sexy burlesque performance will be taking place on the stage, firing up the lusts of the audience and encouraging them to let go of their own inhibitions.

Not that my Kittens have many of those.

Even before the burlesque, there're lots of sexy vibes in the air. A handsome banker in a black suit is queuing at the bar. While he waits to be served, he's caressing a woman next to him, who's passionately kissing her friend.

People are sitting at the tables, drinking and making calls, but nothing really serious is kicking off yet. We're all waiting for the show to get us really fired up. Kitty is on the door tonight, and I'm sitting at a table on my own when Trolley Dolly arrives.

'Darling!' she cries. 'It's so wonderful to see you! How are you?'

'I'm fine.' I return her kiss. 'Where have you been? I haven't seen you for ages.'

She smiles at me and looks a little sheepish. 'Sorry, my sweet. I've been having rather a nice time, actually. I've been screwing your friend, McDreamy.' She sighs.

'Goodness!' I blink, astonished. Have two of my friends that most love playing the field finally settled down – with each other? 'Are you two an item?'

'No.' Trolley Dolly shakes her head with a laugh. 'I think I prefer being single if I'm honest, even if McDreamy is a great guy. I think we're just going to be friends now we've got it out of our system.'

Plaything comes wandering up, but he's far from his usual cheerful self. 'Evening, Emma.' He bends down to kiss Trolley Dolly's cheek.

'Hi! How are you? How's Miss Norwegian Wood?'

He shudders. 'Don't. It's all gone shit-shaped. Have you been getting any weird texts from her?'

I shake my head.

'Good,' says Plaything. 'She's gone well and truly mental this time – a psycho woman, a raving lunatic nutcase.'

'What's she done?'

'She's emailed my boss saying that I'm a thief and that I've stolen clothes from her. Clothes she bought! She messaged my mother on Facebook to tell her she's been a bad parent. And she's sent a poisonous email to all my friends because I won't move to Norway.'

'That's awful,' I say sympathetically. 'I shan't open any messages I get from her.'

'Time to drop her completely,' advises Trolley Dolly. 'Cut off all communication. Now, sit down. I'm going to order a bottle of champagne for us, and we can get down to watching the show. It's just about to start.'

On cue, the lights dim and a voluptuous redhead wearing a strappy black latex bikini comes out onto the stage and introduces herself as 'the hostess with double-D mostess' and urges the crowd to give a 'cheer for cock and tits'.

'Are you ready for something dark and twisted?' she asks the crowd.

'Yes! Yes! Yes!' they roar.

'Get ready for Miss Missy!'

Miss Missy has mastered the art of tease and titillation to perfection. She sashays onto the stage in a long black satin gown with thigh-high splits and wearing killer heels. Her

hair is coiled into a bun. The music plays and Miss Missy
starts bumping and grinding and then peels off her long
black gloves. She whirls them around and flings them away,
then leaves the stage and saunters over to a couple sitting at
a table. They smile nervously as Miss Missy begins to sway
her hips to the music. She lifts the woman's chin with her
index finger and moves in like she is going to kiss her, but
at the last minute she pulls back and sashays sexily back to
the stage to continue divesting herself of her clothes. In one
movement, she slips out of her dress, picks it up and throws
it at the couple. Miss Missy smiles and pouts as she poses in
her underwear and an eye-catching pair of black diamanté
seamed stockings. Then she's off the stage again, going to
another table where she props up her leg and rolls her stock-
ing down it, taking it off along with her shoe. She does the
same with the other leg, steps back into her killer heels and
returns to the stage.

All eyes are on her as she runs her hands over her porcelain skin, then frees her breasts from her black satin bra.
They're magnificent, her nipples huge, pink and erect.
Anticipation builds as Miss Missy's hands go to her black
satin knickers. She slides her fingertips into the waistband
and lifts it away from her hips, smiling seductively. Then
she stops, teasing us all, as she slowly starts removing her
hairpins instead. Waves of copper-coloured hair tumble to
her waist. Then, finally, she slides her knickers down her
legs until she reaches her knees and lets them drop to the
floor. She slowly steps out of them and does a peek-a-boo-
type pose. She's stark naked except for her shoes and very
beautiful.

The switch has been flicked on by Missy's playful, sexy
act. Suddenly, people everywhere are losing their clothing

and soon there is playing everywhere. Men and women are
having sex at the bar, on tables, in booths, on the bed of
giant cushions in the middle of the room. Staff balancing
trays full of champagne, Mojitos and Sea Breezes make their
way through the heaving crowd without batting an eyelid.

Over by the DJ's booth a woman is lying spread-eagled
on a cushion. A man is gently massaging her clitoris, and
he's doing a fabulous job judging by the expression on her
delighted face. His erection is huge, but he's not ready to
slide it into her just yet. Instead, he takes his time, kissing
her and then moving his mouth downwards to lick up her
juices. Finally, as she gasps with pleasure, he slides his
throbbing cock into her. She's instantly hit with an endor-
phin overdose, crying out as she spreads wider to accommo-
date him.

I glance at the bar where two women, both in white
stockings and suspenders and wearing Venetian masks, are
playing together. One rubs lotion onto her lover's breasts,
then starts blowing on the nipples and caressing them with
her tongue. The other woman arches her back, jolting at the
electric sensations of pleasure she is getting. Her friend
spreads her legs and presses her face into her vagina. 'Quite
a show tonight,' murmurs a voice in my ear. It's Trolley
Dolly, watching my face. 'You look like you're taking it
all in.'

'I haven't seen Mr Fox for a while,' I say with a smile.
'But I am later.'

'I'm glad, for your sake. I think you might need to work
off some tension after what's going on in here.'

I notice a beautiful woman waving seductively at us from
one of our champagne stations and smiling at Trolley Dolly,
who waves back.

'Another one of your conquests?' I ask.

'No, but you know me. No doesn't mean never. I've seen her in action and I like what I see. She's flexible and can feed in any number of directions: up, down, backwards and even upside down with a man or woman.'

I wave and look at her again.

'I wish I could remember every member, but I don't. What's her name?'

'Hummingbird. She flits from flower to flower and humms like a hummingbird when she's making love. Her tongue is lightning fast.'

I glance back at her. 'I remember my pa telling me that hummingbirds actually make the humming sound with their frantic wing beat. They flap their wings about 80 times per second.'

Trolley Dolly smiles. 'You should see how quickly she flaps once she gets started. Despite being a little bird, she makes a lot of noise and moves so fast. She is nothing short of impressive.'

Hummingbird's legs are now firmly wrapped around an exquisite Indian beauty and she's kissing her passionately while clutching a glass of champagne. Her other hand is moving slowly to her lover's inner sanctum. A man is watching, his eyes wide and his mouth slightly open. One of Hummingbird's girlfriends drops to her knees beside him and pulls down his trousers, revealing his erection. She looks up, flashes him a wicked smile, then takes him in her mouth and starts sucking hard.

'I'm sure we'll see Hummingbird will be flying high in a pile somewhere soon,' I say, and take a sip of champagne.

Trolley Dolly gets to her feet. 'Will you excuse me, Emma? I've just seen someone I'd like to know better.' She glides off towards a dark stranger across the room who has fixed her with a dark, provocative gaze.

I get up and go to find Kitty to ask if everything's all right.

She nods. 'It is now. I've had to throw out two guys tonight. They think they're so clever, paying for escorts to pose as their girlfriends so as to pass the vetting process.'

I make a face. 'And let me guess – their "girlfriends" leave as soon as the sex starts?'

'Yes. But I'm wise to it.'

'Never underestimate, Kitty!' I say, smiling. 'It's amazing the lengths to which some single men will go to gate-crash our parties.'

'Until we sniff them out.'

'Exactly. Make sure their memberships are terminated.'

I spot a woman standing on her own dressed in a peach crochet dress. I suspect she is a first-timer. She knocks back a generous gulp of champagne and fiddles with her bracelets nervously.

'Hello,' I say. 'Are you enjoying your evening?'

'Yes,' she says with a subdued smile. 'My girlfriend let me down tonight, but I still wanted to come and see what a sex party where women are in control is all about.'

'Good for you.'

'I was worried.'

'There's no need. It's all cool here. Honestly.'

'I can see that. Everyone seems to be having a wonderful time.'

I spot two Asian girls on their knees on the floor nearby. They're both enjoying licking and sucking two erect penises while the men watch, excitement growing on their faces. One of the men stands up and says, 'Let's skip foreplay and tuck into mains. Come on, there's a bed over there.'

His girl stands up and says, 'Uh-uh.'

Her friend stands up too and says, 'We say yes to oral, but no to full sex.' The girls saunter off.

'See?' I say, turning to the first-timer. 'No pressure.'

I leave her chatting away to a couple also on their first time and go back to Kitty.

'I have to go. I'm going to meet Mr Fox. Will you be OK?'

'Of course. Have a great time!'

'I will!' I pick up my bag and head off into the night.

Within half an hour I'm waiting on a stool in a crowded piano bar. I sip my drink and scan the crowd. The light is dim in here and I can't see Mr Fox.

Then, suddenly, he's there, heading my way. My work commitments have kept us apart for too long and I'm in the mood for romance and for reacquainting myself with him tonight. I notice he's in the same suit he wore the night we first met on the boat on the Thames. He's looking *hot*.

I stare at him as he approaches, and he fixes his gaze on me as he makes his way through the crowd. He doesn't take his eyes off me as we play our flirtatious staring game.

'Good evening,' he says in that deep, sexy voice as he reaches me.

'Hi,' I say, kissing him on the lips.

He settles on the stool next to mine and smiles. *God, he's attractive.* 'Can I get you something? What would you like?'

'Sex on the Beach,' I say flirtatiously.

'I'm afraid that's not possible,' he replies.

'Why?'

'There are no beaches in London.'

'Very funny. But I fancy sex on the beach. So if I can't have it right now, I'll guess I'll just have to drink it.'

He orders our drinks and turns back to me. He doesn't say anything. I realize I can read something in his eyes. Something I don't want to see.

Then it hits me.

I know that look – the one that says, 'I'm about to drop a bombshell.'

A knot of fear tightens in my stomach.

No! No! I don't want this, not now! I don't think I can take it. He's going to tell me that it's not me, it's him. I'm going to be a notch on his bedpost after all.

There's an awkward silence and I break it by saying, 'Are you going to tell me what's wrong?'

After all that staring, he suddenly can't meet my eye or find any words, until at last he says to the bar counter, 'Emma – you're an amazing woman, but … I'm sorry …'

I rush in. I can't stand faffing about, even at moments like these. And if something's going to hurt, I want the pain now, fast. Not drawn out like a torture session. 'Are you about to dump me?'

He pauses again, glances at me and says, 'I'm just not ready for a serious relationship.'

A mix of pain and fury rushes through me. 'I guess next you'll be saying it's not you, it's me.'

'Well, that's true. It *is* me, not you.'

I take a gulp of my drink, holding it with a trembling hand. I want to ask him whether he has his paws on someone else or whether it's because he's just not so hungry for me after all. But I don't trust myself to speak.

He's staring at me again, now that the words are out there. I'm breathing fast, trying to control my emotions. Then his face is close to mine, his breath heavy. He stares into my eyes and kisses me passionately.

My heart races, as I can't help opening my mouth to his kiss. What the hell is going on? This man, who I was falling in love with and who has just dumped me, is now kissing me, and it feels beautiful.

Is he doing it just to prove he can? To prove he's still got power over me?

I can't bear it. I pull away, grab my handbag and say, 'Goodbye.'

'Emma,' he says, but I can't look at him now. Instead, I push through the crowd, desperate to reach the open air. When I do, I run as fast as I can away from him, and I don't look back.

Chapter Twenty-One

'Enjoy life. There's plenty of time to be dead.'
Hans Christian Andersen

'Hello, Wonder Woman.'

'Hello,' I pant, knowing only too well who's on the other end.

I'm sweating and on the verge of finishing a 20-kilometre morning run. Usually I never take calls during my gym workout, but I can't ignore this one.

Two nights ago, I got a 999 from Plaything. I nearly didn't answer it, as I was curled up on my sofa trying to deal with the waves of misery washing over me since Mr Fox and I split. During the day, I'm my usual cheery self, but at night, when I'm not out or working, I feel the black cloud of depression descending. It was a good thing I did answer Plaything's call, though, as he'd just got off the phone from Miss D, who had told him she'd tried to break into Mr Kidnap's house. I was on my way to the King's Road in a flash to discover my friend – in high spirits after one too many bottles of bubbly and a little on the hysterical side because neither Mr Kidnap nor Marilyn were on the premises – in the hands of Mr Kidnap's security team. They were only too happy to hand her over to me, keen to avoid any fuss.

Now I feel guilty because I introduced Miss D into Mr Kidnap's life. It's ironic, really, that he pays me to provide manufactured terror and menace. Now I've managed to produce some of the real thing. I only hope he's not too furious.

I'm just about to launch into an apology for Miss D's behaviour when Mr Kidnap says, 'I don't have much time. I'm about to board a private jet with Marilyn. We're escaping to St Tropez for security reasons.'

'I see.' I wonder if fleeing the country is a little over the top. Perhaps Mr Kidnap is enjoying this, in a crazy sort of way.

'I want you to sort out a kidnap. I'll pay you £5,000.'

'When?' I ask, as I hop off the running machine, towelling off the waterfall of sweat on my face. 'I'm flying out to Los Angeles today to host a private party.'

'I need it today.'

Of course. When else?

'What would you like? Is it a Superhero kidnap?' I ask, hoping this isn't going to take place in St Tropez. That would make things considerably more difficult. Two women on the cross trainers are staring suspiciously at me.

There is an awkward silence, then he whispers, 'I want you to kidnap Doctor Sparky.'

'You mean Miss D?' I ask, not terribly surprised.

'Yes. She's great in the sack, but I'm choosing Marilyn.'

I want to laugh. So Mr Kidnap is the superhero in this scenario. I suppose I can't blame him, considering Miss D's drunken antics. I've organized over 30 abductions for Mr Kidnap and nearly as many Marilyn Monroe lookalikes. At last he's found one who's fallen for him, and it's given him a burst of courage.

'It's very short notice,' I say, heading for the locker room. 'And you don't have to worry about D. I've locked her in my flat.'

'Wonder Woman, you're the best!' He sighs with relief. 'Are you taking her to LA with you?'

'No. The flight's fully booked.'

'Are you flying economy?'

'Yes.'

'If you take her with you, I'll book you both seats in first class. I need an ocean separating us. You'll be doing me a big favour, Wonder Woman.'

'I'm happy in economy, but you can book a seat for Miss D if you like,' I reply. The woman may be a liability, but she's always the life and soul at my parties, so I could use her help in LA. 'I am sorry about all this, and I'll make her apologize too.'

'No!' he says, alarmed. 'I'll pay for her never to speak to me again. I'll pay for her manicures, pedicures, hair extensions, boob jobs, facials, Botox, collagen, jewellery, clothes and travel. Anything she wants, as long as she stays away now I've chosen Marilyn. All communication is through you.'

I grin. This would be music to Miss D's ears but perhaps it's better if she doesn't know the extent to which her bad behaviour could be rewarded. 'I don't think you have to go so far.'

'Oh, I do. A golden goodbye handshake, ransom money, call it whatever you like. I'll do anything to get her out of my life. Apart from buying her a house. I don't fancy her as my next-door neighbour. And please ask her to stop emailing me. I've had 20 messages already today, entitled variously "Read this asshole", "Fuck You" and "WTF Fuck Face".'

'I'm so sorry. I'll speak to her.'

'Tell her I'm going to buy a real pistol,' he quips, before hanging up.

Miss D glides across the concourse at Heathrow Airport looking like she's just stepped off the catwalk. Never one to let a meltdown get in the way of being noticed, she's tottering in sky-high wedges, a pink miniskirt and T-shirt and oversized sunglasses for our long-haul flight to Los Angeles. I'm dressed in my black silk sleepwear and worn-down summer sandals and haven't wiped off last night's mascara. Miss D is busy smiling at passers-by, even waving to those who stop and stare, as though they're her fans.

'Is she famous, Mummy?' a small girl asks her mother.

'I don't know, darling,' replies her mother, frowning. 'She looks like she might be an actress, I suppose.'

Miss D has obviously heard this as she says loudly, 'What time is our flight to Hollywood?' and looks at me like I'm her lackey. She's swaying somewhat in her ridiculous shoes.

The little girl and her mummy look suitably impressed. I'm anything but.

'You're going a bit overboard, aren't you? Can you do me a favour and just try behaving? You promised you would if I brought you along.'

'I promise, Ems! Shall I try getting you an upgrade? It's the least I can do. Who bought me this ticket anyway?'

'My credit card paid for it and there's no need for an upgrade,' I reply quickly. I'd rather be alone in economy. I'm desperate for peace and quiet before the big party tonight. 'Just stay off the booze and behave.'

'Consider it done,' she replies as she kisses me goodbye. 'Don't worry about me. I'm fine now. I'm over that little shit. *Au revoir*, Ems. *Vous voir à* Hollywood. It's actually safer sitting in economy if the plane crashes. So enjoy.'

She wiggles off on her high heels, and I watch her lap up the fuss as she's ushered off to the first-class check-in and off to the club lounge, leaving me stuck in the snaking economy queue. By the time I check in, D has texted that she's had a massage and a facial, and is trying to invite a handsome celebrity along to the private beach party. All I want is to be on board so I can settle down and sleep and put the nagging thoughts of Mr Fox out of my mind.

'Ladies and gentlemen, I want to be the first to welcome you to Los Angeles International Airport where the local time is 10.05 in the morning. We hope you enjoyed your flight today. On behalf of Virgin Atlantic, we thank you for choosing us and hope to see you on board again soon.'

I'm one of the last off the plane and I'm finally through US Immigration when I spot a commotion unfolding at the baggage reclaim area. Miss D is attracting the attention of bemused teenage girls as she pouts and poses at the carousel staring at the moving bags. She's dressed up to the max in a totally different outfit to the one she boarded in: a short khaki belted dress, black trilby, oversized sunglasses and sky-scraper heels. The girls snigger when she attempts to drag her Louis Vuitton luggage off the conveyor belt but fails to lift it. She gives up and looks around for help, locking eyes with a strapping LAX police officer walking past in the bustling terminal.

'Could some kind gentleman *please* help me lift my luggage?' she begs, and he strides over at once.

'Let me help you, ma'am,' he says, lifting up her case.

'Thank you,' she says in a soft, beguiling voice.

'You're very welcome, Miss.'

'Miss D,' she says, stretching her hand out to him. 'Lovely to meet you, officer.'

I go over and grab her hand. We haven't got time for Miss D to start on some crazy seduction of an LA cop. I can just imagine how quickly she'd land in jail and I'd be the one left to get her out. 'Come on,' I say. 'Let's get a taxi. I need to get going, pronto.'

I drag her away as she stares wistfully over her shoulder at the hunky officer.

I'm standing in a spacious waterfront mansion perched high above the Pacific Ocean on acres of land. The complex includes guest cottages, a tennis court, a screening room, a swimming pool, a Jacuzzi bathtub and a private beach. My Kittens will have the time of their lives here in the Malibu Colony. It's home to the rich and famous and as private as you can get. Killing Kittens now has more than 3,000 American members, and this is the right time to bring the party across the Atlantic. Katie's invitation to host a party for a movie producer friend of hers was the perfect opportunity to spread my wings stateside.

There are around 200 people coming tonight; some are KK members and others are open-minded friends of the movie producer, Mr Hollywood. I've no doubt that some big movers and shakers will be attending this evening.

Before the flirtation, fun and seductions begin, I need to lay down the rules to Miss D. I don't want her to start acting up on me here, at an important party that could be my entrée into Hollywood. She promises solemnly to be good and goes off to check on the caterers. Kitty Kat comes up looking stunning in a white bikini underneath a loose-fitting kaftan and a butterfly mask with pert silver whiskers, her tousled hair falling around her shoulders. The dress code is white and glitzy, and Kitty fulfils it effortlessly.

'We're almost ready to go.' She hands over the clipboard with the list of names. 'So, I noticed that the door to the second floor is locked. Is that the VVIP room?'

'Yes. It's reserved for one very special guest. I don't know who it is, but I think it's a she.'

Kitty looks intrigued. 'I saw men carrying what looked like a coffin on their shoulders up to the second floor.' She gives me a questioning look. I should remember that Kitty never misses a thing.

'It's not a coffin,' I say quickly. 'It's a kind of long, white and sparkling box with no top. Inside there's a mattress with white satin sheets and there are holes carved in the side.'

'Ah, I see.' Kitty's face clears. 'It's like Snow White's casket – except that a chosen few will be able to put their hands through to touch whoever's inside.'

'Something like that,' I reply, smiling. This was a special request from Mr Hollywood on behalf of a friend of his, and unlike any I've had before. It was hard to source exactly what he wanted, but I managed it. 'Let's get a drink. It'll start kicking off soon.'

'Marvellous idea,' says Kitty. 'We can toast Killing Kittens cracking Hollywood.'

At 7.30 p.m. the valets are parking Bugattis, Ferraris and Porsches and suddenly it's busy, as toned, tanned, beautiful people dressed in white start arriving. It's a glitzy crowd of people who've got rich in the entertainment business, and I've never seen such a collection of perfection. This is a land where any blemish can be fixed and where everybody seems to have the willpower or money to make themselves gorgeous. I'm distracted by everyone's beauty. The masked men all possess that dazzling white Hollywood smile, chiselled jawlines and six-packs from their twice-a-day workouts. The women, whose ages range from 20-something to 40-something, are just as stunning as the picturesque scenery outside. Hollywood women are different to others – they're slimmer, their teeth whiter, their breasts and lips bigger. Despite their smooth faces and immobile foreheads, they give off an aura of pleasure-seeking hedonism.

This soirée looks like it's going to be wilder than I thought.

Two beautiful dark-blonde women with ice-blue eyes are getting into the spirit early outside on the decking. It's not even 8 p.m. and already they're removing their white bikini tops, but they stick to my rules and keep their masks on. A handsome stranger starts spraying a magnum of Cristal champagne, soaking their shapely round breasts with the foam as they shriek and giggle. They let the liquid run in bubbling rivulets over their tanned skin and dark-brown nipples, and open their mouths wide to drink in as much as they can. When their mouths are full to the brim, they lean in and kiss, letting the frothing bubbles pour into each other's mouths. Then they stop, swallow and kiss each other again, this time with more intensity. The handsome stranger watches happily as they caress each other. Then they release one another, gaze at him provocatively and one says, 'Catch us if you can,' before they both get up and run inside. He doesn't need any more of an invitation and strides after them with a determined expression. He wants to get into those itsy-bitsy-teeny-weeny bikini bottoms as soon as he can.

I stroll over to the pool where a group of six gorgeous women are dancing provocatively in skimpy bikinis as music floats out from hidden speakers. Behind the masks, they all have their eyes on the prize. Drawn like moths to a flame, they're waiting for a distractingly beautiful man to emerge from his dip in the swimming pool. He's making them wait as he spins around and does another lap under the water.

When he at last emerges, dripping wet and looking like a sex god, I recognize the famous, brooding face. He's a Hollywood actor. It's impossible not to stare at his tight white swimming trunks as he steps out and dries his muscular body with a towel. His brown eyes turn to see the waiting women and glitter with intensity. 'Do you ladies feel like a game of volleyball?'

'Yes!' they squeal at once.

'I'm talking naked beach volleyball,' he says. 'Down there.' He gestures to the private beach that lies below the house, from where we can hear the ocean lapping the shore.

They certainly don't mind, judging by the chorus of yeses.

'The rules are simple: I'm the only one playing with you six. I'm all yours, do what you want with me.'

He strides off and they rush after him, following him down the steps. I notice they're not the only ones on the beach. It's already quite busy. Some people are still chatting or just kissing. There are a few couples already going further.

I feel a rush of joy. This was my vision when I first set up Killing Kittens: I wanted to provide beautiful places where people could come to enjoy themselves openly and without hypocrisy or deception. Sex is one of life's greatest gifts. Why do we treat it with such hostility and suspicion? It's a natural, essential thing. It's part of our make-up as humans. We've made so many rules about sex to stop ourselves enjoying it. But why? We indulge ourselves with good food, with drink, with massages and dance and plenty of other physical pleasures. So why not sex? I know it's not for everyone, and that for some people sex is too bound up with emotion. They have no wish to do something like this, and that's their choice. But why stand in judgement of those who do? We've accepted for centuries that men have physical needs and that they're able to experience physical satisfaction without involving their emotions. If that weren't true, the vast sex industry wouldn't exist. There would be no need for pornography or prostitutes. But there is a need, and the industry that services men's needs is growing faster than ever. We still haven't fully accepted that women have sexual needs too, ones that might be just as intense and compelling as men's. As a society, we tolerate men's desire but question women's. It might be true that the female is wired differently from the male, but that's what Killing Kittens is all about. The thing that pleases me is that men come to my parties in preference to those darker, harder, male-dominated ones, because they appreciate female desire and the glory of women revelling in sex, doing it because they want to and because they like it.

People have to make up their own minds, but I see no shame in it. We have our bodies for a short time on this earth. They were made to enjoy this divine pleasure. I don't believe we're supposed to deny that need, any more than we should deny ourselves food or air or laughter.

A tangerine blonde kicks off proceedings by ordering the famous man to remove his swimming trunks. The volley-ball net is already being used by a group of naked players, so the game is off for now. Instead, he follows tangerine blonde's instructions and lies down on a luxurious cabana beach bed. His cock is already rock solid. He strokes it slowly when the six beautiful women tell him to as they begin to undress before him. Tangerine blonde is the first to get naked and clambers onto the bed between his legs, taking his erection into her mouth. The others use him in every way they can, stroking, kissing, licking and devouring his god-like form. When they're ready, they take it in turns to climb onto his penis and delight in its movement in their depths. They seem to thrill at the pleasure of sharing him.

As I return from the beach, I see that masks are beginning to come off as darkness falls. The mood is now one of decadence. A rock star is dancing naked on the table while two blondes with the biggest breasts I've ever seen are all over him. His wife is happily chatting to a tall dark stranger who is stroking her fondly, keen to start peeling off her white sparkling top and reveal her breasts, while a foot fetishist on the floor by her wedge sandals is begging to suck her exquisite toes.

Back inside, a naked actress strolls behind the bar to help herself to a drink and then stays to help Miss D serve. As soon as she is there, men suddenly discover a desperate thirst and hurry over for more refreshment. There's a dance floor in one of the large downstairs rooms where a DJ is spinning tunes as people cavort uninhibitedly to the music in various stages of undress. In the corner of the room, I recognize a famous model curling her long legs underneath her, smiling as she watches her girlfriend make love to a voluptuous olive-skinned woman with a strap-on dildo on a giant bed of pillows.

'Ooh, darling,' wails the olive-skinned woman as the other girl plunges in and out of her. 'You like fucking me hard.'

'Just take it. Take all of it,' says her lover, who seems to relish pleasuring the perfectly curvaceous body, thrusting hard and deep with her strap-on. The olive-skinned woman writhes under her, groaning intensely. I can tell this kinky pair will be having wild sex all night long – with each other, and anyone else they meet along the way.

In the huge sitting room, dominated by white sofas, I find a large number of guests having sex in every conceivable position, kissing, licking and devouring each other, communicating in soft moans and groans and whispered entreaties to do more, harder, faster, deeper, just there … Oh *yes* …

I see Katie, who's wearing a long crocheted dress with a white bikini underneath. When she spots me, she beckons me over.

'Hi, gorgeous. Lovely to see you. This party is the greatest thing ever. I mean, *ever*. Now, I want to introduce you to Mr Hollywood. You two haven't met face to face yet, have you?'

Mr Hollywood is short but in good shape. He's dressed in a white linen suit and has the best stubble I've seen in a long time.

'Good evening, sir.'

'It's good to meet you finally,' he says, with a glint of mischief in his eyes. 'Katie told me about the splendid trip you organized for her in Monaco. It sounded so good, I was happy for her to persuade me into holding this.'

'Oh, Monaco was awesome!' cries Katie. 'I think about it all the time.'

'And this party is exactly what I'd hoped,' Mr Hollywood adds.

I'm delighted. 'That's wonderful. I'm so pleased.'

'Yep.' He looks around, clutching his drink to his chest and nodding. 'This is going to take some beating. People will be talking about this one for a long time.' He turns and fixes me with an intense look. 'I was wondering whether you could arrange something for me next time I'm in London.'

'Of course. Any idea of what you'd like?'

'Oh, I've got some ideas. I'll be in touch when I know my dates.'

'Please do. I'd be happy to help.' I give him a beaming smile.

Just then, I see someone walk in and my attention is instantly taken by her. It's one of the world's most beautiful actresses being escorted inside. I realize at once that she is the VVIP guest. Even behind her mask, she looks angelic as she makes her way through the crowd, dressed in a flowing white transparent slip dress with a daisy chain wrapped around her head. She's escorted by a group of masked men who look like rock stars. Just then, she spots Mr Hollywood, smiles and starts walking towards us.

My heart begins to pound as I realize that it's *her*. The woman I first saw in Ibiza, sprawled on a kitchen counter, enjoying every man who wanted her. She's the one who inspired me to set up these parties.

She's even more beautiful up close, and I can hardly breathe as she nears us.

'Hi, everyone,' she says softly when she reaches us. She kisses Mr Hollywood and Katie in greeting.

'This is Emma,' Mr Hollywood says, indicating me. 'She's the organizer of my little party tonight.'

She turns to me, her exquisite eyes glittering behind the mask. I had no idea anyone could have so much impact close up. I can't take my eyes from her smooth skin and beautifully shaped mouth. 'Hi, Emma. It's good to meet you. I'm told you've organized a special playroom for me.'

'That's right,' I say, my throat dry. 'Please, come this way.'

As I lead her towards the staircase, taking the key to the upper floor out of my pocket as I go, I see her nod to her escorts to come with her, and we all mount the stairs together. I open the door and let her in. Tonight, this will be her private playground for as long as she wants it.

In a spacious bedroom with a retractable roof open to the night skies, the large white box is waiting for her.

She peels off her dress quickly and whispers to me, 'Help me get in.'

Her tiny hand lands on my shoulder as I help her climb in, then she lies herself down with a luxurious sigh. 'Thank you,' she says. 'I'm ready.'

She closes her eyes like a Sleeping Beauty and waits. Before long, her male companions are circling the box, observing her naked form – the small pert breasts with their delicate brown nipples, the tiny waist, the beautiful inner sanctum nestling at the top of her long slender legs. All she wears is her mask.

I move to the door and watch for a little longer as the men begin to get closer to her. Now they are sliding their hands through the holes in the box's sides and touching her all over. Not just her breasts, but the neglected places, like the crook of her elbows, her palms, her feet and her armpits. She doesn't stir at first, but slowly Sleeping Beauty comes to life and begins to move gently and moan exquisitely as the hands caress and stroke her, trailing across her thighs and breasts. Her moans become louder when one of her suitors plays at her entrance, toying with her swollen clitoris until she's gasping and moving her legs apart. As soon as she opens her thighs, he inserts his finger into her depths, evidently pleasing her.

I can smell the scent of her arousal filling the room again, just like Ibiza. He wants her but is waiting for her command.

At last she takes off her mask, opens her eyes and says simply, 'Now.'

He scoops her from the box and takes her over to the waiting bed, where he lays her down. She's wild-eyed now, breathing hard, panting with desire. The men surround her, each one burning with lust for her. She's ravishing as she lies upon the white sheets and spreads her long legs open. An olive-skinned suitor kneels on the floor and buries his face in her exquisite love tunnel, his tongue glorying in her. She wraps her legs around his neck and gasps with pleasure. She beckons over a delightfully hard man, who eagerly joins her on the bed and starts pinching her already-erect nipples between his thumb and forefinger. She looks like she is floating across an ocean of bliss. Now her olive-skinned suitor has returned his mouth to hers as he finally presses home his huge erection, sliding it into her welcoming depths. They moan with the delicious pleasure, and those famous eyes grow glassy as she loses herself in the sensation of fucking.

I don't think I've ever seen a woman who adores sex as much as she does. She seems to be made for it, as if every moment she isn't fucking is a moment wasted. It's time to leave her to the private playground I created for her. I'm sure she's only just beginning. I close the door behind me and head back downstairs.

In one of the ground-floor bedrooms, two big-breasted brunettes are whipping a man chained to a bed and ask if I'd like to join them. I shake my head with a smile. In another room, a socialite I recognize is sitting naked on the sofa while a handsome man in a white coat and rubber gloves is playing the part of doctor. He tells her to open up so he can examine her thoroughly.

I'm distracted by familiar giggles coming from the bathroom. *Uh oh. That can only be one person.*

I hurry to the bathroom door and listen. Sure enough, I can hear Miss D. But who's she with? And what's she up to? She's talking to someone.

'I love blow,' she says, slurring her words. 'Seriously, it's my golden secret, which I'm sharing just with you, because you're cool.'

'You're hilarious,' says a man's voice. *Oh no – it's Mr Hollywood!* 'You're really something else. What's your name again?'

'Just call me Miss D,' she giggles. 'D for Dark!'

'You're a very dark, naughty woman.'

'I know. So do you want to enjoy some blow time now and get this party started?'

'Oh yes please, baby! I never say no to blow.'

'Show us what you got then. Get it out.'

There's suddenly a lot of noise and activity going on inside.

I've been here one too many times with Miss D. Maybe it's time to put her on the first flight back to London.

I open the door. There she is, on her knees, devouring Mr Hollywood's erect penis.

'You naughty girl, barging in on us like this,' she says giggling. 'You thought I was doing blow, as in cocaine, didn't you, Ems?'

'Yes,' I say smiling.

Mr Hollywood roars with laughter. 'You English girls are hilarious. Emma, this is the best party ever! You have a talent for this. Now, girls, shall we get this joint really kicking? Come on – let's party!'

'Join me downstairs when you're ready and I'll toast you on that,' I reply, shutting the door behind me.

Chapter Twenty-Two

'Friendship is certainly the finest balm for
the pangs of disappointed love.'
Jane Austen

I'm in a crowded bar, sandwiched between Miss D and
Trolley Dolly, drinking cocktails. We've christened this area
our Bermuda Triangle, because it has three bars in close
proximity and once you're in the triangle, strange happen-
ings occur and it's very difficult to get out.

We've already had to escape the clutches of three elderly
sugar-daddy types who chatted us up by telling us how
many wives they've had between them, as if we'd fancy
adding to the total. I've made Trolley Dolly laugh hysteri-
cally by telling her all about the trip to Hollywood and
Miss D's latest antics. I need them right now. They help me
when I'm low, and both the girls have spotted that I'm
down in the dumps.

'I thought you were getting over Mr Fox,' Trolley Dolly
says sympathetically.

'I was but ....' I sigh. 'I saw him the night before last. I
was in a bar and he came in, and guess what? He just
happened to have some gorgeous eye candy on his arm. He
didn't see me, but I saw him holding her hand, helping her
take her coat off, kissing her, using all the usual tricks. It

made me feel like shit.' I stare sadly into my glass. 'I'm still licking my wounds and he's moved on.'

'Oh, Ems,' says Trolley Dolly. 'I'm so sorry to hear that. What an idiot he is. Bad luck.'

I look up at the other two and shake my head. 'I just don't understand it. Why is it so hard to find the right guy?'

My phone beeps and I reach for it, only for Miss D to grab it away from me before I can look at the incoming text.

'No,' she says sternly. 'I've seen you checking your phone all night. You're still hoping he'll text, aren't you? Sod him, Emma. If it's him, it might be my duty to delete it.'

'No,' I protest. 'Give it back. And don't open it!'

She's already opened the text and is scanning it solemnly. 'Hmm. I'm not sure. Perhaps you'd better not read it. Trolley Dolly, what do you think?'

She passes the phone to Trolley Dolly, who reads the message and shakes her head. 'Oh dear, oh dear.'

'Give it here!' I say and hold out my hand. Trolley Dolly passes it over, her face grave. I'm feeling a little panicked now as I grab it and read the message:

I've realised I lost my favourite pair of Victoria's Secret panties at your Gatsby party. Luckily, some sacrifices are worth it! But do let me know if they're found.
Alexandra x

Laughter erupts at our table at the expression on my face. In a moment, I'm in a fit of giggles too. It's a wonderful feeling to laugh again, and I'm just gasping for breath when a waitress delivers a bottle of red wine with one glass.

'This is for you,' she says.

I look at it, confused. 'I didn't order it.'

'It came from a gentleman at the bar.'

I look up and scan the crowded bar. My eyes lock with those of a handsome man who's smiling at me. I smile back, let my gaze linger on him for a couple of seconds and then look away. I can't resist glancing up again for a sneaky look, to see if he's still staring at me. He is. I flick my gaze away at once.

The waitress brings two more glasses and we pour out the wine. When I look over to the bar again, he's gone. *Oh well. Nice while it lasted.*

Trolley Dolly is kicking my leg under the table and I'm startled to realize that the handsome man is now standing beside us. He smiles at me. 'I have to leave soon, but I wondered if I could share a glass of wine with you before I go?'

I keep my cool, even though I'm fluttering a little inside. 'Why not?'

'It's my favourite,' he says, and I notice his accent is Canadian. 'I hope you like it.'

'Thanks, I'm sure we will.'

He sits down opposite me, oblivious to Miss D and Trolley Dolly, who are smirking away beside me. He's still smiling, his eyes never leaving mine. 'I'm Dougie,' he says.

'Pleased to meet you, Dougie,' I reply, and I can't help wondering if this is the man to help me forget all about Mr Fox.

Today, I'm making fantasy into a reality for two stressed-out high-flying lawyers. They're going to forget about legal conundrums, clients and courts by getting downright dirty instead and spending the day as real-life porn stars. I've taken care of all the usual arrangements: a film crew, a team of hair and make-up artists and a director. Today's backdrop is a stunning red-brick Elizabethan mansion. It's the perfect setting.

John and Lisa have no reservations about going for it when the cameras roll. The sexual charge of being filmed is a thrilling one for them. Lisa is in her mid thirties and wants to star in her own special X-rated movie before things start going south. Right now, she seems to be relishing her role as she and John frolic naked on the manicured lawn. Lisa screams enthusiastically as she sits on top of his erect penis and starts riding him.

'Take all of my garden hose,' he says, sliding deep into her. 'You're so wet. *Dirty, dirty* Lisa.'

She lets out a deep 'ohhhhh!' as he thrusts into her, and her cries intensify as he starts caressing her bouncing breasts. 'Suck,' she orders, putting one erect nipple in his mouth. When he's given it a good, hard sucking, she takes it out and replaces it with the other.

When he can speak again, John says breathlessly, 'Show them how good you are on top.'

Lisa moves up and down on his rock-hard penis, smiling as she takes every inch of him inside her. She moans as they begin to rock back and forth, losing themselves in their desire for each other. Lisa digs her nails into John's flesh as he grabs her hips and makes her grind down on him and ride him even faster. They're both moaning now, louder and louder, as Lisa starts bucking as if her life depends on it. There's no going back; they are set for one almighty orgasm. Lisa closes her eyes and throws back her head, biting her bottom lip as John finally explodes into her, sending her body into total ecstasy as she collapses on top of him. Both of them are exhausted and panting as the director shouts, 'Cut! Well done. That's a wrap.'

Their wild behaviour is catching. I'm distracted by flappings and cooings I hear nearby.

Ha! It's pigeon sex!

Two big fat pigeons are enjoying hot early-afternoon love. There's lots of chirping and wings beating as the lady pigeon lowers her back and the male hops aboard.

John and Lisa hop back aboard as they get busy on scene two, with Lisa in a garden chair this time while John ministers to her. I feel my phone vibrate in my pocket. I pull it out to read the text that's just arrived.

It's another one from Dougie. Ever since that night in the bar, he's been pursuing me relentlessly with texts and phone messages, wanting us to go on a date. The girls are urging me to do it. He's good-looking, gentlemanly and obviously very keen. What have I got to lose?

John is sliding a pair of huge heels onto Lisa's feet, his throbbing erection testament to his adoration of the beautiful shoes. He obviously has something of a foot fetish.

I reread my message, wondering what to do. I've been avoiding all romantic entanglements since Mr Fox and throwing myself into my work. I've already decided that my next relationship will be about sex, if I can manage to find the right guy. Dougie is obviously a romantic. He's after a relationship; I can spot that a mile off.

John is lying flat on his back. 'Walk on me!' he begs Lisa.

She gets up, tottering slightly in the outrageous heels, and then walks nimbly along her lover's torso, managing to hold her balance very well while he's screaming out in both pain and ecstasy. When she's back on solid ground, she teases him with the heel of her shoe, making him suck it and lick it, ordering him to adore it. He loves it. A moment later, he's whipped off the shoe and is licking and sucking her toes instead. As he pays homage to her foot, his hand strays to his huge erection and he takes it in his palm, stroking and rubbing it, occasionally playing with his balls, while Lisa starts to toy with herself. They're having a wonderful time.

I walk over the grass, far away from the cameras and sound equipment. I ring the number that's been left for me over a dozen times now and Dougie answers almost at once, his voice eager. 'Hi, Emma! I'm so glad you called!'

'I had to find a way to stop all those messages,' I joke.

'Oh, I hope you don't mind that. But you're so special, I can't let you go now I've found you. I really want to see you again. What do you say? Will you give me a try, huh? If I promise it's just an old-fashioned date with no funny stuff? You can go at any time, you know!'

I laugh at his puppyish enthusiasm and desire to please. 'OK, OK! What do you want to do?'

'I'm Canadian!' he says, and I can hear the smile in his voice. Over on the lawn, in front of the camera, John is busy taking Lisa from behind. I can hear their distant moans and shouts. 'So I've got a great idea for a date. You're going to love it, I promise!'

Two nights later, I'm skating around a vast ice rink, well wrapped up against the chill air that blows through my hair as I go. Dougie has booked out the entire thing, and we are having a game of ice hockey just for two. As we laced up our skates, Dougie told me he was captain of his school ice-hockey team in Canada and has pulled a few strings to arrange this for us. Luckily I'm good at skating and I loved hockey at school, my long legs helping me to fly across the field and outstrip the opposition, so I'm enjoying the invigorating experience of directing the slippery puck over the ice with my huge blunt-ended stick. Dougie is pretty experienced, though, moving in the long, effortless glides of a practised skater, and he's able to put on amazing bursts of speed when he decides he wants to get that puck out of my possession. We laugh and shout to each other as we tussle to get the puck into the goal net.

At half-time, he produces a Thermos of hot chocolate, which we share at the rink side.

'You're really good at this,' I say, still breathless.

'I've been playing since I was five,' he says with a grin. 'I guess it's kind of shaped my life. And you're not so bad yourself.'

'Well, I was on the hockey team at school.'

He grins at me. 'Impressive. Let's see what we can do in the second half then.'

'Watch out,' I cry as we take to the ice again. 'You won't be skating circles round me, I promise!'

He laughs as he glides off. 'So you're no ice dolly?' he says over his shoulder with a wink. He shoots the puck hard at me and it whizzes over the ice.

I race over to it as Dougie charges towards me in pursuit. He deftly circles me, his stick ready to steal the puck away. I lift his stick with mine, then wedge my body between him and the puck to gain possession.

'Hey!' he protests, laughing. 'I'm playing by the rules!'

'More fool you!' I charge off with the puck and a moment later it shoots into the net. I've scored a goal.

Dougie raises his eyebrows. 'Wow, you shoot like a boy! I'm impressed.'

'And you skate like a girl,' I joke.

'What did you just say?'

'You heard me.'

He skates towards me, drops his stick and kisses me. It's warm and delicious and I like it. When he pulls away, he's smiling. 'I don't kiss like a girl, now do I?'

I answer that with another kiss. Despite being on a cold ice rink, I'm wrapped up in a happy, warm glow. It's strange how people come into your life unexpectedly and change it all over again.

After that date, I find that Dougie quickly becomes a part of my life. He seems to love everything about me, and he's not just accepting but utterly admiring and supportive. I'm wary about explaining Killing Kittens, but I needn't have worried. He loves the idea and thinks I'm amazing for coming up with it and making it a reality. He attends a tropical beach party and he's impressed. It's little wonder. Hot Mama is the life and soul of this party. She's six months pregnant, but she writhes up and down a pole with a group of dancers, while a pile of bodies are tangled up on the bed. Her sex life certainly hasn't shut down, as she beckons her husband to join her on the bed. Dougie is keen to help me with my next party after Hot Mama's performance. He's as good as his word – he calls in a few favours from friends in the events industry and arranges goody bags for all the members to take away. He listens with admiration when I tell him about the Sisterhood and he insists on giving to the cause and drumming up support among his friends. I can't seem to put a foot wrong: he lavishes me with praise and tells me endlessly that I'm beautiful and special and how much he loves being with me. It's a balm to my troubled soul after what happened with Mr Fox and the ongoing despair I feel at Pa's rejection. It's been months since I wrote to him and I've had nothing in response.

'He's brilliant, Ems,' says Miss D, when I tell her about him and how much I'm enjoying this new relationship. 'But ...'

'But?' I echo fearfully. I don't want there to be a 'but'. Not again.

She frowns. 'Well, I've noticed that he's very protective of you, that's all. And when we're out together, he sends all those texts, wanting to know where you are.'

I'm immediately defensive. 'It's true we have the odd squabble, but it would be strange if we didn't. And he's still in the first flush, so it's no wonder that he doesn't want to let me out of his sight.'

'True.' Miss D brightens up.

'Maybe he just cares too much, that's all. I don't think it's a problem.'

'Fine.'

Just then, a text pings into my phone. I pick it up and read it. I frown, not quite believing what I'm seeing.

'What is it?' Miss D asks, leaning over to look.

'Nothing, nothing.' I try to change the subject. But Dougie has just texted me asking where I am. His P.S. says: *People will think you're a slut if you stay out like this all the time.*

I hope you are joking! Goodnight, I text back, then put my phone away and try to put it out of my mind.

Trolley Dolly is more upfront about the fact that she doesn't like Dougie. When we meet up for a drink, she tells me frankly that she thinks he's a bit of an arsehole.

'Why?' I say. I'm having a great time with Dougie. He treats me like a princess.

'He's the life and soul of the party when he wants to be – but have you noticed that he only ever talks to the richest people in the room?'

'You're wrong!' I declare.

'Really?' Trolley Dolly looks sceptical. 'I've watched dear Dougie at a few gatherings now, and he's always the same. Only interested in the most important people there.'

'He's a banker,' I reply hotly. 'He has to make contacts. And guess what? He's only gone and secured investment in my business from a friend of his.'

'Well – that's good news,' says Trolley Dolly, relenting a bit. 'I'm glad to hear it. I like the way he's so into your work. That's a plus point.'

'Yes, and you might be surprised to know where he suggested we have a party to celebrate the news,' I retort. 'If he's so interested in wealth and influence, then why would he ask Plaything if we could party at his flat?'

Trolley Dolly looks impressed despite herself. 'OK then, maybe I'm wrong. I hope I am. Plaything is no millionaire, that's for sure. And he's poorer than ever now that he's finally managed to get rid of Miss Norwegian Wood.'

'Can you come to the party?' I ask, my good humour restored.

'When is it?'

'Friday night.'

Trolley Dolly shakes her head. 'No, I can't, I've got work. But listen, if I'm wrong about Dougie, I'm sorry. You guys enjoy yourselves, OK?'

Plaything pulls out all the stops for the party at his flat that Friday night. We eat, drink and dance, toasting a deal that means I'll be able to continue expanding Killing Kittens. If I want an international reach, I have to be able to access the best venues in the world, have the slickest website and offer the most luxurious, most desirable services. If I've got some investment, I might be able to afford Kitty full time. And that would mean we could really hit the gas and start speeding towards real success.

Plaything opens bottle after bottle of champagne. Miss D is there, and McDreamy, and as many friends as we can fit into his rather compact flat. Dougie is there too, handsome and charming as ever, and sticking to his beloved red wine while we get high on the bubbles.

By dawn, we're all drunk and I'm exhausted. Most people, including Miss D, have left, but the party is still going on. Dougie and I escape the party and slip along the hall to Plaything's spare room. He won't need it tonight. We lie on the bed together, staring into each other's eyes, whispering and kissing.

'You're so beautiful,' Dougie murmurs in my ear.

'Am I?'

'Yes, Ems. So beautiful.'

We kiss again, then he clambers out of bed. I stretch my legs and watch him. He goes to the chest of drawers, where he's left a bottle of red and an empty glass, and starts to pour himself another drink, swaying drunkenly.

'Honey, don't have another drink!' I implore him. 'Haven't we had enough tonight?'

When he turns, I don't believe what I'm seeing. His expression has become one of monstrous hatred. His eyes blaze with fury as he powers at me with his fists flying. He seems almost deranged.

I'm numb with astonishment as he picks me up off the bed and tosses me against the wall. I hit it with a thump and crash to the floor.

'W-what are you doing?' I stutter, gaping at him as I lie crumpled in a heap. The room is spinning and I'm desperately confused. What's happened? Why has Dougie transformed like this? I just don't understand.

My words seem to inflame him. Now he charges at me, like he's taking a strike at goal, and begins to kick and kick and kick.

I shield my face as I take each blow, hunching over to protect myself as best I can. I'm stunned by the vicious pain of his kicks. Agony is spreading through my battered body. I want to scream out loud but fear he'll kill me with a blow to my head. I wonder how much longer he'll go on hurting me like this. Then he stops, picks me up and throws me back on the bed like a sack of potatoes.

Fear is beginning to penetrate my shock and confusion. It's not over, I realize. To my horror, his hands – the ones that have caressed and stroked me dozens of times – are now at my throat. He's squeezing my neck tighter and tighter. I can't move. I lie there in total silence, only able to gasp for breath beneath his iron fingers.

He stares at me, his face contorted with fury, his eyes like those of an enraged wild beast. I can smell the red wine on his breath and feel my lips turning blue and my eyes growing bloodshot with lack of oxygen.

He's savaging me with words now, shredding me to pieces.

'You're a nobody,' he spits in my face. 'Don't you dare tell me when I can drink! Do you understand that, you STUPID bitch?'

I never imagined my Dougie was capable of hitting anyone, let alone me. But now he releases his grip on my neck and starts hitting my arms, my legs and my back hard. 'There's a reason why you've never married, why you're single. You're a nobody!' he snarls.

I lie there in silence, terrified he'll kill me if I say a single word. I pray for it to be over.

'You deserve to die.'

Real fear blasts through me. I've got to get out of here; get away from him. He's out of his mind. He might actually kill me. I muster every ounce of strength I have, force myself to slide off the bed to the floor, then scramble up, making my battered body obey me despite the pain, and dash for the door. I wrench it open and run out into the hall, sprinting as fast as I can into the sitting room.

As he sees me, Plaything gapes in shock, his champagne glass dropping to the floor. Then he charges past me down the hallway and into the bedroom.

But he's too late. Dougie has already vanished.

Chapter Twenty-Three

> 'Anger is an acid that can do more harm to the
> vessel in which it is stored than to anything on
> which it is poured.'
> *Mark Twain*

I've spun myself a cocoon. Apart from going out to Killing
Kittens' parties, I've built my own little universe at home. I
feel safe here, once I've bolted the windows and doors and
shut out the world.

I spend lots of evenings, like tonight, in the bath. I lie
there, soaking up the warmth until the water is too cold and
I'm too wrinkled to stay in it any longer. Then I get out.

Tonight, once I've climbed out of the bath, I go to the
mirror and inspect my neck. The day after Dougie throttled
me, I could see the imprint of his fingers there. After that,
they turned into a mass of purple bruises and then began to
fade. Now they're gone, but I still find comfort in taking
out the bottle of lotion I keep in the cabinet and smoothing
it into my throat, touching it tenderly as I remember how it
felt when he squeezed the air out of me.

My reflection looks back at me. I still seem the same. But
I'm not.

There are no bruises now, but I feel tired and frazzled
beyond recognition. I don't know what's happened to me.
I'm not usually the type of girl who wants to sit at home

alone, drowning her sorrows in a tub of chocolate ice cream and watching a chick flick, but I can't find my energy, my drive, my love of life. No man has done this to me before.

Something has changed. I feel utterly empty and alone. I can't tell Ma what's happened to me, or my brother or sister. They've suffered enough heartache lately and I want to protect them. What they don't know won't harm them. Only Plaything knows the truth. The day after the party, after I'd somehow managed to sleep, Plaything cooked me breakfast while I clutched a blanket round my bruised body and shook. He wanted me to go to the police, but I refused. I couldn't face it. I was ashamed that my lover had beaten me up and that I'd been a victim of domestic violence. Even with a throat so sore I could barely swallow and a body covered in livid bruises, I couldn't admit to myself that a man had done this to me. All I wanted to do was slather on the arnica cream and forget about it as soon as I could. But it wasn't that easy. It's become my guilty secret, and I feel as though it's destroying me. It's not simply Dougie and what he did to me, I feel like it's everything.

Somewhere deep inside me, I'm angry. Resentment is raging within me. I've lost faith and, Aidan aside, I am disillusioned with men. The hurt and the fury are so real that they're becoming all I can think about. I wish I knew how to stop this torment. Is the only answer to run home, lock the windows and board up the door and never let anyone in again?

I wrap myself in my bathrobe and wander through the flat, not knowing what I intend to do. To my surprise, I find myself sitting on the sofa with the phone clutched in my hand. I'm dialling a number. It takes longer than usual to connect, then it's ringing.

Please answer. Please answer.

He picks up on the third ring. There's a huge yawn and then he says, 'Hello, Ems.'

I'm flooded with relief. I wipe away hot tears I hadn't even realized were falling. 'Hi.'

'Do you know what time it is?'

I glance at the clock. 'Yes, it's 8.15.'

There's a laugh on the other end of the line. 'You mean 5.15. In the morning. Is everything OK?'

I try to speak, but I can't manage anything for a moment. When I do it comes out as a weak gulp. 'No.'

'No?' There's concern in his voice. Tenderness. It makes my heart feel like breaking. 'Hey – talk to me.'

I hardly know where to start. 'Everything's awful.'

'Whoever he is, he's an idiot!' Aidan says firmly. 'Take it from me. You're a gorgeous girl, any man would be proud to know you.'

'Aidan, it's not just that. Yes, I've been dumped but ...' I can't bring myself to tell him the truth. Not yet. 'Everything has blown up in my face. Everything. My family ... My father ...'

'Did he reply to that email you sent?'

'No.' I shake my head wretchedly, even though he can't see me. 'He's not been in touch since I sent it. I don't know if I've destroyed everything or what I've done but I can't seem to do anything right ... The man I've been seeing ... he ...'

Aidan's voice is gentle. 'He *what?*'

'He hurt me. I mean, really. Physically. With his fists.'

There's a long pause and then Aidan speaks, his voice strained. 'That fucking bastard! Who the hell is he, Ems? Have you reported the low-life shit?'

'No.' I sniff. I'm crying again without realizing. 'There's no point. I'm never going to see him again. I can't go through all that. I just want him out of my life, that's all.'

Aidan swears under his breath. I can feel his anger coming down the line. 'If I could get my fucking hands on him ...'

'Is it me?' I beg him. 'Am I doing something wrong?'

'Of course you're not! You're a wonderful woman, Emma, I promise. You've had some bad luck. But you can survive this.'

'I've never felt so bad,' I whisper.

There's a pause and then Aidan says, 'You might not be able to cope with this one alone. I want you to do something for me, OK?'

'What is it?'

'I want you to see someone. You need to talk all this through with someone who knows what they're on about.'

'You mean – a shrink?' I laugh despite myself. 'This is your field of expertise, but talk therapy is *not* me.'

'No. I'm talking CBT.'

'CBT? You're suggesting cock and ball torture?' I ask, trying to make a joke of it.

'I'm being serious, Emma. Cognitive behavioural therapy is perfect for you. It's all about reprogramming and releasing bad patterns. Everyone can benefit from it.'

'Go on.'

'The beauty is you don't have to do too many sessions.'

'I like the sound of that.'

'A few sessions of hypnotherapy might help you too.'

'I fancy a deep sleep.'

'Please, Emma. I'm being serious. Your family's been destroyed. You're alone and you feel abandoned. You're

vulnerable to those fuck-awful men who prey on women in
that situation.' His voice is more earnest than I've ever heard
it. 'Will you do it? For me?'

'Maybe.'

'I don't want you alone tonight. Will you call Miss D and
ask her to come over?'

'You mean Miss Selfish? What good will she be?'

'She may be selfish, but you've been friends all your lives.
She can be a pain in the backside, but she's not selfish when
it concerns you.'

'What do you mean?'

'Give her a chance. It's at crisis times like this when the
good guys support you. I think you'll be surprised. Listen,
Emma, I've got to go, but think about what I said. And
remember, love comes to you all the time. Every day. You
just have to see it. I'll talk to you soon, OK?'

'OK,' I say. 'Bye. And thanks.' I put the phone
down.

An hour later, Miss D is at my door.

'Did Aidan send you?' I ask, opening it to her.

'Of course. He knew you wouldn't get round to it. Let me
in.' She holds up a bottle. 'I've brought this!'

Two hours later, after tears and confessions, I've finally
come clean about Dougie. Miss D and I have made a pact.
We're both going to give CBT a go and try to sort out our
issues once and for all.

'I know what my problem is,' says Miss D, swigging back
a mouthful of wine. 'I've got to stop fixating on money,
value myself more and appreciate real love.'

'That's sounds about right.'

'What about you?'

'Hmm. Probably that I date men who want to control me. I need to be shown how to break the habit.' I grin at her wryly.

'You'll get the tools to recognize who those men are,' says Miss D wisely. 'That's what you need. Knowledge and strategy.' She looks at me fondly. 'I'm glad to see the old Emma. We've all missed you. But I knew you'd come out of the dark place eventually. I just want to help you if I can.'

Then she hugs me and I begin to feel a little more normal again.

It's not all doom and gloom for us souls in pursuit of happiness and love in today's fast-paced, crazy world. There is such a thing as a happy ending, and tonight's sex party is the most special one to date for Killing Kittens. I am hosting my soirée at the sauna bar in London where Killing Kittens was first born, a special request from two beautiful members, Lizzie and Mattie.

They first met here when a newly single Lizzie came with her girlfriends, who were hellbent on cheering her up. Mattie arrived with his date, whose ultimate fantasy was to attend a sex party. That night the two groups merged and became friends. During the evening, a strong attraction formed between handsome Mattie and pretty Lizzie, who was shy but stood out with her buxom curves and green eyes. They met often after that at KK parties and eventually began attending as a couple. Then they fell in love and became exclusive. As they became more committed, they changed their rules to suit their needs. They still came to parties and mingled with their friends and other guests, but they never had sex, saving that for when they got home. Then Mattie popped the question and Lizzie said yes – my first Killing Kittens engaged couple! I was as proud as any mother when I heard the news.

Lizzie and Mattie had their conventional engagement party, but they both felt that it didn't quite reflect their whole story, so they asked me to host another one. 'Our real one,' Lizzie called it.

Tonight, Lizzie's pre-wedding present to Mattie is to invite the sexiest women at the party to join them afterwards in a hotel suite she's booked. I have a feeling I know who they'll invite, so when I step out of the cab outside the sauna bar, I go straight inside to Kitty to check the guest list.

'So – she's coming,' I say to Kitty Kat, as I see the name on the clipboard.

Kitty smiles mischievously. 'Yep. She's very nervous, but I told her you'll show her around and that she's in very safe hands.'

'She has nothing to worry about,' I reply. 'I'm sure everyone will want to show her the ropes the minute she walks through the door.' I hand back the clipboard. 'Thanks, Kitty. I am going to make a quick inspection. I'll catch you later.'

Inside, the mood is one of romance and escapism. The bar area is decorated with ornate mirrors, trays of drinks and candles flickering everywhere. The two candle-lit massage rooms smell divine. Tonight, I've hired an erotic massage therapist. He's a real expert with his hands and with oils, and knows how much stimulation a Kitten needs, and which pressure points will deliver the greatest pleasure.

People start arriving as soon as the doors open at nine o'clock, and I'm thrilled to see they've all made an effort for tonight's engagement party, dressed in glamorous evening attire and glittering eye masks. Inside, they chat quietly together while champagne is served. I quickly spot the happy couple; there's a glow of blissful joy around them, and Lizzie is wearing a plunging bridal-style white sequinned dress and white sparkly eye mask. I go over to congratulate them.

'I'm so thrilled for you both,' I say, kissing them.

Lizzie beams. 'If it wasn't for Killing Kittens, our paths would never have crossed. We really owe you, Emma. Thank you so much!'

'That's very kind. Mattie, you look gorgeous.'

'Thank you, Emma,' he says. 'My best bib and tucker.'

'You look like you could both waltz up the aisle right now.' I accept the glass of champagne Mattie pours me. 'All we need is a priest. Would you like me to sort one out for you now? *My* wedding present to you both.' I wink at them.

Lizzie laughs. 'I need someone else entirely! It's Mattie's pre-wedding present night and I have to find the right Kitten to share it.'

'What about her?' Mattie asks, pointing towards the Jacuzzi. We turn around to see a beautiful woman slowly peeling off her dress by the pool, flaunting her figure in a barely-there pink bikini and pair of Jimmy Choos. I recognize her at once.

Hummingbird.

There's already a level of expectation in the air, but Hummingbird steps it up a gear as she smiles wickedly. She takes off her bikini, steps out of her shoes and flicks her glossy jet-black locks. Her humming moans have far-reaching consequences. Couples in the hot tub begin to kiss. One handsome gentleman slowly runs his hands around his lover's breasts back and forth in a circular motion, then squeezes them. He begins to play with her nipples, drops his head and buries his face in her breasts.

Hummingbird grinds her hips and shoots a look at an exotic Oriental beauty standing nearby, one that says: *let's do something*.

Oriental beauty is her opposite. Her tiny frame is wrapped in a long black dress. Her startlingly beautiful face is bare of make-up. She is fired up by Hummingbird and is very happy to oblige. She reciprocates with a smile then strips off her clothes. Her eyes flicker with flirtatiousness as she puts her tiny hand on Hummingbird's shoulder. There's a pause and then Oriental says, 'Take me to the four-poster bed, please.' They walk slowly, swiveling their hips to the left and then to the right before climbing onto the bed. Hummingbird smiles hungrily and reaches out to Oriental's tiny breasts, massaging and squeezing them. Her gaze moves to her lips. The pair start to kiss passionately, humming as they caress one another's golden skin. They're loving the electric charge they're creating.

All eyes are on them as Hummingbird's hand moves slowly down south and she slips her finger inside Oriental Beauty. She pushes her finger in and out, sliding it up to massage Oriental's clitoris before returning to the juicy depths. She adds another finger and then another, finger fucking her harder now as people look on and Oriental starts to writhe under the attention she's receiving. It's obvious she's being hugely turned on, as her legs shake and she groans with delight. Hummingbird begins to rub hard at her clit, darting her tongue into the other girl's mouth, and in a matter of moments, Oriental cries out as she shakes violently on Hummingbird's hand.

The crowd seems to sigh as Oriental's orgasm subsides. Now Hummingbird lies back and opens her legs, trailing her fingers over her glistening clitoris, looking out into the room with big saucer eyes.

'It's my turn now,' she purrs to Oriental. 'Let's get dirty.'

She spreads her long bronzed limbs even further apart, and Oriental slides a humming vibrator deep inside her.

'Oh yes! That's amazing!' Hummingbird writhes in ecstasy as Oriental drives it in and out. After a few minutes, she pushes Oriental's hand away. 'I want to taste your sweetness again.'

Pure wanton lust seems to possess them as they climb into a 69 position. Hummingbird's tongue dances around Oriental's swollen lips and tickles her clitoris. Meanwhile Oriental takes Hummingbird to new heights with her mouth and some fierce probing with the vibrator. The hungry pair have attracted quite an audience as they reach a violent orgasm, shouting and crying out as they come at the same time.

They slowly disengage from their position and sit side by side, holding hands, relishing the way they have set the room alight.

'So, darling, what do you think?' Mattie asks, indicating Hummingbird again.

Lizzie frowns. 'Mmm, she looks exquisite, but I'm not sure. Let's take another good look before we choose.'

I smile at them. 'You still haven't found what you're looking for, have you?'

'No,' says Lizzie, and she turns to Mattie. 'But when I do, trust me, you'll have a night you'll never forget.'

The entire club is in full swing very quickly after Hummingbird's performance. There are naked bodies everywhere and the atmosphere is liberating and fun. There are threesomes, foursomes and group sex everywhere. I spot three couples beginning to get it on. Sprawled on another bed, a beautiful brunette and her partner motion for a young couple to join them. The brunette's hands and mouth are soon all over her new friend's penis, while her partner tends to the other woman. One tall, dark man is having the time of his life giving and receiving oral pleasure with two tall blondes in a corner.

I take a peep into the massage room and smile when I spot Trolley Dolly. By day, she's a rule-follower, but at night she lets the bad girl out to play. She's stretched out on the massage table in all her naked glory as the massage therapist gets to work on her pert bottom, then parts her legs and begins to massage the inside of her thighs.

'Oh, that's gorgeous,' she says. 'I'm in heaven. Please don't make me leave this table tonight.'

'I have no intention of letting you go anywhere if that's what you want.'

'You star. Can I turn over for you now?'

I know exactly what Trolley Dolly wants, and I close the door gently behind me to leave her to it. I open another door to find Miss D pouring lavender oil in a slow trickle onto a stranger's rearing erection.

I close the door. Back in another dark corner, Plaything is busy with three girls.

Then I spot her. She's a luminescent beauty, an American socialite and debutante. She's a proper and well-behaved young lady when she's with Mummy and Daddy in the USA, but the minute she stepped on British soil, where she's studying for a term, she contacted Kitty Kat and told her she wanted to explore some really crazy things. She'd heard that Killing Kittens was the best and safest place to explore the fantasies that have driven her wild.

I head over to her. 'Good evening. Welcome. I'm Emma, the host.'

'Hi,' says the Park Avenue Princess. She smiles, but I can see the nerves in her eyes. 'Are you going to show me around?'

'Sure,' I reply. There's a tap on my shoulder. I turn around to spot Lizzie and Mattie.

'We're more than happy to help you, Ems.'

Lizzie has finally found what she is looking for. Just as I suspected.

I turn to the Princess. 'Do you mind if this lovely couple show you around?'

Park Avenue Princess smiles as she gazes at the other two. 'I'd love them to. Maybe we can hang out for a while.'

'That sounds great,' says Mattie. 'You're American.'

'Yep.' Park Avenue Princess nods, her eyes glittering behind her mask. 'I am.'

Lizzie takes her hand and leads her to the bar.

I look around at my domain. Perhaps a stranger walking in here might see only heaving orgiastic pleasure and endless sordid sex, but they'd be wrong. Everywhere, I see sweetness, affection and even love.

It's restoring my faith that, one day, I'll find that too.

Chapter Twenty-Four

'No great genius has ever existed without some
touch of madness.'
Aristotle

'Claridge's. The Fumoir bar, please.'

I climb confidently into the taxi. I'm wearing a chic
Parisian LBD and killer heels. In the last fortnight, I've
turned a corner and rediscovered my old self. Perhaps the
few sessions of therapy have something to do with it, but I
feel as though I've come through something and learned a
lot. So now it's time to enjoy myself again, and that's what I
intend to do tonight.

My decision: say yes to every invitation and sexual liaison, should I fancy it. But I intend to say no to dating
anyone exclusively for the moment. Another rebound relationship is the last thing I'm looking for now that I've
finally begun to understand why Mr Fox and Dougie acted
the way they did. The problem isn't mine, it's theirs.

As the taxi roars through the London streets, I think
of my mother, who tonight will be going out on her first
post-break-up date. The divorce proceedings have been
horrible for her, but she's decided to embrace life fully and
start dating again. She wasn't up for understand-your-
divorce workshops, and instead said yes to an evening out
with a gentleman who's recently been offering his support.

I wonder how she's feeling, so I pull out my BlackBerry and give her a call. When she answers, I say, 'Hello, Mothership! Are you excited?'

Mothership laughs. 'This is my first date in 30 years. But I'm not nervous now, thanks to a big glass of Pinot Grigio. And being wined and dined beats a microwave dinner for one, as you well know.'

'Just let your hair down and enjoy yourself. But no naughty business on your first date!'

'Watch it, miss, I'm still your mother, you know! I'm going to have a lovely dinner with my Mr Darcy; that's enough for me, thank you very much. Now, what are you up to?'

'Oh, I'm just meeting … a friend.' I stare out of the window as London whizzes by. It's so glamorous in this part of town.

'A special man friend?'

'Ma!'

'I just want you to be happy. Even though my marriage didn't work out, it doesn't mean there's no hope. You do know that, don't you?'

'Yes,' I reply, though I feel like I'm still to be convinced. I've still not told her about Dougie, as she's had more than enough to contend with.

'Now, let's all get together soon. I want a family dinner with my three children. We can put the world to rights.'

'Deal,' I reply.

'Good. Now I've got to dash. I have a charming gentleman waiting for me. I'll fill you in tomorrow,' she says. 'Bye. Have fun yourself.'

I have just enough time to moisten my lips before the taxi comes to a halt in front of Claridge's. I pay the fare and a doorman ushers me inside the hotel. I feel at home here as I stride into the lobby and then go through the tucked-away door into the dark, sensuous Art Deco bar. He's there, sitting at a table waiting for me.

It's been five years since I last saw Silver Fox. Our paths crossed when I worked in PR and right from the start there was a connection. He's a retired Antipodean sportsman now turned media personality and charity fundraiser. A few years ago, Silver Fox moved to the United States to start a new chapter, but since his marriage ended, he's returned to England to live. When he called me unexpectedly and asked if we could meet up, he joked that I could be his 'starter date' while he gets used to being a single man again.

So here I am.

As I walk across the room towards him, I have to acknowledge the attraction I feel towards him. He was, and still is, one of the most handsome and charismatic sportsmen of all time. He's a legend and a beautiful-looking one too. He looks totally relaxed, dressed casually in a white shirt with the cuffs unbuttoned and black trousers. He's engrossed in *The Times*, a glass of red wine on the table beside him.

He spots me walking towards him and quickly discards the paper.

'Do you mind if I join you?' I ask, smiling, as I reach him.

He smiles back as he leans to kiss me on the cheek. 'Emma. My, my! Haven't you blossomed into an even more beautiful, taller giraffe lady?'

I sit down. 'Are you flirting with me now that you're single?'

He sits down too and pours me a drink. 'Yes, I won't lie. That is my intention. So, have you still got a boyfriend?'

'No.'

He flicks me a direct look. 'Good.'

'Thanks for the wine, but I'd like my wake-up call first, please.'

'Your wake-up call?' I have his full attention. 'Do tell me more.'

'It's not what you're thinking,' I reply mischievously, enjoying the innuendo and the flirtation. 'I'd like a Bull Shot. It's vodka with beef consommé.

He laughs. 'Sounds vile, but all right.'

'Think Bloody Mary – but more potent.'

'Coming up,' he replies as he beckons our waiter over. 'But you must have some of this wine afterwards. It's delicious.'

Once we start chatting, time starts to slip away. He's so easy to be with. Silver Fox is cool – a carefree spirit and sophisticated in a macho yet tender way. He brings out the best in me. I smell the strong and sensual musk of his after-shave as he tells me how he and his wife fell out of love. He orders another bottle of red while I talk about my family and being single again after Dougie. Silver Fox has always been a mentor to me, but I can't help noticing he still has a rock-hard physique at 50-something. He is ripped, solid and powerful. A voice in my head whispers that if he looks this hot in clothes, he's probably even better without them.

I'd like to be in his arms.

He brings me back to the moment. 'You look distracted. Are you OK?'

'Yes.'

He gives me a sympathetic look. 'You have to keep moving forward. Soon you'll be surprised to find you don't really care any more.'

I don't right now, as it happens.

I nod. 'I'm trying.'

'My marriage is over. It's been hell. But am I moping around looking miserable? There's no point being reduced to a shell.'

'No, I totally agree.'

He's so compelling. I bet he's amazing in bed. God, I want to go there right now.

The waiter delivers my Bull Shot and I down it in one. It warms me right through. He's looking at me closely now. He's in a playful mood, judging by the glint in his eyes. 'I can tell you have a hearty appetite for life. I'd love to help you satisfy it.'

I smile back. 'What are you suggesting?'

'Well, how about this? Every time I'm in town, let's do lunch, or dinner. I'm here quite a bit. It would be fun to meet up.'

'Sounds fabulous that you want to fatten me up,' I say teasingly.

'I don't want to offend you, giraffe lady.'

'I'm not easily offended.'

He pours me a glass of wine and I take a sip. He's right, it's delicious.

Silver Fox looks at me again, promise in his eyes. 'All right. I'm not really talking about food. It's sex. I want to have sex with you. Or let me put it a better way ... I want to seduce you.'

'Ah, I see.' I take another hasty drink. This is very sexy.

He smiles. 'You're single. I'm single. Neither of us is looking for a full-on relationship. We could have some good old-fashioned fun, with good food and wine, and stay friends forever too.'

I raise my eyebrows as I clink his glass lightly. 'You're a mind reader. I'd be lying if I said the thought hadn't crossed my mind tonight.'

'Well, we can't have a sex entrepreneur not having sex, can we now?'

'I totally agree.' A pleasant shiver is rolling out over my skin. He has an amazing effect on me. 'The more the better. As long as it's good.'

'I think I can promise that,' he murmurs. 'You know we've got some powerful chemistry going on, haven't we? There's no pressure. Make the decision whenever you want. You've got a sex party tonight, haven't you? Maybe that's the best time to decide.'

'But what if someone found out? It would probably end up in the newspapers.'

'We can outsmart them. I am not proposing any rules. I trust you.'

'Can we stay friends?' I ask. 'What if it goes wrong?'

'It won't. I've been in the real world a long time. It will be *our* bit of fun, fair and square. It's just what you and I need.'

He had me before I sat down tonight.

We kiss on the cheek and smile at each other. We both know it's just a matter of when. Then I put down my glass. My party is beginning in 15 minutes.

The venue is my favourite eighteenth-century London townhouse. There are 300 people coming and it's set to be a splendid occasion. Upstairs, Kitty is tightening the brackets around the four black leather beds pushed together in the master bedroom.

'Hi, Ems,' she says. She wrenches the bracket tighter and grins at me. 'Better safe than sorry. We've never broken a bed at a Killing Kittens' orgy, but I don't want to take any risks.'

'Good thinking. We've never broken a bed, but it is Friday the thirteenth and I always get a bout of friggatriskaidekaphobia.'

'What?' she asks, confused.

'It's a term for the fear of Friday the thirteenth – the unluckiest day there is. Apparently, if you change your bed on Friday the thirteenth, you'll get bad dreams.'

'Nonsense,' says Kitty. 'The beds are made, but there's going to be no dreaming. Everything is ready for playtime. Mickey M and the nymphs are on their way and I'll take them down to the Jacuzzi room as soon as they arrive. It's all in hand.'

I leave her, confident in Kitty's ability to get things done. As I walk down the grand staircase and head for the basement, I'm hit afresh by the atmosphere of decadence created by the vast Gothic-style vaulted ceilings in the dimly-lit room. It's empty, but I can already sense something special is going to happen here later this evening. Six poles surround a large bed in the centre of the room, where my Kittens will soon be writhing up and down. The four chaise longues dotted around provide the perfect opportunity for reclining, either to watch or take part. In the Jacuzzi room next door, a tub has been reserved for Mr Kidnap, who tonight will share it with a transvestite dressed as Mickey Mouse. They'll be waited on by beautiful women dressed as nymphs. Marilyn is getting the night off, it seems.

I smile.

You really couldn't make it up.

Upstairs, guests start arriving. It's just gone 9.30 p.m. A dashing masked gentleman dressed in a two-piece tailored suit and diamond-encrusted Franck Muller watch is politely asking my security whether his Lamborghini will be safe outside. I'm busy at the door ticking off names and making sure the crowd is wearing masks. In the ground-floor rooms there is hushed chatter as guests sip champagne and look around for playmates. I spy a picture-perfect group of ladies at the bar. Outside in the real world, they'd be competing with each other, but under my roof, they are happy to share. I notice one gives her companion a come-hither gaze, touches her waist, then leans in towards her plump lips.

Ah, the kiss. They're connected. Now they start the journey.

I look around the room and notice there are lots of beautiful women in groups tonight. There are groups of twosomes, threesomes, fivesomes and an eightsome. All are attractive, some exceedingly so, and they're all more amorous than the guests at an average cocktail party. Two handsome masked men are with a pair of girls in a corner. I recognize them. It's Plaything and McDreamy, back at my parties again after a bit of a break. I can't stop smiling as I stroll over towards them.

'Can I buy you two gentlemen a drink?' I ask.

They don't need any encouragement. 'We'll have a bottle of champagne, please. Long time since we've seen you, Ems!'

I hug them both.

'Are you all right?' Plaything asks, serious for a moment. He hasn't seen me for a while and last time we met, I was deep in the post-Dougie misery.

'Yes, I'm fine. Really.' I smile. 'And you? You can barely hold your neck up. Been up to no good again?'

I sit with Plaything and McDreamy for a while as they regale me with stories of their adventures and a sex position called the Pair of Tongs, which involves a woman balancing in a side plank position while her man straddles her bottom leg and gets inside her that way.

'This girl taught me,' says Plaything. 'She's fabulous.'

'You must have very good muscle control, but not as good as your lady friend's. Tell her to give me a call if she'd like to give my parties a try,' I say. 'She sounds perfect for KK.'

When we've swapped all the news and drained the bottle of champagne, I go upstairs, where the evening has become distinctly less PG. A couple lead two beautiful women into the master bedroom, keen to get to know them better. A stunning blonde in black silk lingerie crawls on the bed and buries her face in her handsome lover's lap. Her hands glide down his muscular legs and she eases them apart and starts caressing his iron-hard penis, stroking it between her fingers and thumb. She waits until he moans and then starts licking and sucking him. He squirms with pleasure when she wraps her lips around his huge erection. Then she reaches for a humming vibrator and rubs it on his testicles as she takes his penis deeper down her throat, until his orgasm explodes into her mouth.

Nearby a masked man is whispering to his companion, a bulge growing in his trousers. 'Are you sure you just want to watch?'

'Yes, darling,' she replies, her lips trembling, her eyes nervous.

I've seen that look in voyeurs' eyes before. Wonder and anxiety turn to arousal as she watches a curvaceous brunette use her mouth on another woman's breast while sliding a hand over the other breast, squeezing it, caressing it, driving her lover crazy.

The masked man sees the change in her expression and smiles down at her. 'So you do want to play?'

'No,' she replies, biting her lip. 'Well, maybe ... I don't know ... We'll see ...'

The party is in full swing and everyone is having a splendid time.

I head out of the master bedroom and find Kitty looking for me.

'What's up?' I ask. Surely Miss D isn't causing trouble already ...

'We've got a situation. The police are here.'

'What? Why?'

'Apparently someone called and told them there's underage sex going on here.'

Now I'm shocked, and indignant too. 'What rubbish! Everyone has been vetted. They're all well over the age of 21 tonight.'

'I know that,' Kitty says helplessly. 'But Jupiter tells me they're determined to look over the premises. I've done a thorough check. I guarantee you there is no underage person here.'

I sigh. 'I knew my friggatriskaidekaphobia wasn't for nothing today. Not to worry. Leave the coppers to me.' I put on my best smile and head to the grand staircase with Kitty by my side, just in time to see Rock on her way down meeting the two Metropolitan Police officers on their way up. She's wearing just a pair of black Agent Provocateur crotchless panties, with pink tassels on her nipples and thigh-high boots.

'Oi, guvnors,' she says, smiling and squeezing her enormous breasts. 'Would you like to stroke these? I love a man in uniform, even if it's fancy dress.'

The officers look flustered and avert their eyes. One says, 'We're from the Metropolitan Police, miss. Can we have your name, please?'

'Rock,' she purrs.

He's taking out a notebook. 'Rock? Can I have your full name and date of birth?'

'Just call me Rock. You boys are as hard as rock, I'll bet,' she teases, her gaze dropping to their trousers. 'I fancy taking you two big boys down. What's your brief, guvnors?'

The other officer coughs. 'We understand that there may be underage sex going on in these premises.'

Rock isn't really listening. 'Do you want to see my briefs, boys? I bet you love sugar holes.'

They don't have time to answer as she slides her legs apart and touches her swollen sugar hole. 'Are you going to arrest me for wearing crotchless knickers?'

'Enough, Rock,' I say in a calm voice as I descend the stairs to meet them. 'Can I help you, officers?'

But there's no stopping Rock. She seems to be possessed by a fervent desire for a threesome. 'Can I help you out of your uniforms, guvnors? I'll give you both a good, hard fucking. Trust me.'

The policemen seem completely at a loss, unsure how to handle this lip-smacking come-on from a beautiful naked woman. It's out of their comfort zone.

'Er,' mumbles one, looking at me. 'We're on duty, miss.'

I turn to Kitty. 'Can you take Rock downstairs, please?'

As Kitty murmurs in Rock's ear and leads her away, I take a deep breath and try to have a serious conversation, despite the moans, groans and squeals coming from all corners of the house. 'How can I help? I'm Emma Sayle.'

One with tired blue eyes sighs and says, 'Yes, we know all about Killing Kittens. We realize you're not breaking any law, but we've had a tip-off that there's underage sex going on in these premises.'

I lift my chin. 'That, I can assure you, is *not* true.'

'So you say. But we have to check it out.'

'Of course. We understand that. I'm happy to show you around. Please, follow me.'

At that moment, Jordie walks down the stairs in just a thong and metal-spike killer heels. Her eyes light up as she sees the policemen.

Oh crumbs, here we go again!

'Ah, lads,' says Jordie, licking her lips. 'I'd love to be locked up with you two! Do you want to come up to a play-room with me? You can handcuff me now if you like!'

I roll my eyes. 'Jordie, these are *real* officers, from the Metropolitan Police.'

She looks astonished for a moment and then laughs. 'No, they're not! Lads, I'm horny tonight and I love a bit of fancy dress. This is a bloody great party, Emma!'

'Jordie, go downstairs. Now,' I command. 'Stop messing. Mr Jordie is the only man for you at my parties. He will sort you out, or you can try Miss D's double dildo. Now go!'

There's no worry about having to disarm these officers; they stand before me open-mouthed.

I can't help laughing. 'I bet you were all drawing straws back at the police station over who got to come here. Have you two been to an orgy before?'

Tired Blue Eyes grins and says, 'Er, no.'

'I can guarantee you this party is all above board. There is *no* underage sex. But I can't guarantee you peace and quiet with a 300-strong orgy going on.'

I smile inwardly as I lead them up the grand staircase into the candlelit bedrooms upstairs. They don't know where to look when they see a tangle of naked human bodies writhing everywhere. A woman gasps in delight as a masked man plunges his rearing penis into her. Next to her, two other women are giving blow jobs in tandem. We walk into another bedroom to find two middle-aged couples and one woman lying naked, sprawled on a bed, chatting nonchalantly about all meeting up for a Sunday roast dinner and whether they should have lamb or beef. In the corner, a woman's head bobs up and down as she strokes, licks and sucks her lover's penis.

'You are a *naughty* wife!' he moans.

'I think we've seen quite enough,' says Tired Blue Eyes.

His colleague starts having an uncontrollable sneezing fit. I suspect that his central nervous system is going into overdrive. His brain is short-circuiting. He's thinking about sex, judging by the burrow of sweat building up on his forehead.

'Are you sure, officers?' I ask sweetly. 'I can show you the basement if you wish.'

'No, thanks,' says the first one quickly. 'We'd best be off.'

'So you don't want to pop down?'

'No. But thank you for showing us around,' he says. He and his colleague are clearly flushed and disturbed and keen to be on their way. 'We've got another tip-off to investigate, but thanks for your cooperation.'

'The pleasure's all mine, officers,' I say as I lead them back downstairs. I try not to laugh. These two officers probably thought they'd seen it all, but I guess they've never witnessed anything like this. I'm not surprised that, when Kitty opens the double doors, they can't get out fast enough.

Kitty and I turn to each other and laugh. 'Crisis averted!' I say with a snort.

'I bet it was a prank call.'

'Now, let's get a drink! We deserve it.'

We head straight to the bar and down a couple of shots of the hard stuff – Stolichnaya vodka.

My BlackBerry rings and I take it out of my bag. I know who it is before I see the name.

'Hello,' I say. 'I thought you'd be asleep.'

His voice is smooth and sexy. 'I'm waiting for your answer.'

I smile down the phone. 'It's yes.'

'You won't regret it.'

'I know.'

'Come back to Claridge's. I'm waiting for you.'

'See you in 20 minutes.' I finish the call and look at Kitty. She's smiling back. She knows me.

'Go,' she says. 'Enjoy yourself.'

'Thanks, Kitty. I will.'

Chapter Twenty-Five

'The good ended happily, and the bad unhappily.
That is what Fiction means.'
Oscar Wilde, The Importance
of Being Earnest

My BlackBerry is ringing and I'm staring at the screen. It's my pa. Despite the way my father walked out on my mother, and the trauma of my parents' separation, I never wanted to lose him. But, without warning, he walked out on my family as I knew it. All my certainties vanished. My email to him vanished as well, and I've waited for so long to hear from him.

Now, at last, he's reaching out to me. My phone is trilling out. I have to answer it soon or it will stop, and my father will find my voicemail on the other end of the line. I don't want that.

I used to feel sick with dread when Pa's name flashed up on my phone in the weeks after he deserted Ma, but it's not so bad now. I've judged, but I've also forgiven, and I've missed my Colonel horribly. I love him and need him. Our relationship will always bind us together. I lift up the handset and say, 'Hello.'

'Hello, Emma,' he says softly. His voice is different. It's gentle now, without that controlling note or the self-righteous tone. 'How are you?'

I swallow hard. There's a lump in my throat for some reason. 'I'm good. And you?'

'I'm well, thanks.'

'It's nice to have the airwaves switched back on again. I thought you didn't like the email I sent. It's been a while since you got it.'

There's a pause and then he says, 'It hurt, Emma. It was hard to read it and to understand what you were saying to me. I can see now that before I only wanted contact on my terms, and that was wrong.'

I feel a rush of happiness. I've longed to hear those words. 'So you want to build bridges?'

'Yes. I do.'

'I would really like that.'

'I'm ready to try, Em. I've missed you. Have you been OK?'

I don't really know where to start with that one. Being led on by men and dumped? Being beaten up? Sorting out sex parties all over the world? Rescuing Miss D from herself and protecting Mr Kidnap? Having an incredibly sexy older lover on tap? CBT and hypnotherapy? 'Er – yeah, it's all good.'

'I see your business is doing very well. It's thriving, isn't it?'

'We're going global, Pa,' I say with pride. I can't help wanting to share my achievements with him. 'Forty thousand members and counting. I'm expanding into loads of new areas – lingerie, accessories. That's just the start of it.'

'I know.'

I'm surprised. 'You do? How?'

'Despite what you may think, I've been keeping tabs on you all,' he says with a chuckle. 'Before you say anything, no clever jokes about me enlisting MI5. It's all thanks to Google.'

'You Google me?'

'Yes, every Friday evening after work without fail.'

I can't help but smile, curling up on my sofa. 'So how are you?'

My Colonel has not given up on me. I'm glad. Whichever way you slice it, divorce is traumatic for children at any age. It hit me like a double-decker bus, but now I have to manage my expectations. I know it can't go back to how it was, and that he's changed. He lives a different life now. I suppose I have to accept that that's what he wants. There would be no more Sunday lunches, or Christmases together at home, or my parents together forever. I've always expected my parents to let me live my life on my own terms, so I have to let them do the same.

There's a long pause as he considers his answer. 'I'm fine, Em. But we can't talk properly over the phone, can we? I don't want to disrupt your life, but I'd like to see you.'

Reconciliation is going to take time and effort. My therapy is helping me deal with my grief and confusion, and the anger that comes along with it. The solid foundation in my life is now *me* and I'm ready to start healing the wounds. 'I'd like that, Pa.'

'I'm delighted, Em.'

'So am I.' I guess we're getting accustomed to the new situation – as much as we ever can. We're all still alive, but existing in a different form. Mothership is dating and looking forward, not back. She's seen Pa again and been able to say a few of the things she needed to. She looked him in the eye and told him that one day he was going to be old and ill, and that they both knew his masseuse would not be there for him. He said nothing, just looked at his feet. He stuck by his choice and, somehow, that helped her to move on. But I don't mention *her* and I don't want him to either. I desperately don't want her to be a part of this delicate time as my father and I move back towards each other.

'So, just the two of us?' he suggests.

Relief washes over me. 'Perfect.'

'Good. How about next Saturday? We could meet for a coffee.'

'It's a date,' I say.

'I look forward to it.'

'I'll call you later in the week to finalize a time.'

'Thanks, Emma.'

'For what?'

'For showing goodwill. For sending that email. It's helped, it really has.'

'I'm glad. See you next week,' I say before hanging up.

I'm taking a luxurious shower in the very bathroom Elizabeth Taylor once used and loved. She and Richard Burton called The Dorchester their second home, and this suite was always theirs. I tilt my head back under the steaming water until I've had my fill, then turn off the water and step out into the bathroom. This is unashamed old-school glamour, the pink Italian marble installed especially for the queen of Hollywood. It was here in the Harlequin Suite that Elizabeth Taylor learned of her record-breaking multi-million-dollar deal to star in the world's most expensive film, *Cleopatra*, the movie that sparked one of Hollywood's greatest romances, when she fell passionately in love with Richard Burton on the set. Accompanied by lashings of diamonds, buckets of booze and an endless procession of famous friends, they ensconced themselves in this suite whenever they were in town. They must have made love in this very bathroom. In fact, according to legend, the couple carved 'RB xxx ET' into the pink marble after one Bacchanalian night, but I haven't found it yet. I've been rather preoccupied pursuing my own pleasure.

'Emma, come back to bed!' It's Silver Fox calling for me. 'It's time for some morning delight.'

'Good things come to those who wait,' I shout back, smiling.

Silver Fox and I have been on an erotic whistle-stop sex tour of London's finest hotels. Luxury suites are where all the best action happens once the 'Do Not Disturb' sign is put up. Hotels are great places for those little extras to heighten pleasure. Every time we step into a new shower, Silver Fox declares that we have to christen it, and he's a master with the kind of showerheads that are detachable and, best of all, come with a massage setting. As for the hotel bedroom, there are plenty of useful props to be found in there. Pillows are not just meant for sleeping; the simple addition of a pillow or two or three can lead to mind-blowing sex. A call to room service provides endless opportunities: ice, strawberries, cream and cold wine are all especially delicious when used on sensitive spots. And afterwards, housekeeping comes and makes everything pristine again. In my opinion, hotels are built for sex.

This exquisite suite is my favourite, though. We've christened most of the non-bed furniture: the sofa, the American walnut floors, the silk rug and the grand dining table underneath the crystal chandelier that made me think of Elizabeth Taylor's dazzling diamonds. We even made love in broad daylight on the large outside terrace overlooking the leafy acres of Hyde Park. It reminded me of the havoc I caused by having sex on the roof of the US embassy in Kuwait – except this time no one batted an eyelid.

My liaison with Silver Fox is no big love affair like Elizabeth Taylor and Richard Burton, but there is passion. My desire for sex is so furious that I may burn Silver Fox out.

He calls from the bedroom again, impatient. 'Emma, are you coming back to bed?'

'I'll be out in a moment!' I shout as I anoint myself with some of the delicious lotions the hotel thoughtfully supplies.

Last week, Killing Kittens increased its worldwide membership by another 5,000, and our waiting list has doubled overnight after one of our provocative members, we've christened Jessica Rabbit, gave an interview in *The Sun*. I suppose it's no surprise given her exhibitionist streak that she should pop up on a reality show, her curves and saucer eyes getting her plenty of attention. The interview ran with the headline 'Why I Love Sex Parties', and in it she cooed about how, with her high sex drive, she loved taking part in Killing Kittens' orgies.

I can't complain, as our website was immediately hit with a surge of internet traffic this morning and our hotline rang off the hook too. I've not seen Miss Rabbit at my bashes for a while as she's hopped off to the world of show-business and more reality TV shows, but I remind myself to thank her should I ever see her again.

I feel as though the tough times are behind me. By letting go of the pain I felt over my father's vanishing act, Mr Fox and Dougie, I no longer feel so lost and alone. My business has stepped up a level. I'm now throwing parties twice a month. Besides those in London, I'm planning more soirées in the South of France, New York, Miami and Los

Angeles. I'm confident my lingerie and erotic toy range will inspire even more orgasms for all man- and womankind. I've no worries about the future now – it looks exciting and full of possibilities.

I'm not sure where my love life is going, but a change has come from within and I'm happily single, enjoying life and making sure I've learned the lessons of my past. I know what kind of guy is best avoided, and I'm waiting for the right one to come along. In the meantime, I'm enjoying the best company and sex to date with Silver Fox. He's helped me get back on track.

I put on a fluffy bathrobe and go back into the suite, where Silver Fox is lying in the bed, propped up against the pillows, waiting for me. When he sees me, he smiles happily and says, 'You were ages in the shower, as usual. Are you coming back to bed?'

I laugh. 'No! You know I can't. I've just had a shower and now I have to get ready to go.'

He makes a face at me. 'And what about my morning delight? Are you denying me?'

'Stop complaining,' I reply, sitting down at the dressing table. 'Didn't I look after you last night?' He's getting out of bed and I can admire his body. He reminds me of a classical Greek marble statue of a man: strong, athletic and the epitome of manly beauty. As he stands there in all his glory, I feel my resolution wavering. Is there time for us to do it all again? He walks towards me, smiling.

'The treat you gave me was particularly enjoyable,' he murmurs as he comes and sits beside me on the broad stool. We gaze at ourselves in the mirror and he brushes the tendrils of wet hair away from my neck. 'I'd love to experience that again.'

'Of course you can.' I smile at him. His nearness is making my stomach go liquid.

'Let's do it now. We can shower again together afterwards.'

I laugh. 'No, I don't have time, you know that.'

'Oh yes.' He nuzzles in and kisses my still-damp skin. 'Later? Maybe tonight?'

'Maybe,' I smile. I start to rub moisturizer into my face. 'I'd like that. But I have to get ready now – I have a wedding to go to.'

I jump out of a cab and spot Trolley Dolly and Kitty Kat looking very glamorous as they stand on the steps of the church. The groom, Mattie, is settling his pre-wedding nerves by smoking a cigarette with his best man. As I go to join the girls, I see Miss D tottering along the road towards us. She's dressed in a floor-length white dress, cut to flatter her curves and draw attention to them. Her hair has been teased into a tousled up-do. She is even wearing cream heels.

I give her a look as she approaches and she tosses her head with an I-don't-care air as she glides towards us.

'Here comes the bride,' I say. 'You're not meant to upstage the bride on her wedding day, Miss D. Have you no shame?'

'No, I haven't,' she replies. She comes up to me and kisses me on the cheek. I spot a blinding rock on her ring finger.

'What's that?' I ask, lifting her hand so I can get a better look. 'An engagement ring?'

She gazes at it happily as it sparkles on her finger. 'No,' she says, 'it's only a five-carat diamond.'

I fix her with a hard stare. 'Do you have something to tell us, D?'

'Do *you* have something to tell *me?*' she asks, touching her earlobes and drawing attention to what look like two-carat diamond stud earrings.

'Er – no.'

'Let me remind you, then, about a certain Mr Kidnap's golden handshake. The one you *forgot* to tell me about.'

I look at the large cushion-cut solitaire diamond sparkling back at me in all its glory. It's impossible to miss. 'Don't tell me he bought you diamonds for alimony.'

'It's not alimony, it's doing the right thing. I called him and he told me about the golden goodbye handshake. He wants me to be happy, he has a big fat wallet, so why shouldn't he indulge me after all I did for him? I insisted on a diamond handshake instead.'

I laugh. 'I didn't tell you because I didn't think it would be good for you. You know why. I don't call you piranha woman for nothing.'

'It's no big deal. If it were bigger, it might qualify as bling.' She looks lovingly at the ring, then takes it off and hands it to me. 'Do you want to try it on?'

She slips it on my finger before I can reply. I look at it sparkling there and I'm hit with an idea.

I see a pile of unwanted jewellery that just acts as a painful reminder of past anguish. Something that could be turned to our advantage …

'I've got it!' I say excitedly.

'Got what?' chorus Kitty and Trolley Dolly.

'What if we create a treasure chest from the gifts we got from our exes?'

'I'm all ears,' says Trolley Dolly, interested.

'Why don't we set up a fund between us? Instead of hurling wedding rings into the River Thames like my mother did, we throw everything into the fund and use the money to *make* money. We could invest it in art, or even buy a house – fix it and sell it and make a profit.'

'I love it, Ems,' says Trolley Dolly, smiling. 'We could call it Cashing Out.'

'Or Ready to Move On? How about the Engagement Fund?' I say.

'I'm in with the Engagement Fund,' says Kitty. She touches a Swarovski crystal dangling from a chain around her neck. 'You can have this when I take it off. I don't know why I'm wearing it. It's from the douche bag who fucked me and then dumped me.'

'I've got a pair of naff earrings from Mr Black to throw in,' I say.

Trolley Dolly says, 'I've got a watch from some scumbag that I can hardly bear to look at. That's got to be worth something.'

Miss D's face is full of horror. She looks like she is about to hyperventilate. 'Emma!' she says. Her eyes are glued to her rock on my finger as her face turns a shade of magenta. 'Give me my engagement ring back!'

'You are *not* engaged!' I reply, laughing as I slide the ring off my finger and hand it back to her.

'You are nuts, D,' says Trolley Dolly.

'No, I'm not,' she replies, looking happy and relieved once her ring is safely back on her finger. 'All women have jewellery they would part with – but not their wedding or engagement ring.'

We chorus: 'But you are *not* engaged!'

An elegant older lady in a powder-blue dress, attracted by our lively chat, comes over and says, 'Ladies, do you mind telling me who you are?'

I smile. 'We're friends of Lizzie and Mattie.'

'I'm Lizzie's mother.'

'Nice to meet you!' we chorus.

'I've never met any of you before,' she says, glancing at all of us and smiling nervously. 'How do you know Lizzie and Mattie?'

I exchange glances with Kitty. 'We all met many moons ago in a private club.'

'Which one?' she asks, interested.

'Oh … just a club,' I say vaguely.

Trolley Dolly says, 'Emma threw a little engagement party there a couple of weeks ago.'

The lady's face clears. 'Ah, it's you! Lizzie and Mattie told me what a wonderful night they had. It's so lovely to meet you.'

'And you,' I say, thinking what a great mother she must be.

She smiles at us all. 'Would you mind taking your seats in church now? Lizzie's going to be here very soon. She's the third generation of our family to be married in this church. I think it's going to be magical.'

'Of course it is!' we chorus, and we head inside.

We are sitting in a beautiful, quintessentially English country church with around 80 of Lizzie's and Mattie's friends and family. We all turn around to catch our first glimpse of Lizzie as she walks down the aisle on her father's arm. She looks every inch the bride in a white satin gown with French-lace sleeves and a dramatic long veil. Her hair is pulled back from her face and curled into an elegant up-do.

'She's copied my hairdo,' whispers Miss D.

'Ssh! Today is *not* about you!'

As she passes us, Lizzie subtly winks from behind her veil, then floats up the aisle to join Mattie. As they stand side by side at the altar, beaming with pure adoration at each other, I know that this is true love. I watch in rapture as they say their vows, promising to love, comfort and honour each other. As they leave the church on a cloud of happiness, the church bells pealing out, I can't stop smiling.

Neither can Kitty. 'It's pretty awesome that they met and fell in love at a sex party, and now they're man and wife.'

'I'm prouder than anyone,' I say. 'Maybe I'm more romantic than I thought.'

'You're the best – a realistic romantic. A pragmatic perfectionist. An honest hedonist.' Kitty grins at me. 'Be proud of yourself.'

I smile at her gratefully. 'Thanks, Kitty. That means a lot.'

Miss D rushes past. 'The reception now!' she squeals with excitement.

I laugh. Some things will never change.

The reception is held in the grounds of a local hotel and as the bride and groom submit to endless photographs, we sip champagne and cocktails on the lawn. Trolley Dolly declares that even though Lizzie and Mattie are a good advert for married bliss, and that Mr and Mrs are another excellent example, she thinks the best of all worlds is having great, no-strings sex with handsome men, while enjoying fabulous, supportive friendships with girlfriends.

'I mean,' she says expansively, 'why do you need the drag of a relationship when you can have the best sex of your life all the time without one?' She sips her drink thoughtfully. 'I wish I could make Emerald Isle see my point of view. Her life could be about a million times happier if she got laid.'

I think about my relationship with Silver Fox. That's working well right now, but I still have worries that one day it will change somehow. 'I agree no-strings is great if it works out, but what if he says one thing but means something entirely different? Take a guy who wants sex and says it's just as friends. Does that mean he just wants sex, or that he might want more once he's made up his mind about you?'

Trolley Dolly nods. 'We need to decode what men say. Claims that men are simple are just not true. It's a misconception. They're just as complicated as we are, maybe even more so.'

Miss D says, 'They lie to us because they think women can't have sex without getting emotionally involved.'

Kitty says, 'It would be much easier if everyone were just honest from the start. I guess men worry they won't get as much sex if they say to a woman that all they want is a one-off shag, thanks very much.'

'Let's make a toast,' says Trolley Dolly. 'Let's say no more to our sexuality being shaped by gender stereotypes. Here's to our sex drives being just as rampant as men's, without the need for an emotional connection. Sex can be just sex for us ladies too.'

'Hear, hear,' says Miss D fervently. 'I just need to feel a physical spark to get aroused and have great sex.'

I grin at her. 'Don't we know it? You all know what I think – no woman should ever feel guilty about her sexuality. We should be able to live the way that makes us happy.'

We all raise our glasses in a toast. I look around at my friends and feel a rush of happiness. They're all smart, sexy ladies living life on their own terms.

Kitty is looking at me. 'But that doesn't mean there isn't room for love in our lives too? Right, Emma?'

I grin at her. 'Of course. When it comes along, when it's the right thing. I think we all agree on that.'

Miss D looks a little wistful. 'I know it's wrong, but I can't help hoping my Mr Right comes with a stucco-fronted five-storey Chelsea mansion.'

'Nothing wrong in dreaming, D,' I laugh. 'But don't mistake love of a house for love of a man, that's all. I mean, did you ever really think you and Mr Kidnap were right for each other?'

'I suppose not. He'll be happier with his big, buxom Marilyn. And if I had my time again, I wouldn't try to break into his house like a bunny boiler.'

'OMG!' I grin. 'Maybe miracles do happen after all and you're learning from your many mistakes.'

'Maybe I finally am.'

Kitty looks at her watch. 'Emma, we're going to have to think about making tracks. We're busy tonight, remember?'

I nod. I'm throwing a private mile-high sex party for a politician and his wife tonight. We'll need to be on our way to the airport before too long for the three-hour round-trip flight.

'I've ordered the car,' says Kitty. 'It'll be here soon.'

I say to Trolley Dolly and Miss D: 'I guess you girls will have to party on without us. Just remember that this isn't a KK party. No stripping off or trying to start an orgy. And stay out of the bride and groom's room – you don't want to scandalize the guests!'

'That's a shame,' says Miss D, her face falling. She opens her handbag and pulls out an exceptionally large double dildo in dark-blue silicon. 'I was hoping to introduce you all to this magnificent creature tonight! Say hello to Tantus Feeldoe.'

'Put it away, D!' I cry, and we all start laughing.

Kitty checks her phone. 'The car's here, Emma. We'd better go.'

I kiss them all goodbye and say, 'By the way, girls, have I told you my new motto?'

They shake their heads. I put my glass down on the tray of a passing waiter and give them all my biggest smile.

'It's this.' I put my hands on my hips and say, 'The aim of life isn't to arrive at the grave unscathed, but to skid in sideways shouting, "Holy shit! That was epic!"'

They laugh and lift their glasses in a toast as Kitty and I head off to find our ride. I hear Trolley Dolly shouting after me: 'I'll toast to that, Emma! Yeee-ha!'

Epilogue

I'm in a silver people carrier on the way to the airport. My phone beeps with a message. I'm expecting some news about the latest Sisterhood challenge. I'm going to go to Istanbul to take part in a 6.5-kilometre race along the Bosphorus Strait, swimming from Asia to Europe. It looks as though the Sisterhood is going to continue performing feats of strength and endurance to raise money for charity. I'm proud of that.

Or, I think, it could be Silver Fox requesting my presence in our glamorous Burton–Taylor suite when I get back from the flight for some more of the delights we share together.

I just hope it's not Mr Kidnap. But I've not heard much from him since he and Marilyn got together.

I check the message.

Hi Emma,
I'm coming back to London. I'll be around for at least a few
months, maybe longer. I've been missing you. I want to see you.
Can we have dinner?
   Aidan

I sit back in the leather seat as the world flies by outside. We'll be at the airport soon. Kitty's checking that the last arrangements are in place. I realize that my heart is pounding.

Aidan's coming back.

My spirits lift. A big smile spreads over my face. I write a message back: *Of course! And I hope it's longer. Call me when you arrive. X.* Then I press send.

'Is everything all right, Emma?' asks Kitty, looking over at me.

'Yeah,' I say happily. 'Everything's just fine.'

Acknowledgements

First of all, my thanks to Mothership, my role model and my inspiration. She's taught me about the fire inside every woman and to *never* let anyone put it out, least of all a man. To all the girls of The Sisterhood, my friends and family, George, JJ and Pa – thanks for keeping me grounded and humouring me regularly. To the arseholes – without you I wouldn't have learnt what I don't want in a man. To my Killing Kittens family who have opened my mind and shown me that life is to be lived. To my agent Diana Beaumont, editor Kirsty Crawford, Anna Valentine and her team at HarperCollins. The job's a good one. Thank you. And finally to Suze, who has magically turned the KK stories into this book while downing vats of wine with me. Without her, this book would still be in my head and the grapes still on the vines.

And not forgetting Rex, my constant four-legged companion who has learnt the art of rolling his eyes more than any other dog I know.